DATE DUE

JE 11 '07		
AP 28 '04		

DEMCO 38-296

Setting
National
Priorities

R

Setting
National
Priorities

BUDGET CHOICES FOR THE NEXT CENTURY

Robert D. Reischauer
editor

HENRY J. AARON
BARRY P. BOSWORTH
GARY BURTLESS
DAVID M. CUTLER
WILLIAM G. GALE
WILLIAM W. KAUFMANN
CHARLES L. SCHULTZE
JOHN D. STEINBRUNER
R. KENT WEAVER
JOSHUA M. WIENER

Brookings Institution Press
Washington, D.C.

ton, D.C. 20036

tion Data:

for the next century /

   p.   cm.
Includes bibliographical references and index.
ISBN 0-8157-7398-6. — ISBN 0-8157-7397-8 (pbk.)
  1. Budget—United States. 2. Government spending policy—United
States. 3. Fiscal policy—United States. 4. United States—
Economic policy—1993–   I. Reischauer, Robert D. (Robert Danton),
1941–
HJ2051.S472   1997
336.3′0973—dc21   96-45888
                                                              CIP

9 8 7 6 5 4 3 2 1

The paper used in this publication meets the minimum
requirements of the American National Standard for
Information Sciences—Permanence of Paper for Printed
Library Materials, ANSI Z39.48-1984.

Typeset in Sabon

Composition by Harlowe Typography, Inc.,
Cottage City, Maryland

Printed by R. R. Donnelley and Sons, Co.,
Harrisonburg, Virginia

Foreword

NOW THAT THE November 1996 election results have reaffirmed the political realignment that occurred when the Republicans assumed the leadership of the House and Senate in 1995, President Clinton and the 105th Congress can turn their attention to the many important issues that crowd the policy agenda. These include fundamental questions about economic growth, the social safety net, the scope of the government's domestic activities, national security in the post–cold war era, the structure of the nation's tax system, and the sustainability of the entitlement programs created for retirees during the New Deal and Great Society eras. As policymakers address these issues they will be constrained by the daunting commitment they made in 1996 to balance the budget early in the twenty-first century.

The chapters in this volume provide concise, clear, and dispassionate discussions of the major issues facing the nation, forthright analyses of the complex and difficult trade-offs that policymakers will confront when trying to resolve them, and frank appraisals of the consequences of alternative policies. Two themes run through the book. First, policymakers should focus their attention on the problems that will significantly affect national life in the first half of the twenty-first century. And second, the last few years of the twentieth century offer a singular opportunity to deal with these long-run problems in a considered manner before they reach crisis proportions. The policy environment is comparatively tranquil: the economy is operating at close to its full capacity, the international environment is relatively benign, welfare rolls and crime rates are down, and the nation is in a favorable demographic period. In short, it is a good time to thoughtfully assess how the nation should meet its national security needs in the post–cold war world, how the major retirement programs should be restructured to withstand the pressures that the baby boom generation's retirement will impose, how the federal government should sort out the myriad domestic activities for which it has assumed responsibility, and how the government should raise the revenues that it needs.

This propitious environment for rational policymaking could come to an end quite suddenly if serious problems arise in the international sphere or the economy falls into recession. Moreover, the favorable demographic situation will end in a decade as the leading edge of the huge baby boom generation becomes eligible for social security benefits and then for medicare and supplementary security income benefits.

Pundits often assume that when one political party controls the White House and the other Congress, gridlock ensues and little constructive legislation is enacted. Instead, divided government should be considered as offering an opportunity to forge bipartisan solutions to the nation's most important problems; these solutions may prove more durable than those crafted by politicians of a single party.

The volume was edited by Nancy D. Davidson. Amanda K. Packel, Melanie L. Allen, Chris M. Furgiuele, Jasper J. Hoek, Christina Larson, Jeffrey J. McConnell, Joseph M. Milano, Susan L. Hardesty, James J. Prescott, and Sheryl K. Zohn provided research assistance for the various chapters in the volume. Kathleen Elliott Yinug provided administrative assistance. The manuscript was verified by Cynthia M. Iglesias and Gerard E. Trimarco. Carlotta Ribar provided proofreading services, and Robert Elwood prepared the index.

The views expressed in this volume are those of the authors and should not be ascribed to the trustees, officers, or other staff members of the Brookings Institution.

MICHAEL H. ARMACOST
President

November 1996
Washington, D.C.

Contents

Tables

Figures

Setting National Priorities

1

ROBERT D. REISCHAUER

The Budget: Crucible for the Policy Agenda

AS THE United States prepares for the twenty-first century, an unusual number of fundamental issues are crowding the agenda of the nation's policymakers. These include basic policy questions involving economics, entitlements, taxes, nondefense discretionary activities, and national security. President Clinton and the 105th Congress will have to decide which of these issues to address in the next two years and which to deal with later. As they grapple with these issues, policymakers will also be attempting to fulfill the bipartisan commitment made in 1995 to balance the budget early in the next century.

On the economic front, the nation's major problem is the slow growth of the economy's long-run capacity, which, because of disappointing productivity growth and smaller increases in the labor force, is projected to expand at a pace that is slow by historical standards. Possible responses include tax reform and tax rate cuts, reduced deficits, increased investment in public infrastructure and education, and further deregulation. The crucial social policy issues center on the need to restructure the New Deal and Great Society entitlement programs in ways that encourage more self-sufficiency, contain costs, and ensure sustainability in the long run. The tax question being debated is whether to replace the existing income tax with some form of consumption tax or to be content with incremental adjustments to the current tax system. Flat taxes, value-added taxes, consumed-income taxes, and national sales taxes have been advocated as alternatives to the income tax. In the domestic arena, the question being debated is what roles and responsibilities the federal government should perform. Should the broad array of activities that Wash-

The author thanks Thomas E. Mann for his significant contribution to the conception of this chapter.

1

ington entered into over the past half century be significantly scaled back, leaving more to individuals, states and localities, and the private sector? Finally, now that the cold war is over and the United States is left as the only power with a global reach, the basic national security questions facing policymakers are how to size our military forces and structure our relations with nations outside the U.S. alliance to meet the challenges posed by the new international environment.

Dealing with any one of these issues in a supportive environment would be difficult. All involve significant redistribution of resources, burdens, powers, or responsibilities. But grappling with several of them simultaneously in the face of inhospitable political and fiscal environments is truly daunting. Different political parties control Congress and the White House, congressional majorities are slim by historical standards, the political loyalties of the electorate are unstable, the public views government and politicians cynically, and fiscal resources are scarce for easing the transition from one policy regime to the next by compensating losers.

For over a decade, the formulation and discussion of almost all major policy initiatives have been shaped and constrained by the federal government's large budget deficits. This situation will persist even though the fiscal 1996 deficit in nominal terms was smaller than any since 1981 and, as a percentage of GDP, smaller than any since 1974. This is because, without further tax increases or spending cuts, the deficit is projected to begin rising again in 1997. By early in the next decade, deficits will return to troubling levels, and in the second and third decades of the next century, when the baby boom generation begins to draw on the government's retirement programs, deficits will reach unsustainable levels.

The bipartisan commitment to balance the budget by 2002 will also force President Clinton and the 105th Congress to pursue major policy issues in a budgetary context. While each issue has its own rationale, each also has important budgetary ramifications. For example, although the reassessment of the nation's security policy is being driven primarily by the changed nature of the post–cold war threats, some policymakers hope that a revised defense policy will contribute to the effort to balance the budget. Similarly, the impetus to cut tax rates and fundamentally reform the tax system arises from desires to spur economic growth, simplify the tax code, and reduce the size of government. Yet any reduction in revenues that results from tax cuts will make the job of balancing the budget all the more difficult because it will entail deeper spending cuts. However, if fundamental tax reform boosted economic growth, federal revenues would increase and the spending cuts needed to reach balance could be smaller.

For procedural reasons, any major policy change with spending or revenue ramifications will be constrained by limitations imposed by the budget process. Under current law, the net budgetary effects of all changes in tax and entitlement legislation enacted after 1993 cannot increase the deficit in any year. In addition to this pay-as-you-go limitation—often referred to as "PAYGO"—annual caps have been imposed on the amounts of budget authority and outlays available for appropriated discretionary programs.

In addition to these restrictive reasons why major policy changes must be handled through the budget process, there is an advantage to dealing with such initiatives through budget legislation. The congressional budget process provides special procedures under which policy initiatives with budgetary ramifications can be considered and acted upon in an expedited fashion. These rules, known as the reconciliation procedures, limit debate and the scope of amendments. They were used by President Reagan in 1981 to secure enactment of his spending reductions. The significant changes in tax and entitlement policies embodied in the 1990 and 1993 deficit reduction packages were also enacted in this manner, as were the procedural changes that established and extended the discretionary spending caps and the PAYGO discipline. The reconciliation procedures were used by the 104th Congress to pass tax reductions and revolutionary changes in medicare, medicaid, welfare, and other entitlement programs—the Balanced Budget Act of 1995—which President Clinton vetoed. The welfare reform bill ultimately enacted in August 1996 was considered under the expedited procedures of reconciliation.

Congressional Republicans and President Clinton have incorporated, explicitly or implicitly, most of their recent major policy initiatives into their respective plans to balance the budget by 2002. These budget proposals have included profound changes in many entitlement programs, major tax reductions, and significant future restraint on discretionary spending. Even though the two sides advanced broadly similar approaches, the volatile political environment of 1995–96 made compromise impossible. Nevertheless, the effort to forge agreement will be renewed in early 1997, when the debate over the fiscal 1998 budget gets under way. This debate will not only

include substantive issues but will also have to address major procedural matters because the PAYGO restraints and discretionary spending caps are scheduled to expire after fiscal 1998.

The balance of this chapter sketches the budgetary context in which
the major issues of the future will be addressed; it reviews the evolution of the current budget problem and recent efforts to resolve it.
This review draws some lessons from past experiences and serves as
a backdrop for the ensuing chapters' discussions of a number of the
major policy issues that President Clinton and the 105th Congress
will consider as the twentieth century draws to a close.

The Roots of the Deficit Problem

From the end of World War II through the mid-1970s, the budget
deficit was not of major concern to policymakers. Although the surpluses that characterized the immediate postwar years occurred less
and less frequently as the 1950s and 1960s unfolded, deficits tended
to be quite modest until the mid-1970s (figure 1-1). Averaged over
1947–74, the federal government's red ink amounted to a bit less
than 1 percent of GDP. Public debt had reached a peak of 114 percent
of GDP in 1946 as a result of the war and depression era borrowing.
During the next twenty-six years the economy grew strongly, causing
debt as a percentage of GDP to decline fairly steadily even though
deficits were adding to the stock of outstanding public debt in most
years. By 1974 public debt had fallen to 24 percent of GDP.

The budget situation worsened significantly after the mid-1970s.
In the last half of that decade, deficits averaged 2.9 percent of GDP;
during the 1980s they averaged 4.0 percent; and during the first three
years of the 1990s they averaged 4.4 percent. As a result of these
large deficits, the public debt grew faster than the economy and the
ratio of public debt to GDP more than doubled, reaching 50 percent
in 1993.

The deterioration in the nation's fiscal situation was brought on
by the interaction of several factors. Some are best characterized as
policy mistakes, while others involved unanticipated and unpredictable changes in the fiscal environment over which policymakers exercised little or no direct control. The first and most significant of the
latter was the unexpected economic slowdown that began in the mid-
1970s. For reasons that economists still do not fully understand, the
trend rate of economic growth slowed by about a percentage point

FIGURE 1-1. Budget Deficit or Surplus and Total Public Debt, Fiscal Years 1946–96

Percent of GDP

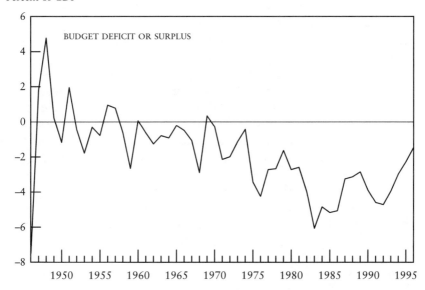

Percent of GDP

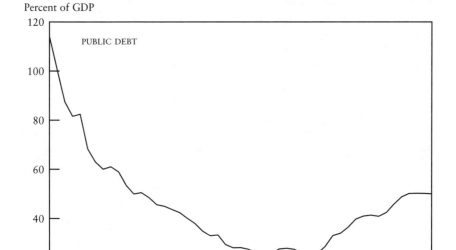

SOURCE: *Budget of the United States Government, Fiscal Year 1997, Historical Tables.*

after 1973. From the late 1940s through 1973, real per capita GDP grew at an average annual rate of 2.5 percent and real output per hour of labor grew at an average rate of 2.1 percent. From 1973 through 1995, real per capita GDP grew at only 1.5 percent a year and output per hour of labor grew at only 0.8 percent a year.[1] Because federal revenues grow as the economy expands, this slowdown had a significant impact on the budget situation.

The entitlement commitments the government made between 1962 and 1972 also contributed in an important way to the growing deficits of the past two decades. During this period, Congress and the president enacted laws establishing the medicare, medicaid, food stamp, guaranteed student loan, title XX social services, and supplemental security income programs. In addition, the social security program was modified to provide automatic annual increases in benefit levels keyed to changes in the consumer price index.

For several reasons, the entitlement commitments adopted during this decade, as well as those enacted earlier, turned out to be far more expensive than anticipated. First, the slowdown in the economy dampened income growth, increasing the numbers of individuals eligible for means-tested programs. Second, unexpected demographic developments—most notably, increased rates of divorce and out-of-wedlock births—boosted the number of people eligible for these programs. Between 1960 and 1980, the divorce rate more than doubled and the fraction of births to unwed mothers more than tripled.[2] These developments were reflected in the poverty rate, which, after declining fairly steadily from 22.4 percent of the population in 1959 to 11.1 percent in 1973, rose to an average of over 14 percent during 1980–95.[3]

A third reason why the new entitlement commitments turned out to be unexpectedly expensive was that health care costs, driven largely by the ever increasing capabilities of medicine, continued to grow at

1. The Department of Commerce revised, chain-weighted NIPA data using 1992 as the base year are available only back to 1959. The growth rates are based on the author's estimates of GDP for 1948–58.

2. Data from U.S. National Center for Health Statistics. The divorce rate rose from 2.2 per 1,000 population in 1960 to 5.3 per 1,000 in 1979. Since 1979, the divorce rate has dropped to around 4.4. The share of births to unwed mothers rose from about 5 percent in 1960 to 17.1 percent in 1979 and over 30 percent in 1992.

3. The first year for which there are official statistics is 1959. U.S. Bureau of the Census (1996).

a rapid rate.[4] After the enactment of medicare and medicaid in 1965, the federal government assumed responsibility for a growing share of the nation's health care bill. In addition, the relentless rise in health expenditures eroded the government's tax base as an increasing share of worker compensation was devoted to the premiums of employer-sponsored health insurance, a tax-exempt fringe benefit.

The costs of the entitlement programs with indexed benefits— social security, supplemental security income, veterans' pensions and compensation, food stamps, and civil service and military retirement—were affected by the unexpected inflationary surges that occurred in the mid- and late 1970s and early 1980s. Prices rose more in the decade from 1973 to 1983 than they did over the preceding twenty-seven years. While real wages and family incomes declined a bit during the decade of rapid inflation, indexed benefits held their own against the ravages of inflation but at the cost of increased federal spending and higher budget deficits.

In 1981 the Reagan administration embarked on an ambitious effort to increase defense capabilities, cut back the domestic side of government, and reduce tax burdens, which had risen to a postwar record level largely because inflation-related wage increases had pushed many into higher tax brackets.[5] The policies that were enacted in response to the administration's initiatives greatly exacerbated the already growing deficit problem. Outlays for national defense rose from 4.9 percent of GDP in 1980 to 6.3 percent in 1986. The non-defense discretionary side of the budget was cut by an equivalent amount, from 5.2 percent of GDP in 1980 to 3.8 percent in 1986. But the Reagan administration was unable to curb the rise in entitlement program spending significantly.

4. Real per capita national health expenditures grew no faster in the thirty years after the enactment of the medicare and medicaid programs than in the fifteen years preceding 1965. Total national health expenditures per capita deflated by the CPI grew at 4.6 percent a year both between 1950 and 1965 and between 1965 and 1994. If the period during which the medicare and medicaid programs were being implemented (1966–70) is excluded, recent (1970–94) real per capita spending grew more slowly (4.2 percent a year) after medicaid and medicare were introduced than earlier. Levit, Lazenby, and Sivarajan (1996); U.S. National Center for Health Statistics (1995).

5. As nominal wage levels rose along with inflation, increasing portions of taxpayers' incomes were subject to higher marginal tax rates. Effective tax burdens increased, therefore, even when taxpayers' real incomes did not increase. This process is known as bracket creep.

In a feeding frenzy that involved congressional Democrats as well as Republicans, taxes were cut in 1981 significantly more than the administration had proposed. The revenue loss was compounded when inflation fell sharply and unexpectedly after 1981, resulting in a commensurate reduction in the growth of nominal incomes. This development reduced bracket creep below projected levels and made the personal income tax cuts of 1981 more generous than policymakers had intended. The new tax law also indexed the code for inflation, fundamentally changing the nature of the tax system.[6] Before 1981, revenues grew faster than the economy as inflation interacted with the progressive rate structure to push individuals into higher tax brackets. Unless policymakers acted to reduce taxes, effective tax burdens rose. Indexation eliminated this inflation dividend. After 1981, revenue growth tended to match that of the economy, and explicit action by policymakers was needed to raise tax burdens. All told, by 1986 the actions of the early 1980s had reduced revenues as a percentage of GDP by about 11 percent (measured on a standardized-employment basis).

A fourth factor that contributed to growing deficits was the weak cyclical performance of the economy after 1974. The economy operated at or above its capacity in twelve of the twenty fiscal years between 1955 and 1974 and in nine of the eleven fiscal years between 1964 and 1974. During the next twenty-two years (1975–96), the economy performed at or above its capacity in only four. The economy's strong performance during 1964–74 gave policymakers an unrealistic impression of how much program spending was sustainable over the long run. It also masked a sharp deterioration in the structural deficit (the deficit that would occur if the economy were operating at full capacity) that took place during the second half of the 1960s. The comparatively poor performance of the economy during the following two decades, along with rising interest rates and the growing size of the structural deficit, added to the burden of debt

6. The Economic Recovery Tax Act of 1981 lowered the top marginal rate to 50 percent, provided a 1.25 percent tax credit for 1981, and reduced rates by 10 percent in 1982 and 1983 and by 5 percent in 1984. Starting in 1985, personal exemptions, standard deductions, and the rate brackets were indexed annually using the CPI. The Tax Reform Act of 1986 held indexing of the tax brackets and standard deduction in abeyance during 1987 and 1988 as new rates and deduction levels were phased in. They were then indexed starting in 1989. The personal exemption was increased in stages over 1987–89 and then was indexed starting in 1990. The 1981 act also contained many business tax provisions, some of which were modified by the 1982 and 1984 tax acts.

service. Federal expenditures on net interest, which had not amounted to more than 1.5 percent of GDP between 1951 and 1977, grew to 3 percent or more after 1984.

In the 1960s, policymakers had been concerned that federal revenues would grow more rapidly than federal spending, producing a dampening "fiscal drag" on the economy. But starting in the 1970s, the situation began to reverse as revenue growth slowed and entitlement spending began to accelerate.

While the overall budget situation was deteriorating, profound changes were occurring in the composition of federal spending and taxes. An ever increasing fraction of the budget was being devoted to entitlements and other mandatory expenditures and interest payments (figure 1-2). In 1955 these purposes constituted less than one-fifth of the budget (3.3 percent of GDP); by 1975 they absorbed a bit over one-half of the budget (11.3 percent of GDP); and by 1996 the share was 66 percent (13.7 percent of GDP). As these activities with their built-in annual increases grew in importance, overall spending became more difficult for policymakers to control over the short run. Unlike discretionary spending—expenditures on activities such as defense, national parks, and health research, which have to be reconsidered each year as part of the appropriations process—mandatory spending and entitlement programs do not require annual attention from Congress. To affect mandatory and entitlement spending, lawmakers have to change basic legislation that sets benefit levels and eligibility criteria. Much of this legislation is either permanent or requires reauthorization only every three to five years. Since most entitlements provide transfers to vulnerable populations or powerful constituencies such as the aged, Congress has little stomach for reassessing these commitments, even when spending and deficits are ballooning. This reluctance to change entitlements—a problem common to many democracies—is exacerbated in the United States by an institutional structure that makes it easier for a determined minority to keep issues off the legislative agenda than for a majority to ensure that an issue is addressed. Without legislative changes, demographic trends and economic conditions drive entitlement spending. Interest rates and the amount of debt outstanding determine net interest expenditures.

On the revenue side of the government's books, the relative importance of social insurance taxes, which support such entitlement programs as social security, medicare, and unemployment compensation, grew steadily (figure 1-2). In 1955 revenues from these sources

FIGURE 1-2. Budget Outlays and Receipts, by Function or Source, Fiscal Years 1955–96[a]

Percent of GDP

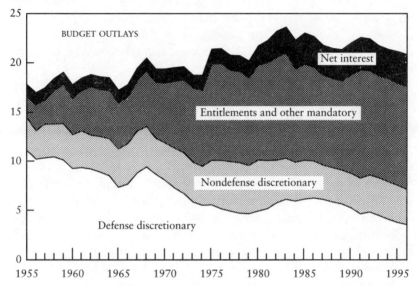

Percent of GDP

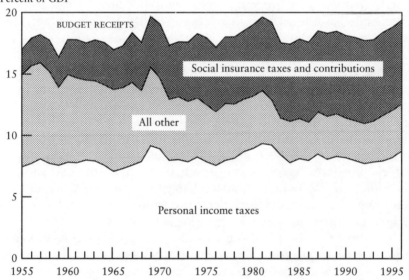

SOURCES line
SOURCES: *Budget of the United States Government, Fiscal Year 1997, Historical Tables*; and estimates by John Cogan of the Hoover Institution.
   a. Excludes FCC Universal Service Fund outlays and receipts.

amounted to 12 percent of federal receipts, or 2 percent of GDP. By 1996 social insurance taxes made up 35 percent of federal receipts and just under 7 percent of GDP. For most individual taxpayers, social insurance taxes (including employer contributions) came to constitute a larger burden than personal income taxes. Other taxes declined in importance, and overall tax collections as a percentage of GDP increased only modestly, from 17.9 percent of GDP in 1955 to 19.4 percent in 1996.

The Response to Growing Deficits

It was some time before policymakers realized that the tectonic plates underlying the nation's fiscal structure had shifted and that some painful responses were called for. This was understandable because the post-1973 slowdown in economic growth could well have been temporary, and there was no way of knowing whether the demographic developments and inflation that were driving up the costs of the entitlement programs would continue. Moreover, the deep recessions of 1974–75 and 1981–82 and the bursts of double-digit inflation in 1974 and again in 1979–81 made economic and budget data difficult to interpret. In addition, with an unindexed tax system, budget projections continually reassured lawmakers by showing them that the deficits would be replaced by surpluses after a few years if policies were left unchanged. What went undiscussed was that for this to happen, tax burdens would have to be allowed to creep up to unprecedented levels.

As the economy recovered from the 1981–82 recession and the double-digit inflation of that era receded rapidly, it became apparent that the nation was facing huge structural deficits that, in the words of former Office of Management and Budget director David Stockman, stretched "as far as the eye could see." These deficits raised concerns among a broad cross section of policymakers. Some viewed them as symbols of the public sector's inherent fiscal immorality, others as a metaphor for the political system's inability to discipline itself. Many were concerned because these deficits were absorbing ever more of the limited pool of private saving that was required for the investment in plant, equipment, and research and development needed to sustain acceptable rates of economic growth. Some recognized that if the increases in the structural deficit were not checked, the budget would be vulnerable to catastrophic instability in the event of a severe economic shock.

The existing budget process, which had been established by the Congressional Budget Impoundment and Control Act of 1974, proved incapable of forcing Congress and the president to take meaningful steps to address the deficit problem despite their professed desire to do so. Responding to growing frustration, Congress passed the Balanced Budget and Emergency Deficit Control Act of 1985, popularly known as Gramm-Rudman-Hollings (GRH). In its sponsors' words, GRH was "a bad idea whose time had come." It established fixed deficit targets that declined each year until balance was reached after six years. The president's budget proposal and Congress's annual budget plan, the congressional budget resolution, were required to meet these targets. Supporters of GRH hoped that the targets would force the executive and legislative branches to propose, debate, and enact significant packages of spending cuts and tax increases each year.

If this did not occur and the deficit for the upcoming fiscal year was estimated to exceed the GRH deficit target by more than $10 billion, the Office of Management and Budget (OMB) was required to cancel sufficient budgetary resources to reach the target. One-half of the savings were to be generated from equal percentage cuts, called sequestration, in the resources of each program, project, and activity in the defense budget. The other half was to come from similar cuts in nondefense activities. Many mandatory programs, such as social security and means-tested entitlements, were exempted from sequestration, and there were limits on the size of the cuts that could be imposed on several others, such as medicare and guaranteed student loans.

The GRH procedure did not achieve its objective, which was not surprising considering that it was more an agreement over desirable future fiscal outcomes than an agreement about how those outcomes should be attained. Obtaining consensus on the desirability of balancing the budget had never been a problem; rather, the difficulty had been deciding which programs to cut and which taxes to raise.

GRH suffered from a number of weaknesses.[7] It was overly rigid, holding policymakers responsible for the budgetary consequences of factors over which they had little control, such as the business cycle.

---

7. See Reischauer (1996, pp. 12–15).

It put a premium on short-term solutions when the problem was long run in nature. Its sanctions were so extreme as to lack credibility and were viewed as unfair because they were imposed largely on discretionary spending, a portion of the budget that had contributed little to the problem of growing deficits.

Policymakers were able to evade the discipline of GRH for several years at a time by relying on rosy economic and technical assumptions and employing a variety of budget gimmicks. When these devices were exhausted and large sequestrations loomed, the GRH targets were relaxed. To do otherwise would have caused programmatic and economic chaos, as is evident from the depth of the across-the-board cuts that would have been required in October 1990: 34.5 percent in affected defense accounts and 31.6 percent in nondefense accounts.

GRH did little to ensure timely enactment of budget-related legislation, did not moderate the degree of budget conflict between the executive and legislature, and failed to achieve the substantial and sustained deficit reduction it promised. Nevertheless, it probably helped to keep the deficit from spiraling out of control. Yet in the five years during which GRH was operative, deficits exceeded the annual targets by an average of $40.8 billion; by 1990 the gap between the target and the estimated deficit had reached $121.2 billion. Both participants and the public became increasingly frustrated and cynical as policymakers turned to ever more transparent budget gimmickry to comply with the GRH strictures.

The GRH procedures were scrapped in the fall of 1990, when policymakers faced the prospect of a sequestration of catastrophic proportions just as the economy was slipping into a recession and the armed forces were preparing to attack Iraq. In its place, President Bush and the Democratically controlled Congress agonizingly crafted the Omnibus Budget Reconciliation Act of 1990 (OBRA90), a multi-year package of spending cuts and tax increases that promised to reduce deficits over the 1991–95 period by a cumulative $482 billion. The policy changes adopted in this package were reinforced by new budget procedures, the most important being the PAYGO restraints and the discretionary spending caps contained in title XIII of OBRA90, the Budget Enforcement Act.

The new procedures reflected lessons learned from the failed GRH experience. Rather than requiring future agreement on yet-to-be identified measures to cut spending or raise taxes, they were designed to reinforce the deficit reduction measures that had already been enacted.

The new procedures were more flexible than GRH. The fixed deficit targets were dropped, and lawmakers were no longer held accountable for budgetary developments over which they had no control. The discretionary spending limits were adjusted (up or down) automatically for deviations from anticipated rates of inflation. Spending for purposes that the president and Congress agreed were of an emergency nature—such as the Gulf War and responses to natural disasters—was exempted from the restraints. The new procedures imposed a multiyear focus rather than the myopic approach encouraged by GRH. The scope of the budget resolution and the related enforcement mechanisms was extended from one to five years. Finally, the new enforcement mechanism was more equitable and therefore garnered more support from legislators. Sequestration would be imposed on discretionary programs only if the discretionary spending limits were exceeded. If the deficit was increased by legislation that reduced taxes or expanded entitlements, the transgression would be offset by PAYGO sequestration of nonexempt mandatory spending programs.

Budget projections made at the time OBRA90 was enacted indicated that it would bring the budget close to balance by 1995. The impact of the 1990–91 recession and unexpected growth in means-tested entitlement spending dashed these expectations. To the lawmakers' consternation, enactment of the largest deficit reduction measure in the nation's history was followed in 1991, 1992, and 1993 by the three largest nominal deficits the nation had ever experienced. This reinforced the public's cynicism about the political system's ability to reduce the deficit and contributed to President Bush's failure to win reelection. He had broken his pledge not to raise taxes, yet the deficit had grown to record levels.

Thus the deficit still dominated the agenda when President Clinton took office in January 1993. Before he could embark on his expansive domestic agenda, the new president needed to show that united government—single-party control of both houses of the Congress and the White House—could break the gridlock and deal effectively with the most pressing problem facing the nation. Together with Democrats in Congress, the president crafted a second multiyear package of spending cuts and tax increases, which squeaked through the Congress with no votes from Republicans and no votes to spare. This legislation, the Omnibus Reconciliation Act of 1993 (OBRA93), was estimated at the time of enactment to reduce cumulative deficits over the fiscal 1994-98 period by $433 billion. Over three-fifths of its noninterest deficit reduction came from tax increases. The programmatic and political significance of OBRA93's deficit reduction is overstated by these dollar estimates because a major portion of the reduction did not involve new measures but instead was achieved by extending through 1998 measures that were adopted in 1990 and were scheduled to expire after 1995.

Democrats lost control of both houses of Congress in the 1994 midterm elections in part because they had supported the tax increases in OBRA93, proving once again the adage that no good deed goes unpunished, especially when it comes to deficit reduction. The Republican-led Congress pledged to finish the job, to balance the budget by 2002. When the Senate fell one vote short of obtaining the two-thirds majority needed to send a constitutional amendment requiring a balanced budget to the states for their ratification, the Republican congressional leadership crafted a seven-year budget resolution designed to achieve the same objective. Unlike the two previous large deficit reduction packages, which imposed only modest modifications in entitlements, this plan called for fundamental changes in the structure of many entitlement programs. Medicaid and aid to families with dependent children were to be transformed from open-ended matching grants to states into capped block grants at reduced funding levels. Limits were to be placed on total medicare spending, and participants were to be offered a range of capitated private health plans in addition to the traditional, unmanaged fee-for-service system operated by the federal government. The system of farm price supports was to be replaced with declining payments to farmers that were not tied to current production or prices.

In contrast with OBRA90 and OBRA93, which together relied on tax hikes for just under half of their aggregate noninterest deficit reduction, the Republican balanced budget plan not only eschewed tax increases, it proposed significant tax cuts. These cuts did not involve tax reform; in other words, they did not alter the fundamental structure of the tax code significantly. However, the plan's proposed spending reductions had to be much deeper than those needed simply to balance the budget in order to offset the deficit-increasing impact of the tax cuts. The Balanced Budget Act of 1995, the legislation embodying the changes called for by the budget resolution, reduced revenues by $218 billion and spending by about $1,200 billion over

FIGURE 1-3. Balanced Budget Act Reductions from the Uncapped Baseline in 2002[a]

Percent

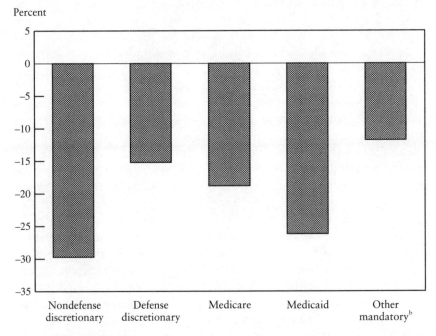

SOURCE: Author's estimates based on CBO data (January 1996).
a. Measured from author's estimates of baseline spending with discretionary accounts adjusted for inflation.
b. Excludes social security.

1996–2002.[8] Compared with the spending levels that would occur in 2002 if policies remained unchanged, these reductions were very deep. Medicare, medicaid, and nondefense discretionary spending in 2002 would have been 18.8 percent, 26.2 percent, and 29.7 percent, respectively, below baseline levels (figure 1-3).

The president vetoed the Balanced Budget Act, arguing that its spending cuts were too extreme and its changes in entitlement programs were unfair and an ill-considered unraveling of the social safety net. Nevertheless, to end the partial government shutdown in November 1995 that had been caused by an impasse with Congress over the fiscal 1996 appropriations measures, he agreed to propose a deficit

8. The spending cuts are measured from the author's estimate of a baseline that is consistent with the Congressional Budget Office's December 1995 capped baseline but is unconstrained by the Budget Enforcement Act discretionary spending caps. The revenue reductions are measured from the CBO December 1995 baseline levels.

reduction package that would balance the budget by 2002 under Congressional Budget Office (CBO) estimates. The president's plan called for smaller tax cuts and less severe reductions in entitlement spending. By 2002, however, his discretionary spending cuts were projected to be every bit as deep as those called for by the Republicans. With the 1996 election campaigns just beginning, the president and the congressional Republicans could not resolve the differences in their proposals. The Republicans were more intent on changing the nature of federal programs than on balancing the budget, while the president wanted to push the sharp spending cuts off until the twenty-first century. Both offered revised versions of their plans for consideration during the fiscal 1997 budget debate, but there never was any realistic prospect that something meaningful would be approved in an election year.

Although the ambitious budget agenda of the 104th Congress was not fulfilled, the Republicans did force the president to accept a modest amount of deficit reduction in the form of lower spending. Discretionary spending was cut below the 1990 Budget Enforcement Act caps through rescissions of fiscal 1995 appropriations and the regular fiscal 1996 and 1997 appropriations. Discretionary budget authority and outlays for fiscal 1997 are some 5.0 percent and 1.8 percent, respectively, below the Budget Enforcement Act limits. The welfare reform legislation enacted in August 1996 will reduce spending on affected programs by an estimated $54 billion over 1997–2002. In addition, the farm bill that was enacted in early 1996 should reduce expenditures over this period by $2 billion, even though it increases spending in 1996 and 1997.

Politics and Public Opinion

The emergence of large and persistent deficits over the past two decades had a significant impact not only on the substance and process of policymaking but also on the character of the nation's politics and on public opinion. President Clinton and the 105th Congress cannot ignore these changes if they hope to deal constructively with the issues on the policy agenda.

Since the early 1980s, the deficit has become more than just another problem to manage or try to solve. Deficits have become symbols. They have been seen as reflections of the moral failure of government, the waste and inefficiency of the public sector, and the nation's insensitivity to the well-being of future generations. Deficit reduction has become a battleground for the clashing of competing views about the proper size of government and scope of federal activity. Some have seen in deficit reduction a window of opportunity to fundamentally restructure several of the federal government's core entitlement commitments. Others have viewed deficit reduction as an occasion to reallocate the division of public-sector responsibilities between the federal government and states and localities. In short, many important but divisive questions involving the philosophy of government have merged into the debate over the deficit.

As this has happened, the public has become deeply confused about the nature and dimensions of the deficit problem and ambivalent about embracing policies that would move the budget into balance. Its schizophrenic attitude is not surprising, considering the information it is provided. Politicians and commentators have used increasingly inflated rhetoric to describe the deficit's causes and consequences. Some truly believe that the nation is in the midst of an immediate crisis; others feel that hyperbole is necessary to jar an apathetic public and calcified political system into action before a serious problem deteriorates into a major societal catastrophe. Daily, the public hears responsible voices warn of the calamitous consequences of persistent large deficits, and yet the economy grows, albeit slowly, and life goes on seemingly unaffected. Nevertheless, the public strongly supports the idea of a balanced budget and endorses, by wide margins, even amending the Constitution to require balance. But when policymakers and others put forward specific measures to achieve that objective, support collapses.

With little more than a fragmentary knowledge of the relative sizes of various components of the budget, most citizens think there must be some relatively painless way of achieving balance. The steady diet of stories of waste, fraud, and abuse in government programs that politicians and the media feed the public has created the impression that tens of billions of dollars can be saved through improving government efficiency and eliminating pork and low-priority activities, and thus that the budget can be balanced without seriously affecting popular programs or ones with powerful constituencies. Political leaders have not disabused the public of this misapprehension, for "sacrifice" has become a four-letter word in the world of politics.

Few among the public are aware that most federal spending—well over two-thirds in 1996—is accounted for by defense, interest payments, and popular middle-class entitlements such as medicare and social security. Most vastly overestimate the proportion of the budget that is devoted to less popular activities such as international affairs and means-tested social welfare programs, which account for 1 and 12 percent, respectively, of all spending. Common discussion of the nature of these less popular programs reflects significant misunderstandings; when these are corrected, reductions seem less acceptable. For example, international affairs spending is not, as many believe, solely bilateral aid to foreign governments. Only 62 percent of the international affairs budget represents such assistance, and 42 percent of that goes to Israel and Egypt. The remainder is spent on U.S. diplomatic functions, export promotion, and international agencies. One-half of social welfare spending is devoted to medicaid, and close to two-thirds of that provides health benefits for the low-income elderly and disabled, groups for whom such support is popular. Widely supported programs such as cash assistance for low-income disabled, elderly, and veterans, earnings subsidies for low-income workers with children, and subsidized postsecondary education loans for low-income students account for an additional one-quarter of social welfare spending. Before its transformation into a block grant in 1996, AFDC, the program the public most identifies with the term "welfare," accounted for only 9 percent of all social welfare spending.

Misinformation is equally pervasive with respect to taxes. A constant drumbeat of propaganda from tax cut advocates has convinced many Americans that they are an overtaxed people. This conviction has effectively removed tax increases from the discussion of ways to reduce the deficit and has made proposals to cut taxes salient. In fact, compared with citizens of other advanced nations, Americans face relatively low overall tax burdens. Estimated total government receipts in 1996 were 31.1 percent of GDP, the lowest level of any of the twenty largest OECD countries.[9] As figure 1-2 illustrates, federal taxes as a percentage of GDP have risen little over the past four decades. They averaged 17.5 percent of GDP during 1955–60 and 18.4 percent during 1991–96. Social insurance taxes, as was pointed out previously, have increased substantially, but so too have the popular benefits these taxes pay for. Personal income taxes have edged up from 7.8 percent of GDP during 1955–60 to 8.1 percent during

---

9. *OECD Economic Outlook*, vol. 59 (June 1996), annex table 29. The comparison is for current receipts and includes all levels of government.

TABLE 1-1. Effective Total Federal Tax Rates, by Income Quintile, Selected Years, 1977–96[a]

Percent

Year	Lowest quintile	Second quintile	Middle quintile	Fourth quintile	Highest quintile
1977	9.2	15.5	19.5	21.9	27.2
1981	8.3	15.3	20.0	23.4	27.4
1985	10.4	15.9	19.2	21.7	24.1
1990	8.9	15.8	19.5	22.1	25.5
1996[b]	5.0	14.9	19.7	22.6	28.1

SOURCE: Congressional Budget Office.
a. Families ranked by adjusted family income, equal numbers of people per quintile.
b. Rates reflect fully phased-in effects of OBRA93.

1991–96, but 79 percent of tax filers face marginal personal income tax rates of 15 percent or less. Other taxes—corporate income, excise, estate, and other levies—have dramatically receded in importance. For most taxpayers, effective federal tax burdens were no higher in the mid-1990s than they were in the late 1970s and early 1980s (table 1-1). Only those with the highest incomes have seen their tax burdens increase, but their pretax incomes have risen the most of any income group over this period.

The public also lacks an appreciation of the recent trends in the deficit. An October 1996 poll found that 70 percent thought that the deficit had increased over the previous five years, 17 percent thought it had remained unchanged, and only 12 percent thought it had decreased.[10] In fact, over 1992–96, the deficit fell from $290 billion to $107 billion, or from 4.7 percent of GDP to 1.4 percent.

With the public uninformed or misinformed about spending, taxes, and deficits and politicians anxious to avoid blame for cutting popular programs in an era of perpetual election campaigns, there is a strong incentive to avoid realistic discussions of the trade-offs and choices involved in achieving a balanced budget while meeting pressing national needs. Instead, the temptation is to turn to symbolic responses to the problem and nonsubstantive measures that purport to be solutions. Prime among these are procedural fixes such as balanced budget amendments to the Constitution and caps on entitlement and discretionary spending. Such measures hold out the promise of deficit reduction without addressing the difficult questions involving which

10. Richard Morin and John Berry, "Reality Check: The Economic Perception Gap," *Washington Post*, October 13, 1996, p. A-1.

programs to cut and by how much. Proposals that hold out the prospect of spurring the rate of economic growth and thereby increasing revenues and reducing the need for spending cuts are another attractive diversion. Comprehensive tax reform and easier monetary policy fall into this category.

Finally, there is the lure of adopting unrealistically optimistic assumptions of how well the economy will perform in the future and how fast spending and revenues will grow under a continuation of current policy. A great deal of uncertainty surrounds such estimates, and very small differences in the assumed growth underlying economic and demographic variables can compound over five or ten years into huge differences in the size of the problem that must be resolved to achieve a balanced budget. An illustration is the contrast between the CBO's spring 1996 estimate that the deficit in 2002 would be $285 billion if policies were left unchanged and the OMB's estimate that, under such a scenario, the deficit would be only $109 billion. The problem is not that some estimates are blatantly biased, but rather that, because of inherent uncertainty, the range of reasonable values for many budget and economic inputs is very wide. This can be illustrated by the fact that well after the fiscal year began the CBO and OMB projected that medicaid would grow by 7.4 percent and 6.5 percent, respectively, in fiscal 1996. The actual growth was close to 3 percent—a difference of several billion dollars. Faced with this uncertainty, policymakers have considerable latitude and a strong incentive to base their estimates of the magnitude of the problem on economic and technical assumptions that are optimistic yet not incredible.

As the effort to balance the budget moves forward, the pressure to succumb to these temptations will mount. The "relatively easy" ways to reduce the deficit have already been tapped, and their ability to contribute to further deficit reduction may be limited. Among these "relatively easy" measures was the significant reduction in defense spending, which fell about 28 percent in real terms over 1990–96. (During this period, nondefense discretionary spending increased by about 15 percent in real terms.) The downsizing of the Pentagon was acceptable because the Soviet Union collapsed and the cold war threats diminished. The tax increases of OBRA90 and OBRA93 were also "relatively easy" deficit reduction measures because they imposed little burden on the vast majority of American families. Over two-thirds of OBRA90's revenue increases and over nine-tenths of

OBRA93's fell on taxpayers in the top one-fifth of the income distribution. These families had benefited the most from the tax cuts of 1981 and 1986, and their pretax incomes had increased the most rapidly over the decade. The reductions that were made in medicare provider payments also were relatively easy for the public and their elected representatives to accept because they did not affect beneficiaries' quality of care or access to it.

Considering the incentives to equivocate or respond in symbolic rather than substantive ways, a remarkable amount of real deficit reduction took place over 1990–96. But this progress exacted a steep political price. President Bush was excoriated by his own party for acceding to a plan that included tax increases; he lost his bid for reelection. Republicans lambasted President Clinton and congressional Democrats for the tax increases contained in OBRA93; Democrats lost control of both houses of Congress in 1995. The Republican 104th Congress, which was the first to propose significant structural changes in entitlement programs and meaningful reductions in nondefense discretionary spending, was labeled as extreme by the president and congressional Democrats; the Republican majority in the House of Representatives was reduced in the 1996 elections.

Lessons for the Future

Five important lessons can be drawn from the experience of the past fifteen years. The first of these is the critical importance of seeking bipartisan approaches to deficit reduction even when one party controls both houses of Congress and the White House. Such cooperation is desirable to ensure that the measures adopted to reduce the deficit are more reflective of the center of the political spectrum than previous efforts and therefore are more sustainable. In addition, a cooperative approach is needed to ensure that both parties share the responsibility for imposing sacrifice.

Unfortunately, bipartisan cooperation on deficit reduction has been next to impossible in the current unstable political environment. In recent years, the minority party has been able to gain political advantage by opposing the other party's proposals and then attacking those who supported the measure that ultimately passes. As long as the public remains unaware that these measures help to reduce the deficit, no rewards await those lawmakers who act in a responsible manner. Given this situation, the majority needs to realize that it has a great deal to gain from involving the minority even if the ultimate compromise that is reached with a segment of the opposition is somewhat uncomfortable for many in the majority party.

Second, budget-balancing packages should not be used as legislative vehicles either for fundamental restructuring of important entitlement commitments or for significant redistribution of responsibilities between the federal government and states and localities, unless these issues have been discussed previously and a broad consensus on them has emerged. It is not that changes of this sort are not needed, but they risk overloading a budget bill. In addition, because reconciliation measures are considered under procedures that limit debate and amendments, some will consider controversial entitlement changes or major governance transformations adopted in a reconciliation bill as less legitimate than similar changes enacted through the normal legislative process. Entitlement restructuring will be viewed as being driven by a need to find budget savings rather than the necessity of modifying programs to achieve greater efficiency and sustainability. Changes that do not reflect bipartisan agreements could remain controversial for years, consuming the valuable energy and attention of policymakers.

A third lesson suggested by past experience is that decisions can be and will be revisited after they are made, and therefore policymakers should not fight over them as if they were irreversible or immutable. President Clinton recognized this when he signed the welfare reform legislation. Deficit reduction is not an event but an ongoing process. It is unlikely that legislation enacted in 1997 that promises to balance the budget by 2002 or some other date will achieve its objective without further adjustments. Unforeseen economic and political developments will intervene. Future midcourse corrections and additional measures will be required to realize the goal of a balanced budget. As the public and policymakers become aware of the consequences, the promises to reduce discretionary spending sharply or to cut taxes may prove impossible to keep. Furthermore, more substantial actions will be required to maintain a balanced budget after 2002: none of the proposals that have been discussed are sufficient to ward off the prospect of record peacetime deficits when the baby boom generation reaches retirement age.

A fourth lesson that can be drawn from recent experience is that procedural changes can not substitute for substantive actions to cut spending or raise taxes. Gramm-Rudman-Hollings showed conclusively that legislated requirements can not force lawmakers to adopt deficit reduction measures in the future if they do not want do so. Constitutional prescriptions are also likely to be ineffectual because the complexities of the federal budget system leave too many avenues of escape. Some of these could be closed, but this would leave the government so hobbled that it could not respond effectively to the constantly and rapidly changing needs of a modern society and economy. Procedural changes, however, can be effective means of reinforcing decisions that have already been made. As the Budget Enforcement Act has proven, rules and limits can keep the political system from fiscal recidivism.

The fifth and final lesson is that political leaders should refrain from using apocalyptical rhetoric to describe the causes and consequences of large deficits. They also need to provide more realistic discussions of the trade-offs involved in balancing the budget and the ramifications of simultaneously pursuing other objectives, such as cutting taxes, building up defense, or expanding education.

Chapter Summaries

The remaining chapters in this volume, which are summarized below, are intended to contribute to the more deliberative discussion of the major policy options that face the nation as it prepares for the twenty-first century.

Economic Growth

If the pace of future economic growth could be boosted a percentage point or even half a percentage point above the projected level of approximately 2 percent, the medium-term deficit outlook would improve markedly and some added public resources might even be available to meet emerging national needs. In chapter 2, Charles L. Schultze examines the various actions that government might take to speed up the rate of economic growth. First, there is the possibility of easier monetary policy. The Federal Reserve, concerned with inflation, may not have allowed the economy to expand to utilize its full capacity. When unutilized capacity is available—that is, when unemployment is high and plants are not operating fully—easier monetary policy can stimulate demand and increase economic growth. When the economy's resources are fully utilized, however, easier monetary policy translates into higher inflation. After examining the evidence, Schultze concludes that, with the unemployment rate fluctuating between 5 and 5.5 percent, there is little likelihood that substantial unutilized capacity exists. Even if this were not the case and looser monetary policy could reduce the unemployment rate to 4¾ percent without increasing inflation, that would permit only a modest ½ to 1 percent increase in the *level* of GDP. After the lower unemployment rate was attained, *growth* would have to slow down to match the long-term expansion in capacity, which is determined by the growth of the labor force and productivity increases. With the former determined mainly by demographic factors, the Federal Reserve would be foolish to pursue an easier monetary policy on the assumption that productivity growth, which has fluctuated narrowly around 1.1 percent for over twenty years, will speed up.

Tax cuts and tax reform have also been championed as ways to stimulate growth. If they increase the incentives to work, save, and invest and, most important, do not lead to larger deficits, such tax policies can boost the growth in the economy's capacity. Schultze's assessment of the empirical evidence, however, suggests that even a large rate cut—a 15 percent reduction in personal and corporate rates fully offset by cuts in federal spending—would raise the growth rate over the next decade or two by only 0.1 to 0.2 percentage point. Politically feasible tax reform would have even smaller effects.

Expanded public-sector investment in education, training, and infrastructure can also expand the economy's potential and growth. There is no reason to expect most of such investment to yield returns higher than those from private investment, and the vagaries of politics make the achievement of even that result uncertain. It would take an increase in current government spending on such activities far larger than the most devoted advocates of such policies ever dream about to boost economic growth by as much as 0.1 percent a year.

Some believe that the nation's economic growth has been hobbled by excessive regulation. While few would advocate scrapping all environmental, workplace safety, and other social regulations, it is likely that the objectives of such regulation could be achieved more efficiently by using economic incentives, such as effluent charges rather than regulatory approaches, and by eliminating regulations whose economic costs exceed the value of their environmental or other benefits. Schultze estimates that if such reforms could reduce the costs of regulation by an optimistic 25 percent, the growth rate would increase temporarily for a few years and the level of GDP would rise by about 0.7 percent.

Looked at over the long run, measures that can increase economic growth rates by 0.1 or 0.2 percentage point a year are worth serious consideration because their effects would compound over time to improve standards of living noticeably. But looked at as ways to help balance the budget over the next decade, such measures are relatively inconsequential.

The Social Safety Net

After decades of acrimonious debate and incremental change, the nonmedical portion of the means-tested social safety net was radically restructured when the president signed the Personal Responsibility and Work Opportunity Act in August 1996. As Gary Burtless, R. Kent Weaver, and Joshua M. Wiener describe in chapter 3, this law transformed the aid to families with dependent children program from a federal entitlement into a block grant to states, placed time limits on federally financed cash assistance for nonaged, nondisabled adults and their children, imposed stricter work requirements on their receipt of cash assistance and food stamps, and eliminated means-tested benefits for most noncitizen legal aliens. While some might have hoped that this reform would take welfare off the policy agenda, this is not likely to be the case. Medicaid, the largest and fastest growing component of the welfare system, was not changed. In addition, the president indicated that he would seek modifications from the 105th Congress when he signed the reform bill. Furthermore, it is not at all clear that the changes called for by the new law can be realized or will leave the nation with a system with which the American people are comfortable.

Although medicaid spending slowed to a crawl during 1996, most experts expect this program, if not reformed, will begin growing in the future at unsustainable rates because of demographic factors, the erosion of employer-sponsored insurance, and the continued expansion of the capabilities and cost of medical care. Thus some structural changes in the current program are probably inevitable if the budget is to be balanced. Change is also being demanded by the states, which want fiscal relief and more program flexibility.

When Congress and the president address medicaid, they will have to decide whether to maintain the federal entitlement or let states decide which of their low-income residents should receive health coverage, whether national standards should be maintained, how federal funds directed at health care for low-income groups should be distributed among the states, how much states should be required to contribute of their own resources to this purpose, and how much spending can be cut back without compromising the health status of the poor. Burtless, Weaver, and Wiener argue that it is important to maintain the federal entitlement, that national minimum standards are vital but in certain areas more state flexibility is appropriate, that the distribution formulas for federal medicaid funds should better reflect differences in state need, that states should not be permitted to reduce their effort significantly, and that federal policymakers should be very cautious as they reduce funding, for there is little hard evidence that efficiencies can significantly reduce the rate of growth of medicaid expenditures.

Under the Personal Responsibility and Work Opportunity Act, new questions will develop that may require reactions from federal policymakers. With hard time limits, significant numbers of people might find themselves cut off from federal cash assistance in five years and subject to significant hardship. The allocation of block grant funds across the states, based largely on past spending patterns, may not reflect the future distribution of need among the states. The incentives inherent in the new system may cause states to ratchet down their benefit levels and tighten eligibility so as not to attract low-income people from more penurious neighboring states. Funding may prove to be woefully inadequate and work requirements unattainable when the next severe economic downturn hits. Burtless, Weaver, and Wiener believe that a number of modifications should be made in the Personal Responsibility and Work Opportunity Act to respond to these potential problems.

The Future of Federal Nondefense Activities

All the plans that have been proposed to balance the budget call for deep but unspecified reductions in the federal government's nondefense discretionary activities. These activities include a diverse array of programs, including international affairs, environmental protection, national parks, space exploration, housing assistance, education grants to states and localities, and compensation for the nondefense federal work force. Chapter 4 questions how realistic it is to promise to cut such spending in real terms by one-fifth below 1996 levels, as all of the balanced budget plans would do. If this were done, by 2002 spending on nondefense discretionary activities, as a percentage of GDP, would fall to levels similar to those of the early 1950s, when the federal government did not engage in many activities that are thought of as routine today. Space science and exploration, environmental protection, extensive subsidization of biomedical research, food assistance to poor pregnant women and children, rental and home ownership assistance for the poor, grants to help low-income students attend postsecondary educational institutions, education grants to states for preschool programs, and much more were not viewed as federal responsibilities.

This chapter concludes that it is unlikely that nondefense discretionary spending can be cut by the promised amounts. Some programs in this portion of the budget constitute essential activities of a modern nation state—customs and immigration control, federal courts and prisons, and public health, for example. Others—such as veterans' health and the National Institutes of Health—are extremely popular. If such activities are not cut or are cut only modestly, the remainder of the nondefense discretionary budget would have to be decimated. Americans are unlikely to accept this. Furthermore, states and localities, which are the direct beneficiaries of over one-third of nondefense discretionary spending, would be faced with difficult decisions if such cuts were made. Would they step in as the federal government withdraws? Even though the proposed reductions are probably unattainable, significant reductions can be made in this portion of the budget and, if done wisely, need not cause severe disruption.

National Security in the Post–Cold War World

The national security challenge facing the United States has changed radically during the 1990s as the Soviet empire has disintegrated and the United States has been left as the sole global power. As John D. Steinbruner and William W. Kaufmann point out in chapter 5, the relative strength of U.S. forces has grown even though the nation's defense establishment has been scaled back significantly. While at first blush this may seem to be a welcome development, overwhelming superiority may not prove to be the best long-run posture if it forces Russia and those outside the U.S. alliance system, many of whom face severe financial constraints and threats of internal social disintegration, to rely excessively on their nuclear forces. Steinbruner and Kaufmann propose gradually replacing the current posture of implicit confrontation with a more cooperative approach, in which the United States, Russia, China, and others agree to limit the size of their forces and the rate of investment in new weaponry and position their strategic weapons so as to reduce the possibility of surprise attack.

Terrorism and the threats from rogue states are not likely to recede in the near future even if more cooperative arrangements are forged between the United States, Russia, and China. Nevertheless, Steinbruner and Kaufmann argue that, especially within a fully articulated cooperative approach, the nation's defense establishment can be scaled back significantly while preserving sufficient capability to meet threats from any potential adversary. If the U.S. force structure is not scaled back, sharp increases will be needed in investment expenditures early in the twenty-first century as expensive equipment is needed to replace the hardware bought during the 1980s defense buildup. If it is scaled back, defense can contribute further to the effort to balance the budget.

Restructuring Medicare

The medicare program, the crown jewel of Lyndon Johnson's Great Society initiative, has been a tremendous public policy success, providing the elderly and disabled with access to high-quality, affordable medical care. The public-sector costs of the program, however, have been growing at unsustainable rates in part because its structure provides few incentives for efficiency. As David M. Cutler lays out in chapter 6, there are three basic strategies for reining in medicare costs: cutting back payments to providers, shifting more of the program's cost onto beneficiaries, and restructuring the program to incorporate market incentives to reward efficiency. In the short run, significant budget savings can be generated only from the first two strategies. Over the longer run, structural reform is inescapable if costs are to be controlled.

The type of structural reform Cutler finds most promising involves converting medicare into a choice-based system in which participants would select from a wide range of competing health plans operating within a fairly tightly regulated market. The government would pay risk-adjusted amounts to plans, and participants would be responsible for the difference between these contributions and the full cost of the plan. Participants would then have an incentive to seek out plans that provided care in the most cost-effective manner. Such a structure would require a number of safeguards. All plans would have to provide a minimum package of benefits and meet minimum quality standards. They would be required to provide prospective participants with the information necessary to make an informed choice. Low-income elderly people would have to be provided with supplemental resources, as they are today through the medicaid program, so that they would not be confined to the least expensive plan. Measures would also be needed to ensure that plans did not seek out only low-risk participants or that participants did not cluster excessively in plans according to their social or economic characteristics.

Cutler reminds policymakers that medicare is an interconnected piece of the nation's larger health care system. Medicare reforms can not succeed if they contradict the trends in the broader health care market. Furthermore, the effort to restrain medicare costs will not succeed if the costs of individual and employer-sponsored health insurance are running amok.

The Lure of Fundamental Tax Reform

Just one decade after President Reagan signed the Tax Reform Act of 1986, which broadened the income tax base and lowered rates significantly, fundamental tax reform is back on the policy agenda. The tax reform movement is being driven again by the desire to simplify the current system and by a conviction that substituting some form of consumption tax for the current income tax will spur economic growth. Some conservatives also hope to use tax reform to scale back the size of government; some liberals hope that a reformed tax system could be used to generate the revenues needed to balance the budget without jeopardizing worthwhile federal programs. In chapter 7, Henry J. Aaron and William G. Gale warn that a reform that substitutes some form of consumption tax for the income tax will confront the American people and their elected representatives with some wrenching choices.

Because the existing tax system is imbedded in the nation's economic, social, and institutional structures, transition from the old to the new regime would involve unavoidable disruption. Tax burdens, asset values, and the financial viability of state and local governments and for-profit and not-for-profit institutions would be affected. The authors' review of several recent empirical studies suggests that substituting a consumption tax for the income tax could substantially affect the value of owner-occupied housing, the prevalence of employer-financed health insurance, the extent of charitable giving, and the competitiveness of businesses with large amounts of undepreciated assets and loss carryovers. There are ways to ameliorate these effects, but all involve narrowing the tax base and raising rates.

The dislocations and inequities associated with fundamental tax reform would be acceptable if the reform greatly boosted economic growth. Unfortunately, a good deal of uncertainty surrounds estimates of the effect of such reform on growth. A pure consumption tax might increase the level of GDP by 6 percent over a decade. However, shifting "cold turkey" to such a tax would be a shock because there would be no personal exemptions, no transition relief for businesses, and no deductions for mortgage interest, charitable contributions, or large health expenditures. A consumption-based tax that accommodated such concerns would have little or no appreciable effect on economic growth over the next decade. As Aaron and Gale conclude, fundamental tax reform looks more attractive from a distance than from up close.

Preparing for the Baby Boomers' Retirement

Balancing the budget by 2002 is a relatively manageable problem compared with the fiscal challenge that will face the nation in the second and third decades of the twenty-first century. If tax and spending policies are not modified significantly, deficits will grow to unsustainable levels primarily because the large baby boom generation will be drawing retiree entitlement benefits and the cost of medical services will continue to grow. In chapter 8, Henry J. Aaron and Barry Bosworth explain that resolving this problem need not be a zero-sum game in which either future retirees bear the burden of the adjustment through reduced benefits or future workers pay through higher taxes. Instead, the nation's resource base, from which future retiree benefits and consumption for nonretirees must be drawn, can be expanded by funding the retirement-oriented entitlement programs to a greater degree than is now the case. This can be accomplished by increasing either public or private saving.

Of these programs, social security represents a smaller financial problem than either medicare or medicaid. At least three broad strategies are available to bring long-run projected social security expenditures more in line with expected revenues. The first would maintain the existing structure but reduce benefits (possibly by raising further the normal retirement age or reducing the amount by which benefits are indexed each year), raise taxes, and invest the trust fund reserves in higher-yielding assets. A second strategy would be to convert social security into a means-tested program, making benefits more like welfare payments. A third approach would be to privatize social security, gradually transforming it from a government-financed, defined-benefit program into a privately financed, defined-contribution program.

Similar types of options are available to limit the future fiscal burden of medicare. The age at which benefits are available could be increased from 65 to 67. Either payroll taxes on workers or some broader tax could be raised. Program participants could be asked to bear more of the costs through increased premium payments, higher copayments, and larger deductibles. Payments to providers could be scaled back. Medicare could also be transformed into a defined-contribution program along the lines discussed in chapter 6.

Aaron and Bosworth conclude that the pension and health costs of future retirees constitute a surmountable problem if the nation plans ahead. If national saving can be increased by a little more than 5 percent of GDP—about as much as saving has declined over the past quarter of a century—the additional growth of GDP would be about the same amount as the increase in government spending on retirement programs over the next thirty years.

Conclusion

Important issues other than those discussed in this volume will also vie for the attention of policymakers over the next few years. Education, urban revitalization, the environment, public safety, immigration, and drugs are just some of these. It will be a challenge for President Clinton and the 105th Congress to focus on only a few of the most important issues. They will face many obstacles and diversions. Time, interparty comity, executive-congressional cooperation, and public involvement—the important intangible inputs to successful policymaking—are in limited supply and can be quickly dissipated.

Unexpected adverse developments, some of which will be regarded as crises, will inevitably arise. A recession could bring the positive economic environment of 1993–96 to an end. Aggressive actions by rogue states, a spread of state-sponsored terrorism, or social disintegration in Russia, China, or a number of smaller nations could make the international environment more dangerous and demand the attention of policymakers.

The issues discussed in this volume are diverse, but taken together they point in one direction, to the future. The energies of policymakers should be concentrated on measures that are most consequential for the nation's long-run well-being. The decade from 1997 to 2007 offers an opportunity—perhaps a final chance—for the nation to deal in a measured but preemptive way with the major adjustments in policy required to accommodate the baby boom generation's retirement in the second and third decades of the twenty-first century. The share of the nation's population 65 or older will remain almost constant at 12.5 percent over the next decade. It will then rise steadily, reaching over 20 percent of the population by 2035.

An important first step in preparing for a future in which a growing portion of the population is dependent on government transfers would be to bring the budget into balance, or even to move it into surplus. This would strengthen the economy and expand the base from which private and public consumption is taken. Modest structural reforms of the retirement entitlement programs in the next few years could contribute to the goal of balancing the budget early in the next century. But such reforms are unlikely unless the president uses his "bully pulpit" to educate the public on the nature of the problem, the alternative ways of dealing with it, and the consequences of inaction. If more modest reforms are not adopted soon, future adjustments will have to be more wrenching. Inaction during the next decade will almost certainly narrow the available policy options and increase the possibility that taxes will be raised significantly. New bipartisan institutions might have to be created to minimize the chances that sensible solutions will fall victim to divisive and destructive political battles to achieve short-run partisan advantage.

The pressures and incentives on policymakers will be to address the problems that seem most immediate—the myriad of day-to-day crises—but history will judge today's leaders according to whether they chose to address the nation's less apparent, but more significant, problems: the ones that will not fully emerge for several decades but will significantly determine the strength of the American economy and quality of life in the first half of the twenty-first century.

References

Levit, Katharine R., Helen C. Lazenby, and Lekha Sivarajan. 1996. "Health Care Spending in 1994: Slowest in Decades." *Health Affairs* 15 (Summer): 130–44.

Reischauer, Robert D. 1996. "Reducing the Deficit: Past Efforts and Future Challenges." Frank M. Engle Lecture. Bryn Mawr, Pa.: American College (May 6).

U.S. Bureau of the Census. 1996. "Poverty in the United States: 1995." *Current Population Reports*, series P-60, no. 194.

U.S. National Center for Health Statistics. 1995. *Health, United States, 1994.* (PHS) 95-1232. Hyattsville, Md.: Public Health Service.

CHARLES L. SCHULTZE

2

Is Faster Growth the Cure for Budget Deficits?

BETWEEN 1992 and 1996, the budget deficit fell sharply, from 4.7 percent of gross domestic product to 1.4 percent. However, the Congressional Budget Office (CBO) projects that without further budget-paring actions the deficit will soon begin rising again, approaching 3 percent of GDP by 2002. The administration's projections are more optimistic but also show the deficit beginning to increase shortly after the turn of the century. Looking further into the future—over the next thirty to fifty years—both the CBO and the administration project a rapid and significant deterioration in the budget situation. A sharp rise in the number of social security retirees starting in about 2010, when the leading edge of the baby boom generation turns 62, together with the expectation that federal health care costs will continue to rise rapidly, raises the specter of federal deficits soaring to unsustainable levels of well above 10 percent of GDP.[1]

Budget projections, however, are far from infallible, especially as they peer into the distant future. The deficit is the difference between two very large numbers—federal revenues and federal expenditures—for which long-term projections contain considerable uncertainty. Although there are many reasons for that uncertainty, two are particularly important. On the spending side, the budget forecasts for the next decade are driven by the assumption, grounded in recent experience, that the costs of federal health care programs will continue to rise rapidly. The critical importance of this assumption is illustrated by the fact that the federal budget would come into balance by 2005 if medicare and medicaid spending grew at a rate that matched general

---

1. When the CBO allows in its projections for the sharp rise in interest rates that would inevitably follow budget deficits of this size, a truly explosive growth in the deficit occurs. In other words, a scenario in which the budget deficit is left to grow unchecked would turn out to be economically unsustainable.

35

inflation plus the growth in the number of recipients, rather than at the expected pace of over 9 percent a year.

The deficit projections are also driven by the assumed rate of growth of GDP, which primarily affects the revenue side of the budget. Despite some modest differences, the CBO and the administration essentially agree on the two critical elements in their economic projections: that the American economy is now operating and will continue to operate at or very close to full employment; and that, at full employment, the economy can be expected to expand by a little over 2 percent a year for the next ten years. This latter figure is derived from assumptions that the labor force will grow at about 1 percent a year, and output per worker by about 1.1 percent. In the years after 2005, output per worker is projected to continue rising as before, but labor force growth will slow (due to a decreased growth of the working-age population) and the annual growth of GDP will fall gradually to less than 1.5 percent.

Under current tax laws, every dollar of additional GDP brings in a little over twenty cents in additional revenue to the federal treasury. If GDP were to grow substantially faster over the next decade than is expected by the Office of Management and Budget and the CBO— say by an additional 1 percent a year—federal revenues at the end of that period would exceed currently projected levels by some $240 billion. As a bonus, the lower annual deficits produced by the extra revenues would slow the growth in the federal debt and also lead to lower interest rates; on both counts, federal spending for interest payments would decline. Lower interest rates would also increase the share of national income going to corporate profits, raising federal revenues even a bit more. Together, the higher revenues and lower spending on interest would be enough to bring the budget into balance by 2006 without policy actions, as long as the higher GDP and the larger federal revenues did not become an occasion to raise federal spending above the levels now projected.

The 2 to 2¼ percent rates of economic growth projected by the CBO and the administration for the next decade are not much different from the average growth the country experienced over the past two decades, but they are substantially below the 4 percent growth the nation enjoyed from 1947 to 1973.[2] This fact has led some ob-

---

2. From 1973 to 1995, GDP rose at an annual rate of 2.5 percent. The slightly slower growth projected by the CBO and the administration for the period ahead arises solely

servers from both sides of the political spectrum to argue that economic policies are available that could generate a rate of growth more like those of the past. On the conservative side, the National Association of Manufacturers, publisher and former presidential candidate Steve Forbes, and vice presidential candidate Jack Kemp take such a point of view. On the liberal side, the AFL-CIO and such well-known figures as Professor Lester Thurow and investment banker Felix Rohatyn come to the same conclusion. Needless to say, the two groups disagree on most of the specific policies they believe would be required to achieve this happy outcome.

The primary reason for adopting policies to speed up growth is not, of course, to come closer to a balanced budget but to improve national living standards. Nevertheless, if it were possible to design policies that would substantially raise the rate of growth, a major side benefit would be the effect on the federal budget. For those on the left, the deficit could be eliminated with much less severe cuts in federal social programs. For those on the right, more of the expenditure cuts could be channeled into lowering taxes rather than having to go toward deficit reduction.

This chapter examines whether there are changes in national economic policies that could reasonably be expected to produce increases in the level and rate of growth in GDP large enough to reduce the deficit significantly. In addition to examining effects in the medium term (that is, by the year 2002), the analysis will consider whether changes in economic policy can help deal with the budget problems that will begin to develop in the second decade of the next century, when the baby boom generation begins to hit retirement age.

The question of whether the U.S. economy could be made to grow substantially faster can conveniently be divided into two kinds of issues. The first of these involves the policies of the Federal Reserve: could an easier monetary policy allow the economy to grow substantially faster than is now in prospect? The CBO and the administration believe that, under current conditions, the American economy has reached full employment and can no longer grow faster than about 2 to 2¼ percent a year without overheating the economy and raising inflation. The Federal Reserve has made no pronouncements on its estimates of the long-term growth potential, but its policies have been

---

because the labor force is expected to grow a little less rapidly; the projected rate of productivity growth is unchanged from its average since 1973.

consistent with the assessments of the CBO and the OMB.[3] Whenever the growth of economic activity threatens to exceed 2 percent or so, the Fed has shown itself ready to boost interest rates to prevent higher growth from being realized. But is the Fed being too cautious? Would a more venturesome policy of easier credit and lower interest rates produce higher output without setting off inflationary pressures, giving American citizens not only the direct benefits of higher incomes but also the side benefit of reduced budget deficits?

Even if the Fed's policy is appropriate, given current limits to economic growth, there are those who argue that national policies can be devised to substantially raise those limits. The enactment of such policies would allow the Fed gradually to relax its caution and accommodate the enhanced growth potential with easier money policies. This is the supply-side issue.

Four major types of supply-side policies have been proposed. The first of these is fundamental tax reform. For example, the recent report of the Republican Kemp commission, which investigated the growth potential of the flat tax and similar radical tax reforms, stated that shifting from income taxes to consumption taxes would "help double the rate of economic growth."[4] Substantial tax cuts are a second supply-side suggestion for boosting economic growth. The third supply-side policy, favored mainly by Democratic liberals, calls for a major expansion in government investment in education and training and much larger public investments in traditional infrastructure. Deregulation is a fourth supply-side policy, favored aggressively by newer Republican members of Congress who have argued that economic potential can be significantly expanded through relaxing and rolling back "excessive" environmental and related regulations.

Before examining the Federal Reserve and supply-side issues, some preliminary discussion of what is meant by "economic growth" is essential to make sure we know what evidence to look for and what questions to ask.

---

3. According to Fed Chairman Alan Greenspan, the Fed does not need to have a firm judgment about the rate of potential GDP growth, since "persistent deviation from that capacity potential would soon send signals that a policy adjustment is needed." (Greenspan, 1996, p. 318). But the Fed's actions in the recent past have been consistent with the view that the nation's long-term growth potential is not much above 2 percent a year.

4. National Commission on Economic Growth and Tax Reform (1996, p. 5).

A Critical Distinction: Stimulating Demand versus Increasing Supply

When the economy is in the midst of a recession, or only partway into recovery from recession, a good bit of economic slack exists. Unemployment is higher than in times of prosperity, and there is unused productive capacity. Labor and capital resources stand idle because aggregate demand (spending)—by domestic consumers, governments, business investors, and foreign customers—is too small to purchase the volume of goods and services a fully employed economy could produce. Since business firms ultimately will not produce what they can not sell, the country's actual GDP falls below its capacity, or potential GDP.

When there is substantial economic slack, a policy of low interest rates can stimulate additional demand or spending—especially for big-ticket items such as housing, automobiles, and business investment, which are often bought with credit. This generates substantial additions to actual GDP as idle workers and industrial capacity are put back to work. But once the economy has reached full employment, additional large increases in spending stimulated by continued easy money policies will cause overheating and increasingly be dissipated in higher inflation rather than creating more output. Beyond the point of full employment, the nation's spending and production can grow on a sustained basis only as fast as its productive capacity expands.

To judge the appropriateness of current Federal Reserve policy, two questions must be answered: how much slack is there in today's economy (or, put another way, how low can unemployment be pushed before inflationary problems arise?); and how fast is the economy's supply potential likely to grow over the near-term future? The answer to this latter question shows how fast the Fed can afford to let GDP grow each year while still avoiding a speedup in inflation.

Figure 2-1 depicts the growth of the country's potential and actual GDP over the past thirty years. When recessions have occurred, substantial slack has developed and actual GDP has fallen below potential. Periods of economic overheating, which are marked by an excess of actual GDP relative to potential GDP, have been associated with rising inflation (although factors other than excessive demand, such as the large oil price increases of 1973–74 and 1979–80, have sometimes been responsible for a rise in inflation). The figure is drawn to

FIGURE 2-1. Actual and Potential GDP

GDP[a]

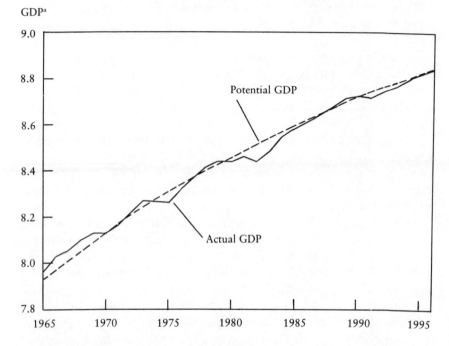

SOURCES: Department of Commerce; Congressional Budget Office; and author's estimates (1996 partly estimated.)
a. Logarithms of GDP in 1992 prices.

reflect the view, consistent with the Fed's current policies, that there is little or no slack left in the economy and that the growth of potential GDP in the near future will remain at about its current 2 to 2¼ percent annual rate. But is that right?

Federal Reserve Issue 1: How Much Slack?

Because wages make up 65 to 70 percent of costs in the American economy, economists concentrate on conditions in the labor market in trying to determine how much slack exists and whether the economy is operating at full employment. The demand for labor can run ahead of supply and wage increases can begin to accelerate when the unemployment rate is still well above zero. Millions of young people start looking for their first job each year, and others (for example, women whose children have reached school age) reenter the labor market. Usually these individuals are unemployed for a period of time as they search for the job they want. Even in booming times, some firms and industries experience falling sales and have to lay off workers, who usually must search a while before finding a new job. The demand for labor may be increasing in locations and for skills that do not mesh exactly with the locations and skills of those who have been laid off. There is, therefore, some minimum level of unemployment that will still exist even when the economy is at full employment and the overall demand for labor matches the supply of labor available for work. But how large is that minimum?

To answer this question, economists have developed a concept called the nonaccelerating inflation rate of unemployment (NAIRU), which is the rate that is consistent with an unchanged level of wage and price inflation. When economic conditions are buoyant enough and the demand for labor is sufficiently strong to push overall unemployment below the NAIRU, the rate of wage and price inflation begins to speed up. When unemployment exceeds the NAIRU, inflation slows down. And whenever economic conditions and overall labor demand keep unemployment about equal to the NAIRU, the inflation rate remains roughly unchanged from year to year.

In theory, economic research can identify the level of the NAIRU by examining historical evidence to see the level of unemployment at which inflation begins to rise or fall. In practice, however, that estimation is fraught with difficulty, for a number of reasons. Twice in the past twenty-five years world oil prices have jumped substantially, pushing up the cost of living and inducing a speedup in wages quite apart from any excessive demand for labor. In the early 1970s the rate of growth in productivity fell sharply, tending to raise the growth of costs and prices even without an excessive demand for labor.

In addition, the NAIRU does not necessarily remain the same over time. Since average unemployment rates among young people are higher than those among experienced workers, a shift in the age structure of the labor force can change the NAIRU. And, if economic conditions develop in such a way that there is a particularly large and persistent mismatch between the locations and skills of the unemployed and the locations and skills of new jobs, the unemployment rate associated with full employment—the NAIRU—is likely to rise. If an unusually large number of workers become discouraged over job prospects and stop looking for work, the official unemployment number will underestimate the degree of slack in the labor market.

Finally, research on the behavior of unemployment and inflation in both Europe and the United States has raised the possibility that long periods of high unemployment may themselves increase the NAIRU, while periods of sustained prosperity may lower it. For example, when unemployment remains high for a long period of time, as it has in many European countries over the past fifteen years, the skills of the unemployed do not keep up with the demands of a changing technology. As a result, when demand and spending rise in an economic recovery, labor shortages and inflation can develop more quickly and at higher levels of unemployment than was formerly the case. Conversely, periods of prosperity and high employment help keep the skills of the labor force more nearly in line with the demands of modern technology and also lower the NAIRU.

Despite the difficulties of pinning down the exact level of the NAIRU, a substantial amount of economic research has been devoted to estimating its value and changes in its value over the past forty years. The consensus is that the NAIRU was in the range of 4½ to 5½ percent in the late 1950s and early 1960s, rose to about 6 percent or perhaps a little higher by the end of the 1970s, and remained there during the 1980s. Judging from the experience of 1995 and 1996, when the unemployment rate has been under 6 percent and inflation has not accelerated, it is likely that the NAIRU has fallen below 6 percent. The latest estimates of Robert Gordon, one of the foremost researchers analyzing these issues, suggests that the NAIRU may have fallen in recent years into a range between 5.2 and 5.7 percent.[5] The Congressional Budget Office has estimated it at 5.8 percent, and the Council of Economic Advisers (CEA) at 5.7 percent.[6]

The postwar years have, on a number of occasions, witnessed the inflationary consequences when unemployment falls below the NAIRU. For example, during the Vietnam War the budget deficit rose sharply, aggregate spending in the economy was not checked by rising interest rates, and the unemployment rate was pushed down well below the NAIRU of that period. Shortly thereafter, inflation began to rise steadily, growing from 1½ percent in 1964 to 4½ percent by 1969. In 1971, with unemployment hovering just about at the NAIRU, President Richard Nixon introduced wage and price controls, which temporarily lowered the inflation rate. But the economic

5. Gordon (forthcoming).
6. Congressional Budget Office (1996, p. 133, table E1); *Economic Report of the President*, 1996, p. 53.

FIGURE 2-2. Unemployment and Inflation, 1992–96

Percent

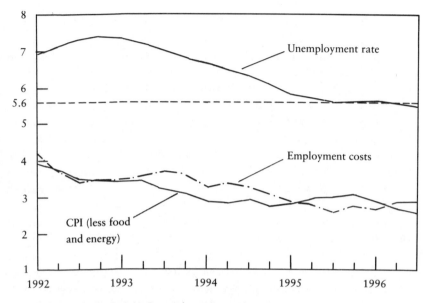

SOURCE: Bureau of Labor Statistics. Data are four-quarter moving averages.

expansion of 1972 and 1973 pushed unemployment below the NAIRU, and when price and wage controls were lifted in early 1973, inflation began rising. In 1978–79 and 1988–90 economic expansion pushed the unemployment rate below the 6 percent level of the NAIRU, which again helped speed up inflation.

Figure 2-2 shows the situation through the third quarter of 1996. Both price and wage inflation fell gently during 1992, 1993, and 1994, when unemployment exceeded 5.6 percent. But more recently, as unemployment stabilized around that 5.6 percent rate and then fell below it, the rate of wage and price inflation fluctuated around a more nearly constant level, suggesting an economy at or near its high-employment level.

An Extreme Case for a More Expansive Monetary Policy

Recently, some analysts and policymakers have argued that this conclusion is wrong and that there are many idle resources that could be put back to work by an increase in demand without increasing inflationary pressures. Typical of this view is the contention of Lester Thurow that the official unemployment statistics vastly understate the extent of unemployment and underemployment in the American economy.[7] He estimates that "one-third of the American workforce is potentially looking for more work than they now have."

A careful analysis reveals a number of reasons to conclude that Thurow's estimates are a massive exaggeration of the slack in the labor market. First, and most important, there has always been a significant number of working-age people who were not counted as unemployed but who might enter the job market or work longer hours, especially during times of low unemployment and tight labor markets.[8] Yet, even though the existence of these workers moderated wage pressures, inflation did accelerate when the official unemployment rate dipped significantly below the values associated with the NAIRU, as occurred in the periods discussed above.

The number of additional workers who typically are drawn into the labor force when unemployment falls can be estimated using statistical techniques to separate the impact of the business cycle on overall labor force participation rates from the longer-term trends in participation. When unemployment was high in the recessions of 1969–70, 1974–75, 1981–82, and 1990–91, the participation rate fell relative to the longer-term trends, which are depicted in figure 2-3 by the dashed line. During periods of low unemployment, it rose. But statistical analysis suggests that these cyclical movements are small. Since 1965 the participation rate has tended to rise only a little over 0.1 percentage point above its time trend for each 1 percentage point fall in the unemployment rate. In the boom years from 1966 to 1969, when the unemployment rate averaged a remarkably low 3.7 percent, the overall participation rate was only 0.3 percent above its trend. There is nothing in the data to suggest that the responsiveness of the labor force (or average hours of work) to reductions in the unemployment rate has become significantly larger in recent years.

7. Thurow (1996, p. 56).

8. When the economy is recovering from recession and unemployment is falling, not only do labor force participation rates and average hours of work rise, but productivity tends to grow a little faster than its trend. This is a cyclical phenomenon, however. As recession occurs, layoffs tend to lag behind the fall in output, and employers build up a temporary surplus of unneeded labor (productivity declines). As a consequence, when recovery starts, output can, for a little while, grow faster than employment (productivity increases faster than normal). But a "permanent" fall in unemployment to a new lower level would not generate a permanent increase in productivity to a new higher level.

FIGURE 2-3. Labor Force Participation Rate, 1954–95

Percent of population aged 16 and over

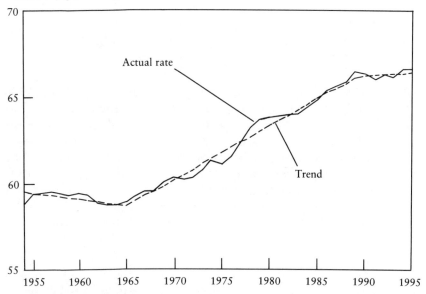

SOURCES: Bureau of Labor Statistics; author's estimates.

(Recall that inflation rose steadily during the 1966–69 period, when unemployment remained substantially below the NAIRU.)

As figure 2-3 shows, the labor force participation rate rose fairly steadily from 1965 through 1989, after which it leveled off through both recession and recovery. Does this imply that there has been a large increase in the number of potential workers who could be drawn back into the labor force if only the Federal Reserve would stimulate the demand for labor with an easier money policy? A close examination of the reasons for the leveling off of the participation rate suggests the answer to this question is "no." Part of the flattening in the overall growth of the labor force since 1989 is due to a virtual cessation in the strong postwar growth of the female participation rate. The causes of this development are still being untangled by researchers, but one natural explanation is that the long-term decline in the number of children per working-age woman came to an end in the late 1980s.

The participation rate of males aged 25 to 54 also fell sharply after

1989. Could this reflect a dearth of job opportunities and the creation of a new pool of available workers who could be drawn into the labor market, thereby dampening inflationary pressures? The labor force participation rate of this group of workers has fallen throughout the last forty years, but at quite different speeds in different periods. It fell very slowly from the mid-1950s through 1966 but then, in a period of very strong labor demand, began to fall rapidly for ten years.[9] (The Vietnam War kept many males in school.) From 1976 through 1989 it once again fell very slowly, but then accelerated its decline after 1989. With this history, it is difficult to interpret the post-1989 decline as an indicator that the labor market is substantially weaker and economic slack is much higher than indicated by the official unemployment rate. On the other hand, it may be possible that the recent decline in the labor force participation rates of adult male workers could be one reason why the level of unemployment at which inflation begins to rise seems to have fallen below the 6 percent level.

Is it possible that the corporate downsizing of recent years has created a large group of workers who took new jobs at substantially reduced wages and would be available for work in higher-skill jobs if the demand for labor were stronger? This would free up their current jobs for the part-time workers who tell the Bureau of Labor Statistics (BLS) surveyors that they would like a full-time job. According to BLS surveys, the percentage of employees displaced by plant closings or downsizing has grown in recent years relative to today's low level of unemployment. But the rise in the displacement rate seems principally to have affected workers who had been on the job for less than three years. And the overall numbers are still modest compared with the roughly 12 million jobs created and destroyed in the United States each year. The major problem with displacements lies not so much in the growth of their numbers as in the fact that productivity and real wages are growing very slowly. It takes a long time for those who suffer a large wage cut after displacement to regain earlier living standards.

Are there other substantial groups of workers who might work more or more productively if the economy were growing faster and

9. Controlling for changes in unemployment, the annual trend decline in the labor force participation rate of males aged 25 to 54 was: 1954–66, −0.08, 1967–76, −0.23; 1977–88, −0.03; and 1989–95, −0.32.

therefore should be included in estimates of slack in the American economy? In building his estimate that "one-third of the labor force" was looking for more work, Thurow counts 8.3 million "self-employed 'independent contractors' (many of whom are downsized professionals who have very few clients but call themselves self-employed consultants because they are too proud to admit they are unemployed)." But this is certainly a vast overstatement of the marginal, self-employed labor force, considering that, in 1995 the *total* number of nonfarm self-employed—including many overworked doctors, lawyers, accountants, and shopkeepers—was only 8.9 million.[10]

Thurow also counts in his estimates of labor market slack the 5 million to 6 million people "who are not working, but who do not meet any of the tests for being active in the workforce and are therefore not considered unemployed." But, according to the BLS, only 1.6 million of this number have both bothered to look for work in the preceding twelve months and are currently available for work. The Thurow "one-third" estimate also includes 4.5 million people who are working part time for economic reasons but tell the census interviewers they would like to work full time. But according to the BLS only one-third of these individuals usually work full time. The Thurow numbers further include 2 million people described as working "on call," but this turns out to be the entire labor force of the temporary help agencies. Why they should be considered as part of the idle or semi-idle labor force is not clear. Having classified some one-third of the labor force as available for additional work, Thurow then says: "Add in another 11 million immigrants (legal and illegal) who entered the United States from 1980 to 1993 to search for more work and higher wages, and one has a sea of unemployed workers, underemployed workers, and newcomers looking for work."

Consequences for the Budget

Although it is indeed necessary to supplement the official unemployment rate with other information to judge the degree of slack in the American economy, the official unemployment rate remains a reasonably good, albeit imperfect, proxy for the complex constellation of circumstances that determine the overall tightness of the labor

10. U.S. Department of Labor (1996, p. 177, table 12).

market. Examinations of the degree to which the labor force participation rate responds to changes in unemployment, together with a
realistic assessment of the number of underutilized workers available
to increase their labor effort in response to a stronger economy, suggest no reason to change that evaluation.

Nevertheless, it is at least conceivable that the NAIRU has recently
fallen below the range of 5½ to 6 percent; if so, the economy could,
for a short while, grow at a faster pace than the Fed seems to be
targeting without triggering a rise in inflation. Moreover, past history
shows that if unemployment is pushed only modestly below the
NAIRU, as in 1988 and 1989, the resultant speedup in inflation is
likely to be quite gradual. For example, the CBO has estimated that
pushing the unemployment rate 1 percentage point below the NAIRU
for a year would lead to an increase of 0.5 percentage point in inflation—say, from 3 percent to 3.5 percent.[11] And Robert Gordon has
estimated that even after three years such a policy would raise the
inflation rate by only about 1 percentage point.[12] The central problem
with a mild and temporary overheating is not that the American
economy would quickly succumb to a spiral of rapid inflation. Rather,
it is that once inflation does take hold in a substantial way, it takes a
large dose of added economic slack and unemployment over a long
time to wring it out.

Given the uncertainties involved in pinning down the current value
of the NAIRU, a reasonable person might argue that the Fed should
carefully probe the possibility of achieving a lower level of unemployment and gently nudge the economy in that direction. If the
assumption of a lower NAIRU proves incorrect, the rise in inflation
would be slow enough to allow the Fed to reverse course without any
great cost. However, the evidence from a large body of economic
research and the simple story told in figure 2-2 are not likely to be
hugely in error. Perhaps the NAIRU has fallen toward 5 percent;
perhaps unemployment can safely be pushed a bit lower without
unwanted inflationary consequences. But it is exceedingly improbable
that the further reduction in unemployment could be greater than
one-half of 1 percent. And the balance of the evidence from the near
and distant past is that even such a gain is uncertain.

11. Congressional Budget Office (1994a).
12. Gordon (forthcoming).

Suppose, optimistically, that the Fed could successfully reduce interest rates and expand the economy sufficiently to push the unemployment rate down another one-half percentage point and hold it at or a little below 5 percent. How much of a contribution would this make to balancing the budget by 2002? First, consider the fact that unemployment would be lowered by one-half percent if for *one year* the GDP grew about 1 percentage point faster than the Fed's apparent 2 to 2¼ percent target. After this, GDP would resume its 2 to 2¼ percent growth, but its level would remain 1 percent higher than the path now projected by the CBO and OMB.[13] By 2002 that 1 percent higher level of GDP and national income would produce about $25 billion in additional tax revenues. Federal spending on unemployment compensation would be a little lower.

Each year between now and 2002 there would be lower deficits, and, correspondingly, a lower level of federal debt and lower interest payments than the CBO and OMB are now projecting. The lower deficits would also bring with them some reduction in interest rates, which would lead to lower federal spending on interest payments. Altogether, the budget deficit in 2002 might be roughly $40 billion lower—in other words, $245 billion instead of the $285 billion baseline deficit projected by the CBO in 1996.[14] This would obviously be a welcome development, but it would only marginally ease the pains of balancing the budget.

In sum, even if the Fed is being too cautious in its monetary policy because it is underestimating the degree of slack that still remains in the American economy, it is not far wrong. No reasonable correction of that underestimate will produce a windfall large enough to make any fundamental difference in what has to be done to achieve budget balance.

13. Following the previous analysis, the estimates in this chapter of the increase in GDP that would result from a reduction in unemployment assume that some marginal workers are drawn into the labor force and there is some increase in average weekly hours of work so that a one-half percentage point reduction in the unemployment rate is accompanied by a 1 percent rise in GDP.

14. This estimate is based on unemployment one-half percent below the NAIRU assumed by the CBO. As noted earlier, the CBO's long-term projections of the budget deficits assume that sometime in the next decade the economy will have a mild recession. They account for this possibility by keeping the unemployment rate each year a shade above the NAIRU. These estimates do not change that assumption.

Federal Reserve Issue 2: How Fast Is America's Economic Potential Growing?

Even if there is minimal slack left in the current system, the economy can continue to grow at the pace set by the expansion of its economic capacity, its potential GDP. An important question that must be answered, then, is "How fast is that potential growing?" Both the CBO and the administration have based their budget projections on the assumption that potential GDP is currently growing, and will continue to grow, at something like 2 to 2¼ percent a year. If they are correct, and the economy is already at or close to full employment, any tendency for actual GDP to rise faster than that would soon lead to an overheated economy and pressures for higher inflation in wages and prices. On the other hand, if those estimates are too conservative and the economy's potential is now or will shortly be growing faster than that, the Federal Reserve could relax its monetary reins, reduce interest rates, and permit GDP to grow at a faster pace. Significantly faster economic growth, sustained over a number of years, would make substantial inroads on the deficit. As was pointed out earlier, an additional 1 percent annual growth would generate enough extra revenues and other budget savings to balance the budget by about 2006. Unfortunately, the evidence seems overwhelming that, under current economic conditions and national economic policies, the CBO and OMB projections are not likely to be far off the mark. (The question as to whether major changes in national economic policies on taxes, infrastructure investment, and regulation could change this outcome is discussed later.)

Growth in the Labor Force and Productivity

The "standard" projection that potential GDP is growing at a little faster than 2 percent a year consists of a 1 percent annual expansion in labor input combined with a growth of a little over 1 percent a year in productivity (output per worker hour). There is little question that the working-age population will grow by about 1 percent a year over the next ten to fifteen years; the level of immigration is the only uncertainty. There is more doubt about the fraction of the working-age population who will participate in the labor force. The standard growth projections assume that the participation rate will remain

FIGURE 2-4. Nonfarm Business Productivity Growth, 1947–95

Output per worker[a]

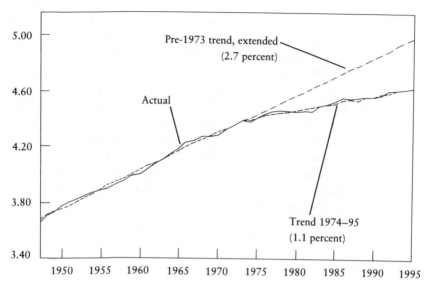

SOURCES: Bureau of Labor Statistics; author's estimates.
a. Logarithms of private nonfarm output per worker.

about where it is now or, at best, creep up very slowly.[15] It is possible that the participation rate might start rising again, but the burden of evidence does not give much hope. Furthermore, the number of hours worked each year by the average American has remained constant for more than a decade, and there is no reason to expect any change in the foreseeable future. Altogether, the standard assumption that labor input is likely to grow by about 1 to 1.1 percent a year seems unassailable.

The second component of the growth in potential GDP is rising productivity. As can be seen in figure 2-4, productivity growth in the nonfarm business sector slowed sharply after 1973, from almost 3 percent a year to a little over 1 percent. Despite a good deal of research, the reasons for this fall in productivity growth, which affected virtually all advanced economies, remain largely a mystery. In the United States, one development that helped keep the rate of pro-

15. *Economic Report of the President, 1996*, for example, assumes 0.1 percent a year future growth in the overall participation rate.

ductivity low was the post-1980 fall in national saving. Private saving shrank, and an increased fraction of that reduced saving was diverted to financing swollen budget deficits. As a consequence, the share of GDP devoted to net new investment declined. It would have declined even further had the United States not supplemented its shrunken domestic saving by borrowing heavily from abroad.

It is conceivable that the information revolution is slowly building a foundation for a new surge in the productivity of American industry. But so far there is no evidence that such a revolution has begun. Indeed, there is some direct evidence to the contrary. GDP grew at an annual rate just a shade under 2 percent from late 1994 to mid-1996. If economic capacity or potential GDP had been growing substantially faster than that during this period, economic slack and unemployment would have increased. In fact, however, unemployment fell in the first six months of that period and then was stable. And so, if productivity and the growth of economic potential are to speed up, it has not yet begun to happen. Although there is no satisfactory explanation for the slowdown in productivity growth after 1973, it is clear that pro- ductivity growth has remained steady at the new lower rate for over twenty years. It would be foolhardy to plan national policy on the simple hope that a speedup will soon be occurring.

A Measurement Error?

There is a widespread view among economists who have examined the issue that the official statistics may be understating the growth of output and productivity in the economy. The real, or inflation- adjusted, growth of GDP is estimated by subtracting the inflation rate from the annual growth in the nominal value of output. If the BLS tends to overstate inflation in consumer prices (because it does not sufficiently allow for improvements in quality of the goods and ser- vices that are produced or for other reasons), correcting that under- statement would show that real growth in the economy has been higher than previously estimated. Projections of future output ought to be raised accordingly. But the average level of prices would be lower by exactly the same amount, leaving unchanged the estimated growth in the dollar value of national output and income. Neverthe- less, the level of federal revenues would increase because certain fea- tures of the personal income tax (personal exemptions, standard de- ductions, and bracket values) are indexed to the consumer price index.

In addition, if the official estimates of inflation were lowered, the growth of outlays for social security and other spending affected by cost-of-living allowances would slow down and the deficit would be reduced.

Although there is wide agreement that official price measures overstate the inflation rate, there is no agreement on the size of that overstatement. Estimates range from 0.2 to 2 percent a year.[16] The Bureau of Labor Statistics, which produces the consumer price index, has made some changes in its procedures and will complete others within the next several years that will deal with part of the problem, but some, possibly significant, overstatement will still remain.

There have been proposals for legislation that, without changing the official CPI, would set future cost-of-living allowances and the inflation adjustment used to index the income tax equal to the growth in the CPI *minus* some percentage adjustment. The budget plan designed by the Senate Centrist Coalition, which received forty-six votes during the debate on the fiscal 1997 budget resolution, proposed an adjustment of one-half of 1 percent.[17] By 2002 this adjustment would have reduced the deficit by about $29 billion a year (plus an extra $5 billion a year in lower interest payments on the debt). But this would be the outcome of a policy decision, like any other policy decision with pros and cons, costs and benefits. It is not a budget dividend from higher growth.

In sum, the evidence is quite convincing that there are no feasible changes in Federal Reserve policies that, on their own, could produce either a large one-time gain in GDP or enough extra economic growth to make a substantial difference in the prospects for the federal budget over the foreseeable future. An effort to raise the level or speed up the growth of GDP to any substantial degree through measures that

16. In 1994 the CBO estimated that the overstatement of inflation in the CPI might amount to somewhere between 0.2 and 0.8 percent a year (Congressional Budget Office, 1994b). Late in 1995, a committee appointed by the Senate Committee on Finance and chaired by ex-CEA Director Michael Boskin estimated that the overstatement might range between 0.7 and 2 percent a year (Advisory Commission to Study the Consumer Price Index, 1995). A recent study (Shapiro and Wilcox, 1996) concludes that the overestimate ranges between 0.6 and 1.5 percent a year, with the most likely estimate a shade under 1 percent.

17. S. Con. Res. 57, amendment 4018, *Congressional Record*, May 23, 1996, pp. S5513-15. A similar proposal was put forward in the House of Representatives by a group of conservative Democrats and moderate Republicans known as "the Blue Dog Coalition." Their plan had an adjustment of 0.5 percentage point for 1997 and 1998 and 0.3 thereafter. The Coalition (1995).

timulate additional *demand* is sure to fail. However, that still leaves open the question of whether there are feasible and realistic policy measures that can significantly increase the level or growth of economic capacity, or *supply*. And it is to that question that this discussion now turns.

Supply-Side Policies to Speed Growth

In the developing economies of the third world, and in the transition economies of eastern Europe, growth can often be significantly accelerated by making fundamental changes in the economic role of government, usually in the direction of dismantling state controls over the economic system and opening the economy to the competitive forces of the world market. But these underlying requisites for economic growth are already present in the advanced nations of the world. Hyperbole aside, the policy proposals that are the stuff of political debate in the United States almost always involve changes at the margins of existing governmental policies rather than radical alterations in the scope of government.

Although the proposals made by the Republican leaders of the 104th Congress were revolutionary compared with recent policy initiatives, they were quite modest compared with the kinds of restructuring going on in eastern Europe or in some developing countries. The downsizing of the federal government envisioned in the Balanced Budget Act of 1995, which President Clinton vetoed, would have reduced federal spending by 2002 from 21.5 percent to 18.5 percent of GDP. Compared with the spending cuts or tax increases amounting to 10 or 15 percent of GDP that some developing countries have had to adopt to eliminate their budget deficits, this is a modest adjustment. A 15 percent reduction in individual income tax rates would reduce those taxes from 8.6 percent of GDP to a little under 7.5 percent, again an important change but not likely to revolutionize economic performance.

Small changes in the growth rate, if they persist for several decades, can have noticeable effects on the incomes of American families. Nevertheless, a central fact about supply-side policies is that even those that have a realistic possibility of making significant long-run improvements in the incomes and living standards of the American people will still not produce effects large enough to make a big dent in the budget deficit over the next decade or two. For example, a 20 percent improvement in the rate at which labor productivity is growing would raise the overall economic growth rate from 2.1 percent a year to 2.3 percent a year.[18] The extra 0.2 percent in the growth rate, if continued for a generation, would raise the income of the average American family by more than $2,000 (in 1996 dollars). That is no small amount, especially at a time when politicians will fall over themselves to take credit for a four-cent cut in gasoline taxes that would save the average family $38 a year. On the other hand, that same 0.2 percent increase in the growth rate would reduce the $285 billion budget deficit in 2002 only from 2.9 percent to 2.5 percent of GDP. Continued for a generation, the same 0.2 percent higher growth would pare the CBO's projected deficit from 8 percent to 5.5 percent of GDP, a sizable reduction but far from sufficient to eliminate the necessity of taking difficult budget-cutting actions.

Most supply-side policies involve either the loss of federal revenue (tax cuts) or additional federal expenditures for public investment in infrastructure, education, training, or research and development. By now even the most enthusiastic supporters of supply-side tax cuts or public investments do not contend that they will pay for themselves— that is, raise economic growth by enough to offset the loss in revenues or increases in expenditures. In a similar vein, "revenue-neutral" tax reforms require that some taxes be raised (usually on consumption or income from existing capital) in order to lower other taxes (usually taxes on the income from saving and new capital investment). And unless the tax increases are large enough to offset most of the initial revenue losses from the tax cuts, the deficit will be worsened.

In other words, supply-side policies are not relatively painless devices that will enable us to grow our way out of the budget deficit, however desirable those policies might be as a means to improve long-run living standards. Here, as elsewhere, we will have to make progress the old-fashioned way—by working for it. To eliminate the budget deficit, there is no substitute for spending cuts or tax increases. And to increase long-term economic growth and future living stan-

18. As noted earlier, the standard projections (CBO, OMB) assume that productivity will continue growing at 1.1 percent a year. A 20 percent improvement would raise that to 1.3 percent a year. With the labor force expected to grow at 1.1 percent a year, the new economic growth rate would be 2.3 percent, compared with the current projection of 2.1 percent.

dards through supply-side tax cuts or public investments, the nation will have to give up some other government spending today, over and above what is necessary to balance the budget.

In practical terms, there are four major types of supply-side policies currently being proposed as means of speeding up the nation's economic growth: tax reform; tax reduction (presumably accompanied by additional spending cuts); increased public investment in education, training, and infrastructure; and a streamlining and paring back of government environmental, health, and safety regulations.

Tax Reform

The potential effects of various tax reform proposals on long-term economic growth are discussed in more detail in chapter 7. This chapter simply summarizes those findings.

The objective of the reforms is essentially to improve incentives for saving and investment by reducing or eliminating the current income tax on the reward for saving, that is, taxes on interest income, dividends, and capital gains. The revenue loss would be paid for principally by shifting the burden of such taxes to consumption. Periodically, proposals to convert some or all of the present income tax to a value-added tax on consumption have been floated. More recently several more complicated proposals have been put forward to achieve the same objective while retaining some of the characteristics of an income tax: the flat tax and the USA tax are the most prominent of these proposals.[19]

Economists differ substantially over the increase in growth that might be expected if one of the tax reform proposals were to be enacted in its "pure" form. The authors of chapter 7, using optimistic assumptions of how saving and investment respond to increased incentives, conclude that the rate of economic growth might increase by as much as 0.6 percent a year if a "pure" consumption tax, unencumbered by the retention of current politically popular deductions, were substituted for the existing corporation and personal income taxes.

However, with the use of more realistic economic assumptions and a recognition that political considerations will burden the "pure" reform with various deductions, exemptions, and transition relief, a

19. Hall and Rabushka (1995); Gale (1995).

increase in labor supply. An elasticity of 0.33 would lead to a 1.7 percent increase in labor supply. Since labor costs constitute about 68 percent of GDP, the resultant gain in GDP would lie between 0.7 and 1.1 percent. While it might take a few years for the higher after-tax wages to affect labor market responses, the gain in GDP from this source should come relatively quickly (compared with the many years needed to realize the full benefits from an increase in the saving rate). But it is important to realize that this expansion in the labor supply will generate a one-time increase in GDP. Thereafter, GDP will grow at the same rate as before but along a higher path.

Effects on saving and investment. As in the case of labor supply, a tax cut that raises the after-tax return from saving has two effects. The higher net return makes it possible for people to achieve any given saving objective (for retirement or other purposes) with a smaller annual saving; they can now consume more without reducing their planned future income. But that same rise in the net return also means that each dollar saved brings higher net income in the future than it did before, which encourages more saving. There is considerable disagreement on the combined result of the two opposing influences. Some believe the overall effect of an increase in the return to saving is close to zero. One prominent macroeconomic textbook summarizes the empirical evidence: "Typically, research suggests the effects [on saving from a rise in the return to capital] are small and certainly hard to find."[25] The experience of the 1980s seems to bear that conclusion out: real interest rates rose to new highs and tax rates on capital income were cut in 1981 and 1986, yet the private saving rate fell substantially. Among the empirically based estimates of the responsiveness of saving to the rate of return, one of the highest was reported in 1978 in a well-known paper by Michael Boskin, who was the chairman of the CEA in the Bush administration. Boskin's results, applied to current data, suggest that a 1 percentage point increase in the after-tax return to savers would induce a 1.2 percentage point increase in the private saving share of national income.[26]

---

tax is about 22 percent (Auerbach, 1996). A 15 percent cut would lower that rate by 3.3 percentage points. The current net wage at the margin, after all taxes (federal, state, and local) is about two-thirds of the gross wage. The additional 3.3 percentage points would thus represent a 5 percent increase in the net wage.

25. Dornbusch and Fischer (1990, p. 289).

26. Boskin (1978) included in his measure of private saving the net investment by households in consumer durable goods. This component of his saving measure is not

The current marginal rate of federal taxation on income from capital, taking into account both individual and corporate income taxes, has been estimated at about 20 percent.[27] This is an average of a higher rate (29 percent) on income from corporate business investment and a much lower rate (6 percent) on the tax-favored housing component of investment. (The total effective tax rate on income from capital is higher than this, since it includes state and local income taxes, personal and corporate, as well as property taxes.) A 15 percent reduction in taxes would shave 3 percentage points off that federal tax rate. On the assumption that the real pre-tax return to additional capital investment is about 8 percent,[28] such a reduction would raise the after-tax return by 0.24 percentage point (that is, 0.03 × 8). In turn, using Boskin's relatively high estimate of responsiveness, the private saving rate would then rise from its current 5 percent of national income to 5.3 percent. An alternative estimate, midway between Boskin's and that of those who believe the response is essentially zero, would yield an increase in the saving rate to 5.15 percent as a result of the 15 percent tax cut.

How much would such increases in the saving rate boost the economy's growth rate over the next ten to twenty years? I assume that the returns to domestic and overseas investment are the same and that 60 percent of additional savings flows into domestic and 40 percent into foreign investment. Given the characteristics of the American economy, the standard economic model of the growth process suggests that, generously estimated, a 1 percentage point increase in the share of national income flowing to domestic investment would add about 0.1 percent to the growth of productivity and GDP.[29]

In recent years, several variants of a "new growth theory" have

---

included in the official (U.S. Department of Commerce) measures of private saving that are used in this chapter. The estimates in the text of the change in saving were first made in terms of the Boskin definition of saving and then adjusted to the official concept on the assumption that the increase was proportionately split between the two components of saving.

27. Auerbach (1996, table 2-2, p. 52).

28. This estimate of the pre-tax return averaged across all sectors (corporate and noncorporate business and owner-occupied housing) was derived starting with the estimate of 7.8 percent for corporate business given by Bosworth (1996) and using the techniques described in his footnote 13 to estimate the other sectors. The overall return (6.5 percent) was then raised to 8 percent to reflect recent increases in the profit rate.

29. This model was originally constructed by Robert Solow. Eventually GDP growth would settle back to its earlier rate, but along a higher path.

TABLE 2-1. Effect of a 15 Percent Tax Cut on the Level of GDP, Selected Years, 2002–17

Percent

Year	Less optimistic assumptions[a]	More optimistic assumptions[b]
2002	0.8	1.4
2007	0.9	1.6
2017	1.0	2.1

a. Assumes a labor supply elasticity of 0.2, an increase in the saving rate from 6 to 6.15 percent, and a 0.1 percent addition to GDP growth per 1 percentage point addition to the saving rate.

b. Assumes a labor supply elasticity of 0.33 percent, an increase in the saving rate from 6 to 6.3 percent (based on Boskin's elasticity; see Boskin 1978), and a 0.2 percent addition to growth per 1 percentage point increase in the domestic investment share of GDP.

proposed that an increase in investment brings with it various productivity-enhancing benefits that are not captured in the return to capital.[30] The new theory, for example, hypothesizes that investments by individual firms indirectly provide increased knowledge and other spillover benefits to the economy at large that are not reflected in the return earned by the investing firm. An increase in investment will consequently speed up productivity and economic growth by more than would be predicted from the standard growth models, which rely on the return to capital as the sole measure of the effect of investment in increasing output. The validity of the new theories is still in dispute. But, in recognition of the controversy, an alternative estimate of the effect of the tax cut was used that doubles the payoff from domestic business investment: each 1 percentage point increase in that investment share adds 0.2 percent to the GDP growth rate.

The estimated effects of a 15 percent tax cut (if enacted in 1996) on GDP, combining increases in both labor input and national saving and investment, are shown in table 2-1. Given the way they were derived, an average of the two estimates would provide a reasonably generous assessment of the potential GDP gain from a 15 percent tax cut fully implemented in 1997. On that basis, by 2002 GDP would be 1.1 percent higher than without the tax cut. Most of the gain would come relatively quickly from a one-time rise in labor input; the tax cut would not raise saving and the growth in the capital stock enough, even using Boskin's relatively high elasticity estimate, to increase the rate of economic growth significantly.

The revenue loss from a 15 percent cut in personal and corporate

30. Romer (1986, 1989). For a discussion, see Congressional Budget Office (1994c); Baily and Schultze (1990).

taxes would amount to about $150 billion a year in 2002. The resulting gain in GDP (based on the average of the two estimates) would produce only a modest offset by way of higher revenues, amounting to about $25 billion. Thus the *net* cost to the budget would be approximately $125 billion in 2002, which would have to be offset by additional spending cuts to keep the budget deficit from increasing above projected levels.[31] If no effort was made to offset the costs of the tax cut, the budget deficit would rise, an increased share of private saving would be diverted to financing that deficit, and private investment would decline. In this case, the end result of the tax cut would be to reduce economic growth.

From the standpoint of economic growth, the $125 billion in spending cuts needed to finance the net cost of a 15 percent tax reduction would be better used to reduce the budget deficit (or, if the budget were already balanced, to produce a budget surplus). The spending cuts would reduce the deficit directly and would gradually produce further large and growing budgetary savings by lowering interest rates and slowing the rise in the federal debt. Initially the tax cut would produce greater GDP gains. But six years after the spending cuts were fully in place, the gain in GDP from deficit reduction would equal the gain from the tax cut, and thereafter would exceed it by a growing amount. After fifteen years, deficit reduction would add about 3.5 percent to GDP, compared with a gain of some 1.5 percent from the tax cut.[32]

During the 1996 presidential campaign, Robert Dole proposed a package of tax reductions, including a 15 percent cut in personal

31. Economists Martin Feldstein (Feldstein, 1993; Feldstein and Feenberg, 1996) and Lawrence Lindsey (Lindsey, 1987) have argued that in addition to inducing more work effort, lower tax rates would lead taxpayers to take more of their income in taxable form rather than in fringe benefits or other tax-preferred ways. To the extent this occurred, it would increase the yield of the tax system and lower the net budgetary cost of the tax reduction. But the magnitude of these reactions is highly uncertain. Moreover, if the tax reduction widened the gap between the tax rate on capital gains and ordinary income, taxpayers would take steps to convert ordinary income to lower-taxed and deferrable capital gains income. I have not included estimates of such changes in income reporting in calculating the revenue offset to tax cuts.

32. The estimated gain from the tax cut assumes a payoff based on the average of the traditional and "new" growth theories. The gain from deficit reduction assumes that national saving rises by 80 percent of the deficit reduction; 60 percent of the additions to national saving flow into domestic and 40 percent into foreign investment; and each 1 percentage point increase in the domestic and foreign investment shares of national income adds 0.11 and 0.08 percentage point, respectively, to growth.

income taxes. The tax cut analyzed here included a 15 percent cut in both personal and corporate taxes. However, the Dole proposal included a 50 percent reduction in the tax on capital gains. There is no reason to believe that the effect on economic growth from these elements of the Dole plan, when fully implemented, would be outside the range estimated above (given the important caveat that the net costs of the tax cuts would be fully offset by spending reductions).

Investing in Education, Training, and Infrastructure

Improvements in the quality of the work force through investment in education and training have long been recognized as a major contributor to economic growth. Edward Denison, in his pioneering studies of the sources of economic growth in the United States from 1929 to 1982, attributes over one-quarter of the rise in the productivity of the American labor force to the increase in the amount of schooling completed by the average worker.[33] Jacob Mincer has provided convincing evidence that on-the-job training in industry has been a major contributor to wage and productivity growth in the American economy.[34]

The widening of the wage distribution over the past three decades, and the accompanying decline in the real wages of the bottom 40 percent of the male labor force, has given rise to a wide variety of proposals for upgrading the education and skills of those who enter the labor market directly out of high school. These include proposals for something similar to the old GI Bill of Rights, a large program of government-provided vouchers for postsecondary technical education, and government requirements that employers devote a specified minimum fraction of their payrolls to worker training.[35] The Clinton administration has given high priority to expansion of federally financed worker training programs and has proposed a combination of tax deductions and tax credits for postsecondary education.

Is it likely that a major infusion of new public investment into education and training could generate a substantial increase in the nation's growth rate, producing enough additional taxable income to offset a large part of the budgetary cost of such an investment? In the private sector, profit data can be used to measure the economic payoff

33. Denison (1985, table 8-4, p. 114).
34. Mincer (1962, 1994).
35. Marshall (1994); Baily, Burtless, and Litan (1993).

to additional dollars of investment. It is much more difficult to do so in the case of public investment in education. The studies of long-term economic growth have generally equated advances in education with increases in average years of school completed and then looked at the earnings premium associated with additional years of schooling to impute the economic payoff to those additional years. But what would the payoff be from providing additional budget subsidies (or tax deductions) for postsecondary education, some part of which will flow to students who would have completed that education without the subsidy? And what is the payoff from public dollars devoted to further reducing student-teacher ratios, or raising teachers' salaries, or providing more computers to schools?

There is a major controversy among the experts (outside of the educational community) about the payoff to increasing educational dollars per student. For a long time the conventional wisdom held that, although individual success stories were not hard to come by, it was difficult to document any systematic gains from widespread increases in educational spending per student. Some recent studies, mainly based on comparisons among states, have challenged that conventional wisdom, however, by arguing that systematic differences associated with spending per child can be found. In turn, the conclusions of these recent studies have been challenged by those holding the traditional view.[36]

There have been many studies of the efficacy of government-supported worker training programs. Given the wide array of different programs carried out at local levels with federal financing, results differed widely from case to case. Several years ago, the Labor Department sponsored a major review of the evidence, and its overall summary of the results suggested a mixed bag. Among adults, especially adult women, training programs on average tended to produce lasting earnings gains that moderately exceeded costs. Among young people, the results of training programs were disappointing and in some cases appeared to be counterproductive. (The Job Corps was an exception, but some question exists about the extent to which this program could be widely duplicated.) Simple programs that primarily teach applicants how to search for a job had the highest *ratio* of benefits to costs, but both the costs and the benefits were quite small.[37]

36. For the latest research and conclusions on the subject from the major participants on both sides of this controversy, see Burtless (1996).
37. Orr and others (1996).

James Heckman has suggested that a good starting place to assess the economic effect of additional investment in human capital would be to use a payoff of 10 percent, not much different from the return to business investment.[38] Since that estimate is heavily influenced by the results of studies that were looking at the payoff from additional years of schooling, it is almost surely on the optimistic side when applied to the widespread investment of additional dollars per year of schooling.[39] Nevertheless, it can be used to estimate the upper bound of the additional economic growth that might be forthcoming from an expansion in federal investment in education and training.

In 1996 the federal government will spend just under $30 billion on major education and training programs, not counting direct and guaranteed student loans.[40] Suppose that a major expansion in the federal education budget were inaugurated, amounting to 1 percent of national income. By 2002 the federal government's education budget would grow from $30 billion to $120 billion. Assume, optimistically, that all of this increment resulted in additional investment in education and training (rather than shifting funds from private or state and local to federal financing). Given the assumption that the return to this investment is about the same as the return to business investment, the rule of thumb developed for net additions to saving can be used: the extra 1 percent of national income flowing into investment would raise economic growth by 0.1 percent a year for several decades.

To the extent that tax deductions or tax credits were the vehicle for increasing human capital investment, the increment to growth would be a good bit less than 0.1 percent. A substantial part of any new tax deduction or credit for higher education would go toward lowering the tax bill of parents who would, in any event, have sent their children to college. These incentives might induce some of them to choose a more expensive college, but even there the evidence is quite slim that this choice would increase average productivity in the nation.[41]

38. Heckman, Roselius, and Smith (1994).

39. Burtless (1996, p. 41) concluded his summary chapter with the statement: "Increased spending on school inputs without any change in the current arrangements for managing schools offers little promise of improving either student performance or adult earnings."

40. I excluded the federal investment in student loans from the total because some significant, but unknown, fraction simply represents a shift from private to public financing, not a net addition to investment in education.

41. Attendance at a more expensive college may well raise a student's later earnings,

On balance, the effects of devoting additional amounts to investments in human capital would have about the same effects on economic growth per dollar of budget cost as growth-oriented tax cuts. The payoff, however, would probably be slower to develop. Sustained for several decades, the additional investments would raise average family earnings by a modest yet noticeable amount. But the growth stimulated by such policies would lower the budget deficit only a little. And so, increases in either public investment (through an expansion in government programs) or private investment (through tax cuts) would have to be paid for mainly by reductions in other areas of government spending.

A substantial increase in the investment in public infrastructure—roads, bridges, airports, sewer and water treatment plants—has often been proposed by liberals as an effective way of increasing economic growth.[42] After examining national and state data on postwar productivity growth and public and private investment, economist David Aschauer concluded that a large part of the decline in productivity growth after the late 1960s could be attributed to the decline in public investment that occurred around that time.[43] His results also suggested that a dollar's worth of public investment yielded a growth payoff three to four times higher than an equivalent outlay for private investment.

Subsequent research has cast substantial doubt on these findings.[44] Productivity growth in the United States was quite high until the early 1970s, when it began to decline sharply. Public investment outlays as a share of GDP also declined at about the same time. Statistically, productivity and public investment are therefore closely correlated. But this correlation does not demonstrate a causal connection. In a 1991 study of the issue, the Congressional Budget Office questioned the estimates of vastly larger payoffs to public investment, finding, for example, that the results obtained from studies like those by Aschauer change dramatically when modest changes are made in the years

---

but much of this advantage comes from the subsequent economic benefits of having associated with more affluent peers. This association could raise the earnings of the affected student, whose chances of being selected for a good job would increase relative to others, but national productivity would not rise.

42. See, for example, Cuomo Commission on Competitiveness (1992).

43. Aschauer wrote a series of articles beginning in 1989 (Aschauer, 1989). For a list of citations on this issue see Congressional Budget Office (1991).

44. See, for example, Holtz-Eakin (1994); Holtz-Eakin and Schwartz (1994).

covered by the analysis or in the specifications of the statistical models. The positive association Aschauer also found between state-level productivity and infrastructure investment could simply reflect the fact that states with higher productivity tend to have higher income and therefore can afford to invest more in public projects.

Given the wide range of potential public investments, it serves little purpose to argue about their superiority or inferiority in general. Some public investments have been uneconomic. For example, the construction and operating costs of many irrigation and power dams have exceeded their benefits. On the other hand, some public investment projects have added substantially to the nation's economic potential—for example, the construction of the interstate highway system starting in 1956. There are undoubtedly areas in which well-selected public investment would strengthen the economy; increasing the relatively low level of federal support for civilian R&D (outside of health and space) is an example.[45] But, if Congress decided to increase public investment, would projects with the highest economic returns be selected?

In the case of private investment, there is a presumption that competitive forces and the search for profits will automatically exert some, albeit imperfect, discipline over the quality of the projects selected. In the case of the public sector, there is no such force operating. The fact that some areas of public life would gain from an infusion of well-selected investments has to be weighed against the fact that political considerations play a heavy role in decisions about both the general areas for public investment and the specific projects to undertake. Examples include the prevalence of congressionally mandated "demonstration" projects in federal aid highway authorizations and the inclusion in appropriation bills of funding for particular research grants for colleges and universities favored by powerful congressional sponsors.

One favorite area proposed for an infusion of additional public funds is federally aided highway construction. Proponents cite surveys that attest to the existence of a substantial "backlog of needs" to bring America's highway system up to standard and to reduce congestion, but the data come from states whose federal highway allocations depend, in part, on the results of the surveys. When Barry Bosworth and Clifford Winston examined this issue in 1992, they did not find

45. See Schultze (1992, chap. 28).

a strong case for a large expansion of federal highway spending. They note that the quality of the highway system has improved since the early 1980s as the level of highway funding has increased, and they argue that a large-scale program designed to reduce congestion is doomed to fail because as new lanes are opened the improved highways attract additional drivers. Bosworth and Winston maintain that the benefits claimed from a large highway building program could be realized at a far smaller cost with an efficient structure of highway fees for trucks and a system that automatically billed highway users tolls based on the degree of congestion.[46]

As in the case of investment in education and training, a carefully chosen program of public investments, financed in ways that did not increase the budget deficit, could help spur economic growth.[47] But there is no reason to assume that the package of public investments would yield, on average, a higher return than that on additional private investment. Indeed, given the likelihood that the menu of public investments would include a significant amount of political pork, there are reasons to expect a lower average return.

Regulatory Reform and Retrenchment

Arguing that excessive and inefficient regulation depresses economic growth, the new Republican majority in Congress set about in 1995 to redesign, restrain, and scale back the regulatory apparatus of the federal government, particularly in the area of environmental protection. How much added growth can realistically be expected from reducing the scope and increasing the economic efficiency of the regulatory apparatus?

In several articles, economists Dale Jorgenson and Peter Wilcoxen estimated that removing all environmental controls would eventually raise measured GDP by 3.2 percent, as labor, capital, and raw material resources devoted to cleanup were shifted to the production of goods and services that are counted in GDP.[48] Adjustment of that estimate—to take into account statistical peculiarities having to do with the net economic costs resulting from the mandated installation

46. Bosworth and Winston (1992, pp. 281, 284).
47. It is popular to argue that public investment expenditures can safely be financed by borrowing. But in today's U.S. economy, further public borrowing would simply crowd out an equivalent amount of private borrowing, much of it for investment purposes.
48. Jorgenson and Wilcoxen (1990, 1993).

of emission control devices—gives a figure closer to 2.9 percent. Of course, no one proposes scrapping all environmental controls. But costs could be reduced by two sets of actions: first, scaling back those regulations for which environmental gains are less than the economic costs they impose; and second, improving the efficiency of environmental controls by relying more on the creation of economic incentives to reduce pollution and less on detailed regulation.

Various research studies have concluded that some environmental laws and regulations have pushed the stringency of environmental controls well beyond the point at which the economic costs begin to exceed the value of the environmental benefits. Other studies have shown that greater reliance on economic incentives as a pollution control device—for example, charging effluent fees or auctioning off effluent and discharge permits—could significantly lower the economic costs of achieving environmental goals.

Realistically, for both substantive and political reasons, we should not expect to achieve all of the theoretically available saving. It would be humanly impossible to fine-tune the environmental cleanup so that all actions whose benefits exceed costs would be undertaken and no actions with costs higher than benefits would be pursued. And in any event, there are widely differing views among voters as to the value of the benefits. A quite ambitious target might be to pare the economic costs of environmental regulation by 25 percent. If one applies that to the adjusted Jorgenson and Wilcoxen estimates, the result would be a gain of 0.7 percent in the level of GDP. In turn, if most of the gains were realized by the end of ten years, this would temporarily raise the growth of GDP by a little less than 0.1 percent a year, after which GDP would grow at its earlier rate, but along a higher path.

A fuller analysis of the potential growth-promoting effects of regulatory scaleback and reform is provided in the appendix to this book.

Conclusion

The currently projected economic growth of 2 to 2¼ percent that underlies the official budget projections seems like a highly disappointing outcome in comparison with the strong performance of the economy in the three decades after World War II, when growth averaged almost 4 percent a year. Higher growth would provide a host of benefits for the American people. The reduction in the budget deficit that would be yielded by substantially higher growth—

although not the most important of those benefits—would be a major boon. I have sought to make a realistic assessment of the extent to which various economic policies that have been proposed might speed up growth, and, as a by-product, how much deficit reduction they might yield.

The first conclusion was that growth is not being unduly limited by excessively cautious monetary policies of the Federal Reserve. I examined and rejected the arguments that the U.S. economy has substantial slack and unemployed resources that could be brought back into production if only the Federal Reserve would lower interest rates and allow markets to expand at a faster clip. While conceivably a bit more could be squeezed out of existing economic capacity, the resulting one-shot increase in output would be quite small, and, in terms of reducing the budget deficit, insignificant. Further attempts to generate faster growth with easier money would be inflationary. With little slack left in the economy, therefore, further growth can only be as fast as the productive capacity of the country expands year by year. And there is no warrant for assuming that the current annual growth in capacity will speed up beyond the currently estimated rate of 2 to 2¼ percent.

I then examined four sets of potential policies that might be adopted to increase growth: fundamental tax reform, federal tax cuts, increased public investments in education, training, and infrastructure, and the reform and retrenchment of environmental regulations. All four types of policies have the potential of speeding up economic growth. However, even with relatively optimistic estimates of their economic payoff, the addition to growth that might be generated is small—roughly 0.1 or 0.2 percent a year. If continued for many years—say a generation—even small increments to growth can cumulate to produce a noticeable, but hardly dramatic, improvement in living standards. Whether, and in precisely what form, some or all of these growth-promoting policies ought to be adopted is surely worth a serious national dialogue and political debate. But the budgetary payoff from the extra economic growth—in the form of higher revenues and lower interest payments on the debt—would not be large enough to alleviate anything but a modest fraction of the projected budget deficits, either in the medium term between now and 2002, or in the context of the more serious longer-term deficit problems that will begin to show up twenty years from now.

The modest size of the growth dividend from tax cuts or increased public investment has one other implication. Those measures will not generate enough additional revenues or reductions in federal interest payments to come at all close to paying for themselves. The budgetary costs of those actions must be largely paid for by cuts elsewhere in federal spending or by tax increases of a kind that do not lower economic growth (which would have to be regressive in nature). If they are allowed to produce an increase in the budget deficit, the overall effect would be to reduce economic growth. The reduction in national saving produced by the higher deficits would exceed the increase in growth flowing from the policies themselves. Moreover, from the standpoint of economic growth, the spending cuts needed to finance a tax cut would be better devoted to improving the federal government's budget balance. After about seven years their application to deficit reduction would produce a GDP gain that would increasingly exceed the payoff from a tax cut.

Discussion of the costs and benefits of measures that seek to raise economic growth ought to be an important part of the political debate. But they should be seen as long-run policies aimed at gradually improving living standards. They are not the way to a balanced budget.

References

Advisory Commission to Study the Consumer Price Index. 1995. *Toward A More Accurate Measure of the Cost of Living*. Interim report to the Senate Finance Committee. Washington.

Aschauer, David A. 1989. "Is Public Expenditure Productive?" *Journal of Monetary Economics* 23 (March): 177–200.

Auerbach, Alan J. 1996. "Tax Reform, Capital Allocation, Efficiency and Growth." In *Economic Effects of Fundamental Tax Reform*, edited by Henry J. Aaron and William G. Gale, 29–82. Brookings.

Baily, Martin Neil, and Charles L. Schultze. 1990. "The Productivity of Capital in a Period of Slower Growth." *Brookings Papers on Economic Activity: Microeconomics*: 369–406.

Baily, Martin Neil, Gary T. Burtless, and Robert Litan. 1993. *Growth with Equity: Economic Policymaking for the Next Century*. Brookings.

Boskin, Michael J. 1978. "Taxation, Saving, and the Rate of Interest." *Journal of Political Economy* 86 (April): S3–27.

Bosworth, Barry P. 1996. "Fund Accumulation: How Much? How Managed?" In *Social Security: What Role for the Future?* edited by Peter A. Diamond, David C. Lindeman, and Howard Young, 89–115. Washington: National Academy of Social Insurance.

Bosworth, Barry, and Clifford Winston. 1992. "Public Infrastructure." In *Setting Domestic Priorities: What Can Government Do?* edited by Henry J. Aaron and Charles L. Schultze, 267–93. Brookings.

Burtless, Gary, ed. 1996. *Does Money Matter? The Effect of School Resources on Student Achievement and Adult Success.* Brookings.

Burtless, Gary, and Jerry A. Hausman. 1978. "The Effect of Taxation on Labor Supply: Evaluating the Gary Negative Income Tax Experiments." *Journal of Political Economy* 86 (December): 1103–30.

The Coalition. 1995. *The Common Sense Balanced Budget Act of 1995: The Coalition Reconciliation Alternative.*

Congressional Budget Office. 1991. *How Federal Spending for Infrastructure and Other Public Investments Affects the Economy* (July).

———. 1994a. *The Economic and Budget Outlook: An Update* (August).

———. 1994b. *Is the Growth of the CPI a Biased Measure of Changes in the Cost of Living?* (October).

———. 1994c. *Recent Developments in the Theory of Long-Run Growth: A Critical Evaluation* (October).

———. 1996. *The Economic and Budget Outlook: Fiscal Years 1997–2006.*

Cuomo Commission on Competitiveness. 1992. *America's Agenda: Rebuilding Economic Strength.* Armonk, N.Y.: M. E. Sharpe.

Dornbusch, Rudiger, and Stanley Fischer. 1990. *Macroeconomics*, 5th ed. McGraw-Hill.

Eissa, Nada. 1995. "Taxation and Labor Supply of Married Women: The Tax Reform Act of 1986 as a Natural Experiment." Working Paper 5023. Cambridge, Mass.: National Bureau of Economic Research.

———. 1996. "Tax Reforms and Labor Supply." In *Tax Policy and the Economy*, edited by James M. Poterba, vol. 10, 119–51. MIT Press and National Bureau of Economic Research.

Feldstein, Martin. 1993. "The Effect of Marginal Tax Rates on Taxable Income: A Panel Study of the 1986 Tax Reform Act." Working Paper 4496. Cambridge, Mass.: National Bureau of Economic Research.

Feldstein, Martin, and Daniel Feenberg. 1996. "The Effect of Increased Tax Rates on Taxable Income and Economic Efficiency: A Preliminary Analysis of the 1993 Tax Increases." Working Paper 5370. Cambridge, Mass.: National Bureau of Economic Research.

Fullerton, Don. 1982. "On the Possibility of an Inverse Relationship between Tax Rates and Government Revenue." *Journal of Public Economics* 19 (October): 3–27.

Gale, William G. 1995. "Building a Better Tax System: Can a Consumption Tax Deliver the Goods?" *Brookings Review* 13 (Fall): 18–23.

Gordon, Robert J. Forthcoming. "The Time-Varying NAIRU and its Implications for Economic Policy." *Journal of Economic Perspectives.*

Greenspan, Alan. 1996. "Statement before the Subcommittee on Domestic and International Monetary Policy, House Committee on Banking and Financial Services." *Federal Reserve Bulletin* 82 (April): 315–20.

Hall, Robert E., and Alvin Rabushka. 1995. *The Flat Tax*, 2d ed. Stanford, Calif.: Hoover Institution Press.

Hausman, Jerry A. 1981. "Labor Supply." In *How Taxes Affect Economic Behavior*, edited by Henry J. Aaron and Joseph A. Pechman, 27–83. Brookings.

Heckman, James J., Rebecca L. Roselius, and Jeffrey A. Smith. 1994. "U.S. Education and Training Policy: A Re-evaluation of the Underlying Assumptions behind the 'New Consensus.'" In *Labor Markets, Employment Policy, and Job Creation*, edited by Lewis C. Solomon and Alec R. Levenson, 83–122. San Francisco: Westview Press.

Holtz-Eakin, Douglas. 1994. "Public-Sector Capital and the Productivity Puzzle." *Review of Economics and Statistics* 76 (February): 12–21.

Holtz-Eakin, Douglas, and Amy Ellen Schwartz. 1994. "Infrastructure in a Structural Model of Economic Growth." Working Paper 4824. Cambridge, Mass.: National Bureau of Economic Research.

Jorgenson, Dale W., and Peter J. Wilcoxen. 1990. "Environmental Regulation and U.S. Economic Growth." *Rand Journal of Economics* 21 (Summer): 314–40.

———. 1993. "The Economic Impact of the Clean Air Act Amendments of 1990." *Energy Journal* 14 (1): 159–82.

Lindsey, Lawrence. 1987. "Individual Taxpayer Response to Tax Cuts: 1982–1984 with Implications for the Revenue Maximizing Tax Rate." *Journal of Public Economics* 33 (July): 173–206.

Marshall, Ray. 1994. "Job and Skill Demands in the New Economy." In *Labor Markets, Employment Policy, and Job Creation*, edited by Lewis C. Solomon and Alec R. Levenson, 21–58. San Francisco: Westview Press.

Mincer, Jacob. 1962. "On the Job Training: Costs, Returns, and Some Implications." *Journal of Political Economy* 70, pt. 2 (October): 50–79.

———. 1994. "Investment in U.S. Education and Training." Working Paper 4844. Cambridge, Mass.: National Bureau of Economic Research.

National Commission on Economic Growth and Tax Reform. 1996. *Unleashing America's Potential: A Pro-Growth, Pro-Family Tax System for the 21st Century*. Washington (January).

Orr, Larry L., and others. 1996. *Does Training for the Disadvantaged Work? Evidence from the National JTPA Study*. Washington: Urban Instititute Press.

Romer, Paul M. 1986. "Increasing Returns and Long-Run Growth." *Journal of Political Economy* 94 (October): 1002–37.

———. 1989. "Capital Accumulation in the Theory of Long-Run Growth." In *Modern Business Cycle Theory*, edited by Robert J. Barro, 51–127. Harvard University Press.

Schultze, Charles L. 1992. *Memos to the President: A Guide through Macroeconomics for the Busy Policymaker*. Brookings.

Shapiro, Matthew D., and David W. Wilcox. 1996. "Mismeasurement in the Consumer Price Index: An Evaluation." Working Paper 5590. Cambridge, Mass.: National Bureau of Economic Research.

Thurow, Lester. 1996. "The Crusade That's Killing Prosperity." *American Prospect* 25 (March–April): 54–59.

Triest, Robert K. 1996. "Fundamental Tax Reform and Labor Supply." In *Economic Effects of Fundamental Tax Reform*, edited by Henry J. Aaron and William G. Gale, 247–78. Brookings.

U.S. Department of Labor. Bureau of Labor Statistics. 1996. *Employment and Earnings* 43 (January).

GARY BURTLESS
R. KENT WEAVER
& JOSHUA M. WIENER

3

The Future of the Social Safety Net

PROGRAMS OFFERING ASSISTANCE to the poor are seldom popular. Consequently, welfare reform has repeatedly been on the agenda of the nation's policymakers. Over the years, three recurrent criticisms of the welfare system have combined to generate a consensus that fundamental changes were needed in its structure. First, there was the feeling that the means-tested safety net programs cost too much, that they placed an undue burden not just on the federal budget but also on state budgets. Second, there was the criticism that federal rules and regulations did not give states, which administer a number of these programs, the flexibility they needed to design programs that best met local conditions and values. Finally, there was the conviction that the incentives inherent in the programs did little to encourage recipients to become self-sufficient and instead rewarded behavior that perpetuated dependence.

Despite these criticisms and the unpopularity of welfare, the means-tested safety net has expanded, and spending on welfare programs has increased almost without interruption since the early 1960s. In the two decades before 1980, the federal government launched a number of entitlement programs to help low-income families, including medicaid, food stamps, supplemental security income, the earned income tax credit, and guaranteed student loans. In addition, a number of older programs, such as aid to families with dependent children (AFDC) and housing assistance, were expanded. The growth in spending slowed briefly during Ronald Reagan's administration, but expenditures on these programs resumed their rapid rise in the late 1980s, fueled largely by burgeoning medicaid expenditures.

The election of a conservative Republican Congress in November

75

1994 represented the strongest challenge to social safety net programs in almost a generation. Harsh critics of the welfare state arrived in Washington determined to reduce social expenditures and curtail the influence of the federal government in regulating and administering safety net programs. Conservative critics of the American welfare state argued for four kinds of fundamental change.

First, they recommended a reallocation of governmental responsibility for social safety net programs. This reallocation, known as devolution, would shift programmatic control to the states, sharply reducing federal control and oversight. Second, conservatives wanted to remove the federal guarantee of individual entitlement to benefits for most means-tested programs, including cash assistance payments and medicaid, replacing it with block grants to the states. This change would give the federal government almost total control over the level of its welfare expenditures, while it would transfer to the states the financial risk posed by economic downturns and demographic change. It could also result in sharp reductions in, or even elimination of, benefits for some low-income people who met all of the asset and income tests used to determine program eligibility. Third, they urged limits on the duration of cash and food stamp assistance going to the working-age poor. From their creation in the Great Depression, federally supported assistance programs were designed to provide cash and in-kind aid to low-income families for as long as they remained poor enough to qualify for benefits. Under the alternative favored by conservatives and many moderates, benefits for able-bodied recipients would be limited to a specified period and would be tied to an adult recipient's efforts to find and keep a job. Fourth, conservatives hoped to couple these structural changes with large reductions in federal spending from the levels required to support existing programs. Budgetary considerations dictated many of the program changes they endorsed.

In late 1995, President Clinton, who had promised to "end welfare as we know it," vetoed a bill that contained a fundamental restructuring of the safety net along with other measures and then a stand-alone bill containing the welfare changes. But in August 1996, the 104th Congress passed and President Clinton signed the Personal Responsibility and Work Opportunity Act, which restructured and cut back cash assistance and food stamps. This legislation gave to the states much of the responsibility for providing cash assistance to needy children and their parents, placed time limits on federally financed cash assistance, imposed stricter work requirements on non-aged, nondisabled recipients of food stamps and cash assistance, and eliminated means-tested benefits for most legal immigrants who are not U.S. citizens. The president and Congress were unable to agree on reforms that would restructure medicaid, even though it is by far the most expensive and fastest growing means-tested program.

The nature, organization, and financing of an important part of the American safety net changed when the president signed the Personal Responsibility and Work Opportunity Act. The remainder of this chapter evaluates the implications of this measure and other suggested reforms for social protection of the poor.

The Social Safety Net for the Poor

The American safety net consists of two kinds of programs. The first, which includes social security and medicare, is based on social insurance principles: benefits are paid to people who have made payroll tax or premium contributions. Most benefits from these programs, which are discussed elsewhere in the volume, are received by middle-class and affluent families. The second group of programs, which are the focus of this chapter, are the means-tested ones that distribute money and other resources directly to poor or near-poor families.

Means-tested assistance is provided in two principal forms: cash payments and in-kind transfers. Until 1965 most means-tested aid was provided in the form of cash. In the decade after 1965, however, public spending on medical care for the poor, food stamps, and subsidized housing rose dramatically, altering the balance between cash and in-kind benefits (see figure 3-1). Nowadays the most costly means-tested programs are those that provide in-kind assistance. Such aid is provided in three main forms: as food (through food stamps, subsidized school meals, and food commodity distribution), housing (through public housing projects and rent and home-ownership subsidy programs), and medical care (primarily through the medicaid program).

Table 3-1 shows trends in federal spending on the major forms of means-tested aid, both cash and in-kind assistance. The table provides an incomplete summary of total public spending on the poor because state and local spending, as well as some smaller federal income transfer programs are excluded. In 1995 state and local governments paid

FIGURE 3-1. Federal Means-Tested Spending, Fiscal Years 1965–95

Billions of 1995 dollars

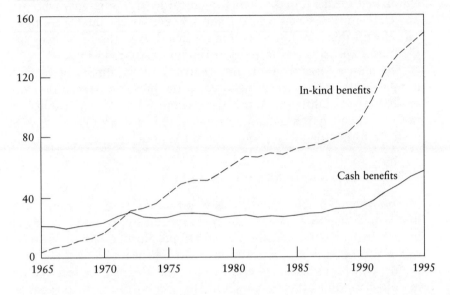

SOURCE: Office of Management and Budget.

about $70 billion of the cost of medicaid and about $12 billion of the cost of AFDC, or roughly 45 percent of the total cost of the two programs.

Cash Assistance Programs

Established in 1935 as part of the Social Security Act, AFDC was one of the first federally supported assistance programs. The program, which provided federal grants to states for family support payments and child support enforcement programs, was essentially abolished by the welfare reform legislation of 1996 and replaced by block grants to states. Before the 1996 reform, the federal government offered states open-ended grants, which the states were required to match, to pay for cash welfare payments to needy children and their adult caretakers. States were free to define need, establish basic benefit levels, and determine eligibility as they saw fit. As a result, there was a great deal of interstate variation. For example, in 1994 the basic monthly grant for a three-person family in AFDC ranged from a low of $120

TABLE 3-1. Federal Spending on Major Means-Tested Programs, Selected Fiscal Years, 1965–95

Billions of 1995 dollars unless otherwise indicated

Program	1965	1970	1975	1980	1985	1990	1995
Cash programs							
Aid to families with dependent children	12.5	15.4	14.2	13.7	13.1	14.1	17.1
Supplemental security income	7.9	7.5	11.9	10.7	12.4	13.3	24.5
Earned income tax credit	. . .	. . .	. . .	2.4	1.6	5.1	15.2
In-kind programs							
Food and nutrition	1.3	3.8	18.3	24.6	23.7	24.6	33.5
Housing assistance	1.0	1.8	5.8	10.2	15.9	18.4	25.5
Medicaid	1.3	10.1	18.9	26.3	32.3	47.5	89.1
Total	24.0	38.6	69.1	87.9	99.0	123.0	204.9
Total as percent of GDP	0.8	1.0	1.6	1.8	1.8	1.9	2.9

SOURCES: Office of Management and Budget; *Economic Report of the President, 1996*, p. 367.

a month in Mississippi to a high of $923 a month in Alaska, with the median state offering a little less than $370 a month, or a bit more than 38 percent of the federal poverty line.[1] Benefit levels were higher than average in states on the West Coast, in the upper Middle West, and in the Northeast, but were lower than average in the Southeast. Because the new family assistance block grant allocates funds to the states based largely on historical funding levels, this pattern of uneven benefit generosity will almost certainly continue or grow when the 1996 law is fully implemented.

A crucial feature of AFDC was the method used to determine federal payments to states. By matching state spending on an open-ended basis, states were encouraged to devote more of their own resources to cash assistance. In all states the federal government paid 50 percent of the cost of program administration. It also reimbursed each state for a percentage of its AFDC benefit costs. The percentage varied inversely with the state's per capita income. The lowest matching rate, available to states with high per capita incomes, was 50 percent. States with low per capita incomes received higher federal reimbursement, up to a maximum of 83.33 percent of benefit payments. Even after the 1996 reform is fully implemented, the old matching formula will continue to be used to determine federal pay-

1. U.S. House of Representatives, Committee on Ways and Means (1994, pp. 366–67).

ments to state medicaid programs and a portion of federal funding for child care subsidies for low-income families, although it will no longer be used to calculate federal payments for state cash assistance programs.

Supplemental security income, or SSI, is available to people aged 65 or older and to disabled and blind adults and children who meet federal eligibility standards. To qualify for benefits a person must have assets and annual countable income below very low limits. Unlike cash assistance for needy dependent children, the SSI program is federally funded and administered. Most states provide modest state supplements to the basic federal benefit.

While most cash assistance is received by people who do not work, the earned income tax credit (EITC) goes only to low-income people who *do* work. Enacted by Congress in 1975 to offset social security taxes and encourage low-income people to work, the EITC provides cash subsidies or income tax reductions to wage earners and self-employed people with low or modest incomes. As a worker's income rises above a certain threshold (about $12,000 in 1996 for a family with one child), the credit is gradually phased out. It is eliminated altogether when a family's income reaches about $24,000 a year if the breadwinner has one child and about $28,500 a year for breadwinners with two or more children. Liberalized in 1986 and twice again in the 1990s, the EITC in 1996 provided as much as $3,556 in refundable income tax credits to a breadwinner with two or more dependents.

In-Kind Transfer Programs

Although the federal government supports a number of assistance programs aimed at improving the diets of low-income Americans, by far the most important is food stamps. Before the 1996 welfare law became effective, this program was unique in offering assistance to all categories of the poor: working and nonworking, disabled and nondisabled, young and old, and families with and without children and single individuals. The 1996 legislation restricted food stamp eligibility for childless adults between the ages of 18 and 50 to three months of benefits over a three-year period, unless they are working or participating in a workfare, education, or training program. In addition, it denied eligibility to legal immigrants who are not citizens (previously, only illegal immigrants were denied benefits).

Food stamps are provided as coupons (or as electronic debit card balances) that can be used to purchase food in most grocery stores. Benefit levels and eligibility rules are determined by the federal government, which pays the full costs of the program. State and local welfare departments, however, administer the program and are reimbursed by the federal government for this service. A person who has no other income is eligible to receive a monthly allotment of food stamps that will permit the purchase of an inexpensive but nutritionally adequate diet. People who have other income are expected to spend roughly 30 percent of their counted monthly income on food. If that amount is not sufficient to buy a nutritionally adequate diet, the food stamp program provides enough coupons to purchase the additional food needed. In effect, the food stamp program is a negative income tax or guaranteed income plan in which the marginal tax rate is relatively low (roughly 30 percent), the guaranteed income amount is generous enough to buy a basic diet, and the payment is issued as food coupons rather than cash. Benefits provided in the food stamp program, like those available in SSI and medicaid (and, formerly, in AFDC), are an entitlement. That is, persons or families with incomes and assets low enough to be eligible for benefits have a right to receive coupons.[2]

Over the past few decades, the nation has established a number of programs to assist low-income families with their housing needs. Unlike food stamps, SSI, and medicaid, housing assistance has never been available as an entitlement to all eligible families. The majority of low-income households do not receive any earmarked government aid to help them pay their shelter costs. The federal government has instead appropriated money to build and operate publicly subsidized housing projects and to help pay the rents of a specified number of families living in private rental housing and the mortgage interest of a set number of low-income home owners. In 1996, about 5.1 million households received rent subsidies. Another 670,000 low- and moderate-income families received direct government subsidies to reduce

2. Technically, the food stamp program is referred to as an "appropriated entitlement." Funds for the program must be appropriated annually by Congress. If Congress does not appropriate enough money to fund the program for a full fiscal year, food stamp benefits could, in principle, be suspended toward the end of the year when funds for the program are exhausted. In the past, however, Congress has always acted as though food stamps represent an entitlement. When funds have been low, Congress has appropriated supplementary funds so that full benefits are available throughout the year to all eligible applicants.

their mortgage interest cost.[3] Each year Congress appropriates funds for a number of new commitments. These commitments used to run from five to fifty years, so appropriations were spent gradually over several years or decades. In recent years, however, most commitments have been for only one to five years, and the number of new commitments, which increases the number of subsidized households, has been reduced sharply.

Medicaid is by far the most costly income-tested program, as well as the one with the most sustained and spectacular history of spending growth. Established in 1965 along with medicare, medicaid is a joint federal-state program that provides health care for certain low-income persons. State programs must cover a minimum federally determined package of medical services; additional services may be covered at state option.[4] Under current law, all states *must* offer medicaid coverage to people receiving (or eligible to receive) family support payments for dependent children and almost all receiving federal SSI benefits; children under age 6 and pregnant women with family incomes below 133 percent of the official poverty thresholds; and all children born after September 30, 1983, with family incomes below 100 percent of the federal poverty line. In addition, states *may* offer benefits to certain other needy children and pregnant women; to certain aged, blind, and older people whose incomes are somewhat higher than the federal standards for SSI benefits; to low-income people who are confined to nursing homes and other institutions; and to other people who are deemed by the state to be "medically needy." Nearly all states offer benefits to one or more of these optional groups.

In 1996 almost 36.8 million Americans, including 4.3 million elderly, 6 million blind and disabled, 18.6 million dependent children, and 7.8 million adult caretakers of children, were covered by medicaid.[5] Outlays on the aged and disabled absorbed 68 percent of total medicaid expenditures, whereas spending on other adults and their children accounted for the balance.[6] Compared with children and their adult caretakers, the aged and disabled receive medical care more

3. Data from Congressional Budget Office.
4. Federally mandated services include inpatient and outpatient hospital services; physician, laboratory and x-ray services; nursing facility and home health services for adults; prenatal care; early and periodic screening, diagnosis and treatment (EPSDT) services for children under age 21; family planning services and supplies; rural health clinic services; and nurse-midwife services.
5. Data from Congressional Budget Office.
6. Data from Congressional Budget Office.

frequently and require care that is typically much more expensive. Nursing home care for the elderly is particularly costly. Medicaid— unlike the medicare program—will pay nursing home bills for an indefinite period. The cost of nursing homes is so high that even middle-class Americans can rapidly become impoverished during a stay. Private health insurance rarely covers the cost of lengthy nursing home stays. Thus many older Americans become eligible for medicaid sometime after entering a nursing home, even if they were not poor when they were admitted.

Two features of the haphazard system made up of the programs just described are notable. The first is that the federal government's role in initiating and financing policies to help the poor has expanded over time relative to the states' role. Indeed, by the 1980s, the federal government had assumed almost complete responsibility for providing food assistance to all groups and cash assistance to all but the working-age, able-bodied poor and their children. Even for this group the growth of the earned income tax credit has increased the federal role in recent years. The expansion of the federal role has reduced effective benefit differentials across states.[7] Second, even as its role has increased, the federal government has refrained from directly administering most of the programs that actually dispense aid to the poor. Usually it has relied on state governments or local public welfare agencies to determine eligibility, calculate benefit payments, and distribute federally financed aid to the needy. The three exceptions to this general pattern are the EITC, SSI, and veterans' pensions, which are administered by the Internal Revenue Service, the Social Security Administration, and the Department of Veterans Affairs, respectively. The remaining means-tested programs are administered by state and local agencies.

Rethinking the Federal Role in Safety Net Programs

The safety net programs described above were not developed under a coherent or carefully considered plan. The programs were introduced on a piecemeal basis and have been modified under a wide variety of political circumstances. As a result, they share no common philosophy or administrative rationale. Moreover, with separate

7. Pierson (1995).

transfer mechanisms for different consumption goods and special cash programs for different categories of the poor, there is little administrative efficiency in the system.

Four issues are central in current debates over reform of the safety net. First, should the entitlement to benefits be retained? Second, what national standards should be preserved and what, if any, new ones should be imposed on the states as a condition for receiving federal funds? Third, how should funds be distributed among the states? And, finally, if large budget savings are achieved, what will be the consequences for beneficiaries? Although the Personal Responsibility and Work Opportunity Act may have appeared to have settled, at least temporarily, these issues for some programs, political pressures and implementation problems could soon put these issues back on the congressional agenda. In fact, even as he signed the welfare reform bill, President Clinton promised to introduce legislation to change some of its aspects in 1997.

Entitlement Status

A key issue in many income transfer and health safety net programs is whether individuals, under state or federal law, should have a statutory right to benefits, that is, whether eligibility ought to be subject to legal enforcement in federal or state courts. The federal law that established medicaid, for example, creates an individual entitlement to benefits both by enumerating certain categories of persons who must be covered by the states and defining a package of services that must be offered to eligible persons. It also guarantees payments to the states according to a matching formula, thereby creating a state entitlement to federal reimbursement. The welfare reform legislation passed in 1996 did not affect the individual entitlement to medicaid, adult SSI, and food stamp benefits. SSI eligibility for children was restricted, although the principle of entitlement was retained. The federal entitlement to cash assistance payments for needy children and their adult caretakers, in contrast, was eliminated. If they choose to do so, states can establish a legal entitlement for state cash assistance payments under the new system.

People who favor ending the individual entitlement to benefits argue that spending for public programs should be decided as part of a deliberative process in which all programs compete for resources within an overall spending limit. If funds are depleted because of a recession, for example, federal and state legislators can always appropriate additional money if that is a high priority. In this view, an entitlement provides safety net programs with a blank check that inevitably leads to higher spending levels than policymakers or the public would consciously choose.

Those who would retain individual entitlements argue that they provide the population with an important sense of security. Individuals know that if they become destitute under certain circumstances, they can obtain specified benefits. Under an entitlement, public resources flow automatically to individuals in need and are distributed equitably because governments are required to treat persons in the same circumstances in the same way. None of this is true with block grants or appropriated programs. Aggregate funding may fail to adjust in timely fashion to changes in the size of the needy population or in the cost and use of services. The distribution of resources among states may be determined more by political considerations than by need. The end result may be that some needy people will be denied assistance, or assistance levels may be suddenly reduced just when the need is greatest.

National Standards

Although states have substantial flexibility to set eligibility and benefits in some shared-responsibility safety net programs, detailed federal statutes and regulations restrict state freedom in many respects. In theory, conservatives favor eliminating federal restrictions. In practice, however, many do not always favor greater state flexibility, fearing that some states would not impose tough restrictions unless required to do so by federal law. For example, many wanted to impose strict time limits on eligibility for federally supported cash benefits to needy children and detailed work requirements for their adult caretakers. Others argued for family caps that would prohibit increased federally supported benefits for children conceived while the mother was receiving welfare.

Those who favor reduced federal regulation point out that restrictive and uniform national rules do not work well, given the wide variation in economic circumstances and voter preferences across states. Restrictive national rules place federal lawmakers or regulators, who lack a thorough understanding of the situation in each state, in the position of micromanaging safety net programs. Even though the federal government pays at least half the cost of safety net programs, states deplore the imposition of nationwide rules—sometimes referred to as unfunded mandates—that oblige them to spend at least some of their own money on measures they oppose. Governors and state legislators often view federal regulation as unwarranted interference in "their" programs.

Allowing states broad discretion to experiment with safety net programs may lead to better policy designs by allowing innovations to be tested without running the risks that would arise if an untried initiative were implemented on a nationwide basis. Selectively devolving policymaking authority to the states may also allow states to reduce their paperwork burdens and integrate different safety net programs so the programs can work more effectively and efficiently. States may, for example, create integrated eligibility requirements for means-tested programs such as cash assistance and food stamps. Between January 1993 and October 1996, some seventy-nine waivers were granted to forty-three states to test large and small changes in their cash assistance programs. For example, state experiments are shedding light on the effects of a variety of welfare-to-work schemes. In addition, several states are examining behavioral responses to innovations such as the family cap.

Opponents of devolution believe that since Washington provides the lion's share of funds, it is only reasonable to expect federal legislators and administrators to retain a major voice in how the programs are run. If federal oversight were scaled back, Congress and the president might see less reason to support the programs adequately. If they had little say in how that money is used, it would be politically more difficult for federal lawmakers to raise taxes, cut other programs, or increase public borrowing to appropriate more money when the need for social protection increases, as it does in recessions.

Another important argument made in favor of at least some minimum national standards, especially in the context of a block grant, is that they are necessary to ward off a "race to the bottom" in eligibility and benefits. Without federal cost sharing at the margin, states will become more concerned about the relative generosity of their programs. A state that provides more generous benefits than its neighbors may fear that it will attract poor residents of neighboring states. Paying benefits to a larger number of poor people costs money and requires higher taxes, which may make it harder to attract the job-creating businesses and affluent taxpayers that every state wants. To avoid becoming a "welfare magnet," some states may cut their benefits to less generous levels than they feel are appropriate. This could touch off a negative competition in which neighboring states repeatedly cut back their benefits. Although there is little convincing empirical evidence indicating that significant numbers of low-income people move to states because of high welfare benefits, many governors and state legislators are convinced that such migration is important.[8] Furthermore, such migration could become a greater problem under the five-year time limit on benefits mandated by the restructured family assistance block grant. Because there are no plans to develop a national system to track the length of time individuals have received assistance from different states, people who have exhausted their time-limited assistance in one state will have a strong incentive to move to another state where they can obtain assistance again, like nomadic people looking for a new supply of food. The new welfare law also allows states to set time limits of less than five years, which could set off migrations from states with short durations.

Federal involvement in safety net programs can restrain this interstate competition through two mechanisms. First, open-ended federal cost sharing of the type that characterizes medicaid and the old AFDC system reduces the costs to a state that has relatively generous benefits, wants to raise its benefits, or experiences an influx of low-income families. This is so because at least half, and for most states more than half, of the marginal cost for new residents or expanded benefits is assumed by the federal government. Second, the federal government can reduce interstate variation by establishing minimum (and less commonly, maximum) benefits and eligibility conditions for receiving federal aid. For example, because all states must provide medicaid to children under age 6 and pregnant women with incomes below 133 percent of the federal poverty line, states cannot compete on whether they provide such coverage. Although state policymakers chafe at the suggestion that they may act in harmful ways if given discretion, it is prudent to ask why they want the flexibility to adopt policies that will harm beneficiaries if they do not intend to use this freedom.

Funding Formulas

The federal funding formula is another area of disagreement. Two kinds of issues are particularly important. The first involves the allo-

8. Kenyon (forthcoming).

cation of funds among states. The second revolves around the question of whether the total amount allocated by the federal government should vary with economic conditions.

Conflicts over allocations among states are inevitable when an open-ended matching grant program such as medicaid or AFDC is converted into a block grant program. Under a matching formula, the federal government simply pays a fixed percentage of the allowable costs incurred by states. The amount each state receives is determined by its actions and is unaffected by the amounts received by other states or by any federal budget limit. Under a block grant, however, total federal funding is fixed, and, therefore, if one state receives more, other states must receive less. Some mechanism must be established to divide the total federal appropriation among states. Equity considerations suggest that block grant monies should be distributed according to some measure of need—such as the number of poor residents in a state—possibly with an adjustment for the state's fiscal capacity. Such an allocation would involve a wrenching redistribution of federal funds because states with high average incomes and few poor tend to have far more generous benefits and coverage than lower-income states. The allocation formulas proposed for initiatives that call for replacing entitlement programs with block grants almost always divide the block grant resources among states according to historical distribution patterns. This, however, can lead to striking inequities in which wealthy states receive substantially more federal support per poor resident than low-income states. Such a distribution of federal resources can be rationalized under a matching grant formula because it arises from decisions made by each state. Low-income states could increase the size of their federal grants by spending more of their own money, but most choose not to. In fact, benefited by high federal matching rates, low-income states have to spend far less of their own funds per poor resident than rich states do to obtain the same amount of federal money per poor person.

Other than the political rationale of avoiding conflict, there is very little justification for giving wealthy states larger federal grants per poor person after federal financing has been converted to block grants. Over time, as the populations of the states grow at different rates, the use of historical allocations is likely to become increasingly unsatisfactory and the allocations will become a source of growing political conflict. States with poor populations that grow rapidly can be significantly disadvantaged under such a system. They are likely to react by cutting benefits, aggravating the situation described above.

The second issue, dealing with adjustments based on economic fluctuations, is less likely to pit states against one another than it is to cause conflict between the federal government and states as a group. A block grant financing scheme gives federal budgetmakers certainty about their spending commitments, but it also places the risk of economic downturn squarely on the states. Under a system of fixed block grants, states must either pay for all the additional costs of their recession-related increases in caseloads or tighten eligibility or reduce benefit levels at a time when need is greatest. If state governments reduce benefit levels or restrict eligibility during a recession, they can increase the severity of the recession by reducing the purchasing power of the state's consumers. The same would be true if they tried to maintain benefits by cutting other spending or boosting taxes.

Unlike the federal government, most states are prohibited by their constitutions from major borrowing to pay for spending in their operational accounts. The federal government, which faces no constitutional restrictions on its borrowing, has been able to maintain public spending during recessions. The countercyclical effect of federally supported safety net programs has helped to reduce the severity of postwar recessions. In theory, a block grant can be structured so that additional federal resources automatically become available when the economy weakens. However, the measures available for triggering additional federal funds, such as state unemployment rates, are likely to be poorly correlated with the level of need experienced by individual states. More appropriate measures, such as the number of poor in each state, are available only after long time lags.

When available federal funds are fixed or shrinking, the likelihood of conflict over funding formulas increases. The political fight over the funding allocation then becomes a zero-sum game, in which one state's gain is another's loss. Although it is possible to design new formulas that compensate perceived losers from the programmatic changes, those payoffs require that the federal government put in more money, thus reducing the budget savings from devolution. The stakes in obtaining a favorable funding allocation when a block grant is established are very high, because experience has shown that block grant funding formulas are hard to change once they are put in place.[9]

9. A GAO study of the nine block grants created by the Omnibus Reconciliation Act

Cutting Spending

Although devolution and restructuring do not logically require reductions in federal spending, the reforms considered by the 104th Congress were coupled with substantial cuts designed to contribute to the effort to balance the budget by 2002. Some advocates of a smaller federal role argue that the elimination of federal requirements will permit states to administer their programs more efficiently and effectively, reducing the adverse effect of smaller budgets on beneficiaries. Some even claim that beneficiaries will enjoy gains in well-being compared with their situation under the old system. Finally, many people who urge lower federal spending believe that a smaller and balanced budget will have wider economic benefits that will improve the circumstances of low-income as well as middle- and high-income families.

There is little evidence to support the argument that safety net budgets can be reduced significantly without hurting beneficiaries. Most of the specific policies recommended by those who advocate lower budgets are untested, have been shown to produce small budget savings, or are known to reduce the net incomes of beneficiaries.

The 1996 Reforms and Issues for the Future

Making choices about the structure of safety net programs inevitably involves both trade-offs among conflicting values and a great deal of uncertainty. Since many of the policies that have been proposed or enacted go well beyond historical experience, it is difficult to offer reliable estimates of their costs, benefits, or consequences. Under these circumstances, it is prudent to tailor policy changes to the level of risk they involve and to our knowledge about those risks. Where the benefits of policy change are almost certainly large, the federal government should move boldly to change current policy. Where there is a major risk of harm to the nation's poor (for example, by setting off a race to the bottom in family assistance payments), the federal government should move more cautiously—through sponsored state experimentation and state waivers, for example. And

---

of 1981 notes that three of them—community services, maternal and child health services, and preventive health and health services—are "still largely tied to 1981 allocations" rather than changing to reflect changes in population, need, and fiscal capacity. U.S. General Accounting Office (1995a, p. 9).

where the risks of potential innovations clearly outweigh their likely advantages, the federal government should prohibit states from taking those actions.[10]

Unfortunately, most advocates of reforming the social safety net have not tried to link their proposals for policy change to the degree of risk they may impose or to the uncertainty surrounding the issue. Radical policy changes have been adopted for cash and nutritional assistance without giving much consideration to the problems that might be encountered when trying to implement them. Little thought has been given to what might happen if developments do not unfold as the advocates of reform have assumed. All of this suggests that some of the reforms that have already been enacted may have to be revisited over the course of the next few years. Moreover, medicaid, the portion of the safety net that was not affected by the Personal Responsibility and Work Opportunity Act, is projected to experience rising costs and therefore is likely to be the focus of future policy action.

Cash and Nutritional Assistance

The recent policy debate on cash and nutritional assistance programs was dominated by the conflicting visions offered by President Clinton and congressional Republicans. As this debate unfolded, states initiated numerous innovations, some of which were fairly radical, under research and demonstration waivers granted by Washington.[11] The principal change contained in the reform bill that the president proposed in 1994 was a two-year limit on the length of time an adult AFDC recipient could draw cash benefits without engaging in work. Under that plan, states would have had to phase in work requirements for all families in which the custodial parent was born after 1971, but were allowed some flexibility. In addition to substantial leeway over the number of hours of work to require, states were given the flexibility to impose tighter time limits and apply their limits to a broader group of recipients.[12] Cognizant of the uncertainty of

10. For a more complete development of this argument, see Weaver and Dickens (1995).

11. See Douglas Besharov, "Waivers Change the Face of Welfare," *Los Angeles Times*, June 20, 1996, p. A11.

12. States could require participants in the administration's WORK program to work no less than fifteen and no more than forty hours per week. U.S. House of Representatives (1994).

such a change, the administration's plan did not impose a "hard" time limit—that is, a flat prohibition against providing cash benefits or job guarantees after the two-year limit elapsed. Additional benefits could be provided, but only if the adult recipient engaged in significant public or private work.

Republicans in the 104th Congress took a very different approach to reforming cash and nutritional assistance, one that was reflected in the Personal Responsibility and Work Opportunity Act of 1996.[13] This law converted the AFDC program into the temporary assistance for needy families (TANF) block grant program. With the exception of some minor adjustments for low-income states with rapidly grow-ing populations and states in recession, the size of each state's TANF grant will be determined by its federal AFDC payments in recent years. The law abolished the individual entitlement to benefits. While giving the states additional program flexibility in many areas, the new law also confronts them with new federal requirements.[14] For exam-ple, states must meet escalating work participation requirements in their family assistance caseloads. The head of each family on welfare will now be required to work within two years of the date that welfare payments begin.[15] The work hours requirements imposed on assis-tance recipients are stringent, and states face increasingly harsh pen-alties for failing to meet them.[16] The Congressional Budget Office

13. On development of the Republican welfare reform legislation in Congress, see Weaver (1996).

14. A state with a waiver will have the choice of following the particular requirements in that waiver until it expires or adhering to the requirements in the Work Opportunity and Personal Responsibility Act. Thus for several years some states may choose to operate under the less restrictive terms set out in their waivers.

15. The fraction of family heads that must be working rises gradually from 25 percent in 1997 to 50 percent in 2002. The percentages are reduced commensurately if a state's case load has declined since 1995. In mid-1996, caseloads had declined since 1995 in all but three states.

16. Participants from single-parent families would be considered working if they worked at least twenty hours a week in 1997 and 1998. By 2000, participants would have to work at least thirty hours a week. For two-parent families, the requirement is even more stringent. Thirty-five hours a week is the minimum effort required to be counted as a worker. Penalties for a state failure to meet work participation rates can be up to 5 percent of the block grant for a state that had not been in violation the previous year, with an increase of up to 2 percent for each succeeding year, with a cap of 21 percent. The secretary of HHS may impose penalties for less than the full amount; in its budget estimates, the Congressional Budget Office estimated that penalties imposed by the secretary would, following historical practice, be much less than the maximum allowed. For provisions of

(CBO) has estimated that states would have to invest $13.7 billion of their own money over the 1997–2002 period to meet the new work participation requirements. In view of the high cost of compliance, the CBO predicts that most states will "simply accept penalties rather than implement the requirements."[17]

States are prohibited from using the TANF block grant to pay benefits to families for more than sixty months (consecutively or nonconsecutively). They are, however, permitted to use existing federal social services block grant payments to provide vouchers or other noncash benefits to families who have exhausted family support payments. Up to 20 percent of a state's caseload can be exempted from this hard time limit for hardship reasons. Unlike earlier versions of the Republican welfare bill, the reform legislation did not mandate, but rather allowed, states to impose family caps and to exclude unmarried teenage mothers from eligibility. Under waivers issued over the past few years, many states have already imposed family caps.

Although the Republicans' 1995 welfare reform proposal allowed states to convert the food stamp benefits received by their residents into a nutrition block grant, thereby ending the federal entitlement to nutrition assistance, this option was dropped from the legislation enacted in 1996. The new law does, however, contain strong work requirements for able-bodied adults without dependent children, limiting that group to three months of food stamp benefits every thirty-six months unless they are actively engaged in work. In effect, this eliminates food stamps as a source of continuing aid for the long-term unemployed who have no dependent children. A variety of changes will gradually trim the amount of food coupons available to most recipients. By 2002 the average recipient's food stamp allotment will be reduced by one-fifth below the amount projected under the prereform law.[18]

On certain elements of welfare reform, the president and Congress did agree. Both thought it important to increase collection of child support payments from absent parents. The 1996 law attempts to do this by establishing uniform state tracking procedures, promoting automation of states' child support procedures, pushing states to es-

---

the welfare reform legislation, see U.S. House of Representatives (1996); Greenberg and Savner (1996); Super and others (1996).

17. Congressional Budget Office (1996b, p. 5).

18. Super and others (1996, p. 17).

tablish child paternity, and ensuring tough measures to enforce child support orders. Since these measures are broadly popular among voters, they aroused little controversy in the 104th Congress.

Many questions remain about the effects of the new welfare reform law. The following discussion addresses some of the most important problems and uncertainties and describes possible legislative changes that address these issues.

Entitlement status. The conversion of AFDC into a block grant probably settled the federal entitlement issue with respect to family support payments for the foreseeable future. It is unlikely that even a Democratic Congress and president would revisit this issue within the next few years. Nevertheless, certain problems will arise as a consequence of ending the entitlement. Even greater disparities than now exist might develop in who is eligible for cash benefits from one state to the next. Some states may decide to vary eligibility criteria from one area to another within their borders, as is the case with state-financed general assistance today. In such an environment, low-income families will have no assurance that they will be able to receive assistance in states that do not establish state entitlements. Even in states with state entitlements, benefits may fluctuate if the state decides to operate within a fixed welfare budget. The distribution of cash assistance could become quite capricious.

Although the entitlement issue may have been settled in the case of cash assistance, it is possible that future efforts to wring savings from entitlement programs will rekindle the effort to allow states to transform the food stamp program in their area into a block grant. Such an initiative would be a serious mistake, especially in light of the elimination of entitlement status for federal cash assistance. Food stamps are now the only program providing a uniform level of assistance throughout the nation without categorical restrictions that limit aid to the aged, disabled, and families with children. Moreover, this program is also highly responsive to the increases in need that come from economic downturns, natural disasters, or demographic change. While it would be desirable to improve the integration of food stamps with the other safety net assistance programs, the proliferation of state programs under the new welfare law will make this objective unattainable unless other important goals of the safety net are sacrificed.

Hard time limits. The hard time limit of the new TANF block grant has some advantages as well as potentially detrimental consequences. On the positive side, a hard time limit sends a clear signal to recipients that they must seek to be self-sufficient in the labor market and sets an unambiguous timetable for achieving that goal. The stark reality, however, is that a significant percentage of adult assistance recipients will not become self-sufficient in the foreseeable future. Some lack the necessary skills, others have no work experience, and still others face family circumstances or health problems that make work problematic. A number live in areas—rural counties and Indian reservations, for example—where jobs are scarce. Moreover, the inherent instability of many jobs in the low-wage labor market makes it inevitable that many of these individuals will suffer repeated spells of unemployment, some of long duration. If current recipients are provided no government-financed cash assistance, the effects of strict time limits should increase hardship and homelessness among the least skilled single parents and their children.

Allowing states to set hard time limits with durations even shorter than five years, as permitted under the new law, is a particularly risky policy. Some states may be tempted to export their welfare problem by establishing more restrictive time limits than those of their neighbors, expecting to encourage an exodus of welfare recipients. Early evidence from states that have tried to implement time limits also suggests that these limits pose severe administrative challenges for state welfare agencies.[19]

To mitigate the hardship and adverse incentives of hard time limits, the law could be changed in several ways. States could be allowed to provide cash assistance after five years to those who were willing to engage in workfare or subsidized jobs in exchange for benefits. In addition, states could be required to obtain federal approval if they wanted to impose time limits of less than five years. Similarly, federal waivers could be granted that would allow states to extend the five-year time limit under certain circumstances.

National standards in work requirements and illegitimacy reduction. In addition to time limits, the recent debate about national standards in means-tested cash and nutrition programs revolved around work participation requirements for individuals and states, guarantees of child care for those required to work, and mandates that states impose specific measures to help reduce illegitimacy.

Political competition between President Clinton and congressional

19. Bloom and Butler (1995).

Republicans ensured that the new welfare law would feature stiff work requirements. Work requirements enjoy overwhelming support among the public and surprisingly strong support among assistance recipients themselves.[20] Thus work requirements are likely to be essential to maintaining public support for cash and nutrition assistance programs over the long run. But it is important to be realistic about what such programs can and cannot accomplish and about the capacity of the low-skill labor market to absorb large numbers of new workers. Research evidence indicates that, although welfare-to-work programs can significantly increase both earnings and work participation of welfare recipients, most of those recipients are unlikely to earn enough to become economically self-sufficient and many will endure lengthy spells of unemployment after completing the programs.[21] Without access to publicly provided jobs and supplemental aid, such as child care assistance, some single mothers will find it impossible to support their children.

On the detailed issues of work requirements—how many hours of work to require and how much of the caseload to cover—it is tempting for federal policymakers to be overly prescriptive. This permits them to score easy political points, but it may not give states the flexibility they need to design effective long-term programs. Evidence from welfare-to-work experiments suggests that the highest short-term earnings gains are achieved by programs that move recipients into work quickly. But these findings are still preliminary and may not be valid for mothers of very young children, who increasingly will become subject to stiff work requirements. Considerations such as these suggest that states should be given much more flexibility than the new law provides to set the required number of hours that welfare recipients must work and the mix of work and training that they will be offered.

With respect to initiatives to reduce illegitimacy, the new law requires teenage mothers to live with a parent or responsible adult in order to receive cash benefits. As long as a provision is made for exceptions in the case of parental abuse or other hardship, this requirement is appropriate. The law also offers modest incentives for states to reduce their out-of-wedlock birthrates. In addition, states were given discretion to impose family caps. Giving states flexibility

20. See Weaver, Shapiro, and Jacobs (1995); Farkas and others (1996).
21. See, for example, Friedlander and Burtless (1995); Nightingale and Haveman (1995).

on this issue is sensible because evidence on the impact of family caps on additional births to welfare recipients, drawn almost entirely from an experiment in New Jersey, is still being gathered and analyzed.

Many social conservatives favor a federal mandate that would preclude states from providing cash assistance to teenage mothers who bear children outside of wedlock. The new family assistance block grant does not require this but gives states discretion to implement such teenage mother exclusions. It would be far more prudent to allow such initiatives only in strictly limited trials, with a requirement for careful evaluation. Although there is little question that teenage pregnancies impose large costs on society and on the children themselves, there is no evidence that illegitimate births will be reduced significantly if teenage mothers are denied benefits.[22] The effect of such a ban has never been tested, and the harm to poor children from such a policy could be immense.

State fiscal effort. Another problem with the new block grant is that it imposes weak requirements on states to maintain their funding levels. States are permitted to reduce their current welfare spending significantly, which could set off a race to the bottom in eligibility and benefits. To qualify for their full federal block grant funds under the new law, states that meet the work participation targets are required to spend only 75 percent of the amount they previously devoted to assistance benefits. States that fail to meet the work targets must spend 80 percent of the amount previously spent on assistance payments.[23] The maintenance-of-effort requirements are even less restrictive than these percentages imply because states are permitted to spend part of their TANF block grants on services that may not be received by low-income dependent children or their parents.[24] In addition, inflation will erode the value of previous state spending, making the requirement less onerous over time.

The shift to block grant funding for family assistance payments, combined with continued availability of federally financed food stamps, will present states with a powerful inducement to save their own money by reducing cash benefits. If a state cuts its cash assistance benefits and spends some of its TANF grant on other services previ-

22. For evidence on the costs of out-of-wedlock births to teenagers, see Maynard (1996).

23. States that do not spend the required amount will have their federal TANF block grant reduced dollar for dollar for their shortfalls.

24. Super and others (1996, pp. 8–9).

ously supported with state tax dollars, the state could free up money for tax cuts or other nonwelfare spending. The amount of its block grant would remain unchanged, while the cut in assistance payments would be partially offset by increased federally financed food stamp payments because food stamp benefits are calculated based on families' cash income, including family assistance payments.[25]

In the first few years of the new program, the temptation to reduce state fiscal contributions for cash assistance and shift the funds to other purposes or tax relief will be great. This is because the AFDC caseloads in many states declined significantly in 1995 and 1996, while their future block grant amounts have been set equal to the federal AFDC payments they received when they had larger caseloads. With more federal money than they need to maintain benefits for their current caseloads, many states will be able to shift some of their state welfare spending to other needs. When welfare again becomes a pressing fiscal problem, however, they will find it politically difficult to recapture these monies.

A strong case can be made for tightening the state maintenance-of-effort provisions. Effective programs that move recipients toward self-sufficiency are going to cost money. Moreover, it is not going to be cheap to set up the new administrative structures needed to implement the time limits and other aspects of the new system.

Funding issues. The new family assistance block grant has three major funding shortcomings: it provides very uneven levels of federal support to children in rich and poor states; the amount each state will receive is not very responsive to its changing demographic needs; and a state's grant may not respond much in the event of a severe economic downturn. The first two flaws are the result of the decision to base state block grant allocations primarily on historical distribution patterns. States are allowed to choose the highest of their 1994, 1995, or average 1992–94 spending levels for their allocations. This formula was chosen not because of compelling policy considerations but rather because of the political need to avoid an allocation with highly visible winners and losers. The allocation mechanism will lock into place a distribution of federal funds that benefits wealthy states

---

25. When AFDC benefits (or benefits under a family assistance block grant) to a family are reduced, federally financed food stamp benefits automatically increase. Thus under a family assistance block grant, cutting families' cash assistance would leave the family with lower total (cash assistance plus food stamp) income, but would lead to a greater inflow of federal funds to the state. For a detailed discussion, see Reischauer and Weaver (1995).

rather than poor ones. In 1994, for example, the federal government through the AFDC system gave about $1,800 per poor child in Connecticut and only about $300 in Mississippi. In time, the allocation mechanism will be advantageous to states that are losing low-income residents and disadvantageous to rapidly growing states. If the block grant approach is to be retained, an improved allocation mechanism, one that distributes funds more equitably, must be developed. For example, over a ten-year period the allocation mechanism could gradually be transformed into one in which funding was based on the number of poor children in a state.

The problem created by recessions could be dealt with by increasing federal appropriations for the contingency grant fund. Monies in this fund, which are budgeted at $2 billion for the fiscal 1997–2001 period, will be made available to states with high and increasing unemployment rates and to those whose food stamp caseloads have jumped by at least 10 percent.[26] To compensate for the additional burden imposed by a moderate recession, the size of this fund should probably be doubled or tripled. Furthermore, states drawing money from the contingency fund should be required to match any federal dollars they draw from the fund.

It should be recognized that any effort to increase the size of the contingency fund or the basic block grants will face the same obstacle that sank the Clinton administration's welfare reform initiative in 1994: the requirement that it meet the deficit neutrality test under the Budget Enforcement Act of 1990. Increasing taxes or cutting other programs to fund increased spending for family assistance is likely to be politically difficult, just as it was when policymakers tried to reform the old AFDC program.

Will the new welfare policies increase poverty? Forecasting the impact of the 1996 welfare reform law is not easy. It is not clear, for example, how quickly or effectively states will implement welfare-to-work and workfare programs. Furthermore, under the new law, states may choose to follow the structure called for in any operative federal waivers they have recently obtained rather than move to the new system.

There are many questions to which no one knows the answers. How many welfare recipients, faced with the threat of a five-year time limit, will find work in the private sector? How many states will use

26. Super and others (1996, pp. 9–10).

their own resources to pay for cash benefits or vouchers to recipients who exhaust five years of eligibility for federally supported benefits? Will competition among the states lead to even more stringent time limits? How many states will implement a family cap or exclude unwed teenage mothers from benefits? Will family caps and teenage mother exclusions have a noticeable effect on illegitimacy and caseloads? How will future recessions affect states' willingness to pay for family assistance?

There is little doubt that the policy changes will, in time, result in an increase in poverty and—equally important—deeper distress among Americans who are already poor. A July 1996 report by the Urban Institute, using fairly optimistic assumptions, estimated that the version of the welfare bill that passed the House would increase the number of poor persons by about 2.6 million, of whom 1.1 million would be children.[27] The Urban Institute estimated that the poverty gap—the total amount of money required to bring the incomes of all poor families up to the poverty line—for families with children would rise by almost 25 percent. The potential effects of the new law on poverty and distress during a future recession are much greater than these figures suggest because federal funding would not increase substantially and state resources will shrink.

Medicaid

In 1995 Congress passed legislation that would have converted medicaid from an open-ended entitlement program with a number of federal requirements into a block grant (called medigrant) with few national standards.[28] The legislation would have eliminated the federally enforceable entitlement to a comprehensive range of medical services. The individual right of action would have been limited to state courts, where the concerns of state governments carry substantial weight. Lawsuits by providers would have been specifically prohibited. The block grant would have been capped each year and allowed to grow at a rate far below that projected for expenditures of the existing medicaid program. Over the 1996–2002 period, $133

27. Urban Institute (1996). The Urban Institute estimates include both cash income and noncash income from food stamps, housing assistance, and the EITC, less taxes paid.

28. Although widely referred to as a block grant, the plan was technically a capped matching program and not a block grant. That is, federal funds were to be available to match state expenditures up to a ceiling.

billion less would have been distributed under the medigrant block grant. By 2002 federal medigrant expenditures would have been 26 percent below projected expenditures under the current law.[29]

President Clinton proposed a different approach to curbing medicaid. His plan called for establishing limits on the growth of average per beneficiary expenditures (per capita caps) while giving states somewhat greater flexibility to contract with managed care organizations (such as health maintenance organizations), set reimbursement rates for hospitals and nursing homes, and organize long-term care services.[30] The individual entitlement to services would be retained. Although a far less radical proposal than the medigrant block grant, the president's plan would have established, for the first time, a mechanism to cap federal, if not state, expenditures. The proposal would have cut federal medicaid expenditures by $52 billion during 1996–2002, substantially less than the congressional medigrant plan.[31]

President Clinton vetoed the Balanced Budget Act, the budget bill that included the medigrant block grant. Following his veto, the National Governors' Association (NGA) developed an outline of a bipartisan proposal that attempted to marry the block grant approach of the medigrant program with limits on the growth of average per beneficiary expenditures proposed by the Clinton administration. Under the NGA approach, certain categories of individuals would retain an entitlement to services, but states would have almost complete control over the "amount, duration and scope" of benefits that these individuals were provided. This degree of flexibility raised the question of whether the entitlement would be a meaningful guarantee of access to services. Congressional Republicans drafted a bill, based roughly on the NGA proposal, that would have saved $76 billion over 1996–2002. Democratic governors, however, disavowed this legislation, calling it a repackaged medigrant plan. Similar provisions were included in the welfare and medicaid reform bills that were reported by the House and Senate committees in the early summer of

29. Congressional Budget Office estimates. For another set of estimates, see Holahan and Liska (1995). This study estimates that in eighteen states, federal expenditures would have been cut more than 30 percent.

30. Although widely referred to as a "per capita cap," the proposal takes as its denominator the number of medicaid beneficiaries rather than the number of people living in the state.

31. Congressional Budget Office estimate. Also see Executive Office of the President (1996).

1996, but the medicaid provisions were stripped from the final bill—which became the Personal Responsibility and Work Opportunity Act—to head off a certain presidential veto.

The radical changes in welfare embodied in the Personal Responsibility and Work Opportunity Act of 1996 could have had a major impact on medicaid eligibility because individuals who are deemed eligible for cash assistance benefits are usually automatically entitled to medicaid. To mitigate the impact of the new restrictions on cash assistance eligibility, the welfare reform legislation decoupled eligibility for cash assistance from medicaid eligibility. For adults and children in dependent families, medicaid eligibility will be based on the AFDC criteria in effect as of July 1996.[32] Adults, but not children, may lose medicaid if they fail to meet welfare work requirements.

Decoupling the two programs could increase the workload of those who determine eligibility because there could be separate applications and determinations for TANF and medicaid. Separate applications could reduce the number of persons covered, since some cash assistance applicants will not bother to fill out the second application. The overall number of applications for welfare is also expected to decline because some low-income persons will presume that they do not qualify for assistance; this in turn is likely to reduce medicaid applications.

The welfare reform act also makes it very hard for legal immigrants to receive medicaid. New immigrants are barred from receiving anything but emergency medical services during their first five years in the country. After that, states can choose to bar immigrants from eligibility for medicaid; if they do not, then they must include the income and assets of the alien's sponsor in determining eligibility, effectively precluding eligibility in most cases.

Because it was not reformed in the 1996 legislation, medicaid remains on the nation's policy agenda. Medicaid spending slowed markedly during 1996, and the Work Opportunity and Personal Responsibility Act should dampen the growth of future spending somewhat. Nevertheless, the Congressional Budget Office and the administration projected in mid-1996 that medicaid spending would grow by 9.6 and 7.5 percent a year, respectively, over the 1996–2002 period.[33] In a future effort to balance the budget, medicaid will be expected to

32. States may reduce eligibility to 1988 standards and may update income and asset criteria by the consumer price index in future years.

33. Congressional Budget Office (1996a, p. 434); Office of Management and Budget (1996).

make a significant contribution. The issues that were contested but not resolved during 1995 and 1996 will be debated again. These include whether medicaid should remain an entitlement, what national standards should be retained, and how federal funds should be allocated among the states. The impact of a reformed program on state budgets and on those who depend on the program will also be matters of great concern.

Should the entitlement be retained? The medigrant proposal is an indicator of how far the social policy discussion has shifted in just a few years. In 1993 and 1994 the nation was caught up in a debate over how to provide a guarantee of health insurance to all Americans. The medigrant plan, however, would have eliminated a long-established entitlement to health coverage for low-income Americans.

The main rationale for ending the entitlement to medical benefits is straightforward. Advocates of this position contend, first and foremost, that doing so is the only way to control spending and provide needed budget predictability at both the federal and state levels. Medicaid expenditures are hard to control under an entitlement because the program is obliged to pay for covered services for all eligible individuals who obtain services. Many of the services they use are very expensive. Neither the federal nor state government can permanently afford to have medicaid expenditures increase faster than revenues without squeezing out other desirable spending.

Advocates of ending the entitlement also argue that changing medicaid into a program with a fixed annual budget could change the nature of the program in beneficial ways. States would no longer have an incentive to manipulate the medicaid financing system in order to maximize federal reimbursement.[34] In addition, a capped program would put states in a much stronger bargaining position with providers regarding reimbursement rates and the provision of services. All parties would know in advance that only a fixed amount of money

34. According to the General Accounting Office, "Beginning in the mid-1980s, states were allowed to use revenue raised from 'provider-specific' taxes—that is, taxes imposed on hospitals serving Medicaid patients—and 'voluntary contributions' (called donations), as part of the state share eligible for federal matching funds. States then returned to providers the funds collected from such taxes and donations along with part of the matching federal payments. In some cases, a portion of the federal matching funds was then redirected to state general revenues and spent on nonhealth-care services. This swapping and redirecting of revenues among providers, the state, and the federal government resulted in increased federal spending, increased funds for providers, and—in some cases—additional revenue for states' treasuries." U.S. General Accounting Office (1995c, p. 34).

was available to pay for services. For individuals, ending the entitlement would eliminate the notion that the government "owed" them benefits. Finally, without the constraint of providing services on an entitlement basis, states could tailor services to local needs and individuals. States that have been reluctant to entitle needy residents to certain services, such as home and community-based long-term care services, because the definition of need is hard to establish or the number of people who meet the criteria is large, might be willing to offer at least some of these services in a nonentitlement framework. The conflict between coverage of a broad range of long-term care services and an open-ended entitlement led even the Clinton administration to propose a major expansion of home care without an entitlement to services as part of its health reform plan.

Those who favor retaining entitlement status for medicaid point out that eliminating the entitlement could result in an increase in the number of people without health coverage. This would be unpopular with the public, which generally supports expanded access to health care regardless of financial status.[35] It would also reverse the trend established by the expansions of medicaid eligibility enacted in the 1980s and early 1990s that have moderated the growth in the number of uninsured.[36]

With less policy control, Congress may not have much interest in increasing or even maintaining block grant funding in the future. Abolishing the entitlement would do away with the mechanism that links expenditures to need, that is, to the number of beneficiaries and the cost of care. Once the entitlement was eliminated, funding could be set at any desired level and Congress could easily reduce federal spending without deliberating on how cuts would actually be implemented at the state, local, or facility level. The proposed level of funding for the medigrant block grant provides an example. It was probably inadequate to cover all medicaid beneficiaries who would be eligible under existing law and would have resulted in a loss of coverage for millions of indigent Americans by 2000. One estimate

35. In a recent public opinion poll, 60 percent of respondents thought the government should "take some action to ensure that all Americans have health insurance coverage" and 24 percent thought that the government should "make a start by helping some groups to get health insurance." Only 13 percent thought that the government should "leave things the way they are now." Kaiser-Harvard Program on the Public and Health/Social Policy (1996).

36. For a listing of eligibility expansions, see U.S. General Accounting Office (1995c, pp. 56–62).

concluded that the trend toward less employer-sponsored health coverage combined with these medicaid cutbacks could have resulted in a growth in the number of uninsured from about 40 million in 1995 to between 50 million and 68 million by 2000.[37] Since medicaid spending is sensitive to economic conditions, even more might lose health insurance coverage in a recession. The U.S. General Accounting Office found that in at least twenty-two states, including eight of the ten largest ones, medicaid spending is sensitive to state economic conditions. On average, medicaid spending rises by 6 percent for every 1 percentage point increase in the unemployment rate.[38]

Block grant proponents counter that states are not heartless and will not turn their backs on the poor.[39] But without federal requirements for states to provide specified services to particular groups, it is not obvious what they will do if the federal and state money runs out before the end of the year. Would a state deny medicaid eligibility to a nursing home patient who had impoverished herself and had no place else to go? Or would it find that it had to spend additional funds, even though medicaid was no longer an entitlement? One of the attractions to states of making capitation payments (fixed per capita reimbursement) to health maintenance organizations is that it allows them to shift the responsibility for living within a budget from the government onto providers. However, managed care organizations have had little experience with long-term care or with low-income elderly and disabled beneficiaries, who account for the bulk of medicaid expenditures.

More than 36 million persons are currently receiving medicaid benefits. As a practical matter, it seems highly unlikely that states could establish programs tailored to the needs of individuals. The administrative complexities of implementing such programs would be overwhelming. Furthermore, basic legal standards prohibit states from being "arbitrary and capricious" in their determinations of who will and will not receive services. The Americans with Disabilities Act may also deter states from limiting the enrollment of persons with disabilities. If states used their block grants to establish discretionary

---

37. Holahan and Nichols (1996)

38. U.S. General Accounting Office (1995b, p. 2).

39. Jim Edgar, "Testimony," presented to Health and Environment Subcommittee of the House Commerce Committee, June 8, 1995; and Michael O. Leavitt, "Statement on State Perspectives on Medicaid Reform," presented to Health and Environment Subcommittee of the House Commerce Committee, June 8, 1995.

health programs for the poor, they might find themselves faced with an avalanche of litigation, especially in the early years of the program. It is probable, therefore, that states would establish standard administrative rules about who will be eligible and would run their new programs as state quasi-entitlements. If this is the case, it would make more sense to retain the federal entitlement, which brings with it funding that fluctuates with need.

What national standards should be imposed? Perceptions of how much freedom states have had to design and operate their medicaid programs vary greatly. Federal policymakers believe that medicaid is essentially a federal program over which they have little control because of the enormous amount of state flexibility. On the other hand, state policymakers believe that medicaid is essentially a state program over which they have little control because of extensive federal requirements. Whatever the actual balance, there is little doubt that federal rules and mandates that shifted power toward the national government proliferated in the 1980s and early 1990s.

In reaction to the expanded federal role, the medigrant block grant passed by Congress would have eliminated most national standards. For example, it would have repealed current requirements that states provide coverage for all children below the poverty level and almost all cash welfare recipients, that a minimum benefit package be provided, that nursing home standards be enforced by the federal government, that reimbursement rates to hospitals and nursing homes be adequate to cover the costs of an efficiently operated facility that meets the quality standards, that beneficiaries have freedom of choice of provider, and that services be available statewide.[40] Although President Clinton's proposal did not go anywhere near as far, it too provided states with substantial additional flexibility. Indeed, there is now a broad, bipartisan consensus on the principle that states ought to be given more freedom to run the medicaid program as they want, although there is not much agreement on which requirements should be repealed and which should be retained.

While states argue that additional flexibility will allow them to tailor their medicaid programs to meet local and individual needs, most of the requirements that the medigrant plan would have repealed were designed to protect beneficiaries and providers of services. In an odd echo of the health care reform debate of 1993 and 1994, the

40. Rosenbaum and Darnell (1996).

states argued in 1995 and 1996 that they wanted the flexibility to do all sorts of things that would benefit their low-income residents (such as covering additional groups of uninsured persons), while at the same time they contended that program expenditures were so out of control that drastic cuts were necessary. These are inconsistent messages, and advocates for beneficiaries worry that states would use any new flexibility they obtained to implement changes that would harm low-income people. Thus the debate on this issue has centered on the extent to which states can be trusted to do the "right" thing without federal requirements.

There is no simple answer to the question of whether states should be given additional flexibility. Much depends on which issue is involved—eligibility requirements, covered services, service delivery, reimbursement, or quality assurance.[41] In some areas it makes sense to allow a good deal of variation from state to state because of particular subnational conditions. In others it is best to have a degree of uniformity throughout the country or at least minimum national standards.

The case for uniform minimum national standards is probably strongest regarding who should be covered and what services they should be provided. For example, since all low-income children need health insurance, there is no compelling reason why children below 100 percent of the federal poverty line should have medicaid coverage in California but not in Mississippi. Because not all states covered such children before there was a federal mandate requiring them to do so, there is strong reason to believe that at least some states would cut back on this coverage if they were not required to provide it. A similar logic applies to covered benefits. For example, since there is widespread agreement that all children should visit a physician for periodic checkups and when they are ill, no health care purpose is served by making physician services optional.

On the other hand, there are many acceptable ways to organize and deliver care, reimburse providers, and assure quality of care. The case for uniform national standards with respect to these issues is less obvious. But even here strong arguments can be made for retaining some federal rules. Take, for example, the question of whether states

41. We are indebted to Alan Weil, executive director, Colorado Department of Health Care Policy and Financing, for suggesting this point at "Devolution and Medicaid: A View from the States," a conference sponsored by the Brookings Institution and the Nelson A. Rockefeller Institute of Government, May 23, 1996.

should be given greater freedom to require beneficiaries to enroll in managed care organizations.[42] While there is relatively broad agreement that this should be the case, many of the states that have been granted waivers to expand their use of managed care have run into problems, especially when they have tried to expand quickly in order to meet budget targets.[43] In some cases, the access to and quality of services have been compromised. State medicaid staffs, data, and technology are largely unequipped to measure quality of care and access to services in managed care organizations. Given this situation, it may be appropriate for the federal government to retain oversight responsibility in order to ensure that an acceptable quality of care is provided.

Federal requirements regarding reimbursement of nursing homes and hospitals imposed by the Boren amendment are another area where arguments can be made both for and against allowing more state flexibility. The Boren amendment requires that states "meet the costs which must be incurred by efficiently and economically operated facilities in order to provide care and services in conformity with applicable State and Federal laws, regulations, and quality and safety standards."[44] The medigrant, Clinton, and NGA proposals all called for the repeal of this amendment, which has proven difficult to operationalize in ways that both the states and the courts find reasonable. But if states paid less than the amounts called for by these regulations, quality of care in nursing homes and hospitals might decline below acceptable levels.

Finally, there is the issue of federal nursing home regulations. Largely in response to concerns about inadequate care in nursing homes, the Omnibus Budget Reconciliation Act of 1987 (OBRA87) dramatically revised and strengthened the medicaid and medicare quality standards and the survey and certification process. Facilities that do not meet the standards are not eligible for medicaid and medicare reimbursement. Many states and providers chafe under

42. Although under current law states may obtain waivers of the freedom-of-choice requirement in order to enroll beneficiaries in managed care organizations on a mandatory basis, they are limited to managed care organizations in which at least 25 percent of enrollees are not medicare or medicaid beneficiaries. 1903(m)(2)(A)(ii) of the Social Security Act. This rule is based on the theory that health maintenance organizations that have to compete for the privately insured population will have to provide a higher quality of care than if they provided services solely to public beneficiaries.

43. Sparer, Gold, and Simon (1996); Gold, Frazer, and Schoen (1995).

44. Section 1902(a)(13) of the Social Security Act.

these very detailed requirements and would like to see them changed. The standards were retained in the medigrant proposal, but federal enforcement was eliminated. But before OBRA87, quality standards and their enforcement were weak in many states.[45] Moreover, it is the threat of losing federal funds that motivates states to insist on quality improvements. There is strong evidence that the nursing home quality standards imposed by OBRA87, while not perfect, improved quality of care and may even have saved money.[46] Weaker enforcement of the nursing home quality standards combined with lower reimbursement could result in reduced quality of care.

How should funds be distributed and how much state effort should be required? Federal medicaid funds are currently provided to states on an open-ended basis.[47] Each state is reimbursed for a fraction of its eligible spending on health care for qualified low-income people. The federal matching rate varies from state to state, depending on each state's per capita income. The federal government never pays less than half of a state's costs and can bear as much as 83 percent of the burden. Like cash assistance spending, federal medicaid spending per poor person varies dramatically among the states, reflecting the wide diversity in state policies. In general, higher-income states receive more federal dollars per poor person than lower-income states because the former choose to provide coverage for more of their low-income residents, offer a wider range of services, and pay providers more. For example, in 1993 New York and Connecticut received $3,200 and $4,300, respectively, per person below the federal poverty line while Florida, Mississippi, and New Mexico received less than $1,400.

Reformed allocation systems, especially block grants, could create significant inequities if they are based on historical spending patterns. They would lock in place very low levels of spending in low-income states while leaving high-income states with comparatively generous federal funding. These inequities would be compounded over time because medicaid expenditures in many states (mostly in the South)

45. Institute of Medicine (1986); Wiener (1981).

46. An evaluation led by Research Triangle Institute, Inc., found that the OBRA87 standards reduced the use of physical and chemical restraints, lowered hospitalizations, reduced use of indwelling catheters, and decreased the number of dehydrated patients. Catherine Hawes, "Statement," Research Triangle Institute, Research Triangle Park, presented at a forum on the impact on long-term care of proposals to alter medicaid, Washington, D.C., October 6, 1995.

47. This section draws heavily from Holahan and Liska (1995).

with historically low levels of spending have increased very rapidly in recent years as a result of rapid population growth and federally mandated coverage expansions. Barring changes in the allocation formula, this expenditure growth is projected to continue. In contrast, medicaid spending in the Northeast and Midwest has been increasing more slowly because of sluggish population growth and more aggressive efforts to contain costs. In short, block grants that are not adjusted to reflect state differentials in the growth of the population in need and disparities in spending per recipient will disproportionately hurt states with low benefits and rapidly expanding populations.

The medigrant proposal attempted to address this problem by adopting an allocation formula that included the number of state residents in poverty, an enrollment mix factor that included both the state's caseload distribution (for example, proportion of children, elderly, and persons with disabilities) and expected spending on each group relative to the national average, and an index of input costs. If unconstrained, this distribution formula would have led to redistributions of resources, with states like Connecticut losing large sums and states like Mississippi gaining greatly. Political and policy considerations dictated that limits be placed on the amount of money that any state could gain or lose relative to its previous year's allocation. As a result, the amount of leveling that would have occurred across states under the medigrant program would have been quite modest.

These adjustments addressed only how each year's funds would be allocated and did not affect the aggregate amount that would be distributed in any year. The legislation specified the aggregate amounts to be allocated among the states each year through 2002. After 2002, the amount allocated would have been permitted to grow at the rate of inflation, as long as it was below 4.2 percent. The aggregate amount allocated among the states would not have increased had there been a burst of inflation that pushed up costs, a period of economic weakness that swelled the number of uninsured poor, or technological developments that made health care more expensive.

President Clinton's proposal for limits on the growth in average per beneficiary expenditures handled these issues in a more equitable fashion. A state's allocation would have been automatically adjusted for enrollment growth whether caused by demographic trends, changed economic circumstances, or decisions by the state to expand or shrink eligibility. The per capita cap distribution, however, would have done nothing to even out the large disparities across states in expenditures per covered person. If a state with a limited package of benefits decided to expand its package or reimburse its providers more generously, it would have had to pick up all of the marginal costs from state resources.

If policymakers decide that limits must be placed on the growth of medicaid spending, probably the most equitable solution to these problems would be to marry the two approaches. In other words, per capita caps for which levels were set according to a measure of each state's per capita need rather than according to historic per capita expenditure levels would be the most appropriate way to allocate funds while constraining total federal spending. A simple alternative would be to lower the federal matching rates. Any such change in the allocation formula would have to be phased in over a decade so as to avoid undue disruption.

A related issue that was part of the reform debate of 1995 and 1996 was the extent to which states should be required to contribute their own resources to obtain federal medicaid grants. For years, some states, in particular industrial states with large poor populations such as New York, have argued that they are burdened unfairly by having to pay half of the costs of medicaid. They contend, with some justification, that per capita income is a very inadequate measure of state fiscal capacity or the ability to raise resources.[48] Furthermore, they believe that large concentrations of inner-city poor impose burdens that more rural states do not experience. The medigrant proposal responded to these pressures by allowing states to choose the higher of their current federal matching percentage (FMAP), a rate determined by a new matching formula, or 60 percent. The new matching formula would have taken into account total taxable resources and need. The effect would have been an increase in the FMAP for most states and a significant reduction in the amount of their own money states would have had to spend to draw down their federal block grant.

This change could have had a dramatic impact on total (federal and state) medicaid spending. In an open-ended program, higher federal matching rates will induce more total spending on medicaid because a state can obtain more federal money than before for each dollar of state money that it devotes to medicaid. With a fixed block

48. U.S. General Accounting Office (1993).

grant the effect is the reverse. A higher federal match means that the state can draw down a fixed amount of federal money with less of its own money. This will lower the total amount devoted to medicaid because after it has drawn down the federal funds, any money the state spends will not be matched by a federal contribution. One analysis of this issue estimated that the reduction in spending under the medigrant program would be 25 percent larger using the new matching rates than using the existing FMAPs, assuming states did not spend beyond their federally matched funds.[49]

Given that any medicaid reform is likely to reduce federal medicaid spending, there is little compelling reason to compound the effect by reducing the effort states would have to make to obtain their federal grant. A good case can be made, however, for improving the FMAP formula so that it better reflects the differences in state fiscal capacity and need. This would lead to some states facing higher FMAPs and other states lower ones and therefore is likely to be politically controversial.

The challenge of reduced spending. A key question for policymakers is, "How far can medicaid spending be reduced without imposing unacceptable hardship on low-income groups or excessive burdens on providers and state and local taxpayers?" The answer to this question depends very much on the extent to which states can slow the growth of medicaid spending by implementing cost containment measures designed to make the financing and delivery systems more efficient. If such initiatives do not generate enough savings, states will have no option but to cut eligibility, services, and provider reimbursement rates, or raise taxes or cut other programs.

The 1995 medigrant proposal, the 1997 congressional budget resolution, and President Clinton's 1997 budget all envisioned significant reductions in medicaid spending over the 1996-2002 period—$133 billion, $76 billion, and $54 billion, respectively. No one knows whether states, even if granted new flexibility under reform legislation, could generate savings of these magnitudes solely from greater efficiencies. Much of the anticipated savings are expected to be realized by enrolling more beneficiaries in managed care. However, there is a great deal of uncertainty concerning how much managed care could save and whether it can reduce the rate of growth of spending over a sustained period.

49. Holahan and Liska (1995, p. 13).

Roughly 40 percent of medicaid-eligible children and nondisabled adults were already enrolled in managed care as of mid-1996. Expanding this penetration significantly will have only a limited effect on spending. Research suggests that managed care for this population generates relatively modest savings, usually in the 5 to 10 percent range. Moreover, this population accounts for only about a quarter of medicaid expenditures, even though it constitutes almost three-quarters of beneficiaries.[50]

The potential saving from providing acute care for aged medicaid beneficiaries through managed care organizations is not known but is probably limited. Medicaid spending for this type of care is relatively small and consists mostly of payment of the medicare part B premiums, deductibles, and coinsurance, and reimbursement for prescription drugs. Enrolling substantial numbers of elderly medicaid beneficiaries in managed care organizations would be a complex undertaking because they are also eligible for medicare. Nevertheless, some states will try to surmount the hurdles.

Acute care costs for younger persons with disabilities are high and will undoubtedly be the target of future cost containment efforts.[51] Such care is often provided in a fragmented delivery system that could benefit from the kind of coordination that is theoretically possible under managed care. Health maintenance organizations, however, have almost no experience with younger persons with severe disabilities, and advocates for the disabled worry that quality of care and access to specialists may be compromised by managed care organizations.

While there is broad consensus on expanding enrollment in managed care to control acute care expenses, there is a good deal of uncertainty about how best to control expenditures on long-term care—nursing home care, home care, and intermediate care facilities for the mentally retarded. Long-term care currently accounts for about one-third of medicaid spending. With an aging population projected to increase the demand for nursing home care by 1.9 percent a year over the next thirteen years, this is a critical issue.[52]

Some have argued that home and community-based care should be

50. Rowland and others (1995).
51. In 1993 acute care spending per blind and disabled medicaid beneficiary was $4,471, compared with $1,804 per nondisabled adult beneficiary and $980 per child beneficiary. Liska and others (1995, pp. 61–63).
52. Wiener, Illston, and Hanley (1994).

substituted for institutional care. However, the bulk of research has found that expanding home care for the aged raises rather than reduces overall expenditures.[53] This is because large increases in home care use more than offset relatively small reductions in nursing home use. If the entitlement to services were eliminated, some states might be able to force a substitution of home care for nursing home care by explicitly limiting the expenditures for institutional services. However, this may be impractical because nursing home residents tend to be extremely disabled and lack strong informal support. As a result, they can be very expensive to care for in the community.

Some indication of the potential for reducing expenditures in this area will be provided by Oregon's experience.[54] That state has aggressively moved nursing home patients who need supervision and personal care, but not much medical care, into smaller, cheaper, less medicalized residential settings, including adult foster care and assisted living. These innovations are promising, but their cost effectiveness has not been rigorously evaluated.

Significant savings might also be realized from more efficient provision of services to those with mental retardation and developmental disabilities who are now served through intermediate care facilities for the mentally retarded. Such facilities are extremely expensive because of extensive regulatory requirements, antiquated physical plants, relatively highly paid staff (many of whom are state employees), and padding of reimbursement rates for state-run facilities. There are reasons to believe that moving these beneficiaries into community-based services might save significant amounts of money. Average per person costs for those who have been moved into home and community-based care under medicaid waiver programs are about half those for intermediate care facilities.[55] There are, however, limits to these savings because the most severely disabled and most costly residents will probably remain institutionalized.

Even if states restructure their financing and delivery systems to place a maximum emphasis on managed care and community-based care, they may find themselves falling far short of the savings necessary to meet the budget targets.[56] If this is the case, states will have to either increase their own spending on medicaid or cut eligibility,

53. Wiener and Hanley (1992).
54. Kane and others (1991).
55. U.S. Department of Health and Human Services (1994).
56. Holahan and others (1995); Wiener (forthcoming).

reimbursement levels, covered services, or quality standards. Such cuts would reduce expenditures, but they are likely to be painful to beneficiaries and providers. Moreover, some steps could be taken only if existing federal regulations were relaxed. Among the measures that states could take under existing regulations are eliminating or reducing medically needy coverage for persons with high medical expenses who are not eligible for cash assistance; freezing or cutting reimbursement rates, which are already substantially below medicare and private insurance rates; eliminating coverage of certain services that are not mandated (such as dental services, physical therapy, and eyeglasses); and reducing the "amount, duration and scope" of covered services (for example, limiting the number of prescriptions to two a month). If states were given the flexibility to do so, they might reduce eligibility for cash assistance recipients, decide not to cover all disabled persons who qualify for the SSI program, reduce the amount of income and assets that community-based spouses of nursing home patients may retain, and reduce coverage of qualified medicare beneficiaries (low-income elderly for whom states are now required to pay medicare premiums, deductibles, and coinsurance).

Such measures would not just increase hardship but also would increase the number of uninsured and inadequately insured persons. These individuals would still receive some of the care that was once paid for by medicaid. Much of it would be provided on an uncompensated basis by public institutions. State and local taxes would have to rise to pay for some of this uncompensated care. This problem could be compounded if reduced medicaid reimbursement rates made private providers more reluctant to serve medicaid patients, thereby concentrating more of their care in public institutions.

The considerable uncertainties that surround the question of how much savings states might realize from improved efficiencies achieved by increased flexibility suggests that policymakers should exercise considerable care as they try to reduce federal medicaid expenditures. Arbitrary deficit reduction goals should not determine how much the medicaid program is scaled back.

Conclusion

Few public functions arouse as much passion—or antipathy—as assistance to the poor. Many Americans believe that although some of the indigent deserve help, others are poor because of indolence or moral defects and deserve their poverty. Poor children, the elderly, and the disabled arouse sympathy, but impoverished able-bodied adults, even parents of young children, are often the target of scorn. This attitude profoundly affects Americans' views toward assistance. They object to offering healthy working-age people pay without work but are more willing to provide in-kind assistance such as food stamps and medical care.

Broad dissatisfaction with assistance programs has led to numerous reform initiatives over the past quarter century. Some reform efforts yielded modest adjustments in the structure of public aid, but none produced fundamental change. Politicians were unable to craft a compromise between those who believe social protection of children is the paramount public interest and others who regard public aid as a narcotic that subsidizes idleness and illegitimacy among adults who are capable of self-support.

The Personal Responsibility and Work Opportunity Act represents a decisive break with the past with respect to cash assistance. It removes the guarantee of federal support to indigent children and their parents, thus eliminating a pillar of social protection that survived more than six decades. It places primary responsibility on governors and state legislatures to devise programs to protect child welfare. At the same time, it sharply limits states' ability to use federal funds for income or work assistance that lasts longer than five years for any adult recipient. It constrains state governments to offer aid to poor families with children in a form that is tied to work. It abolishes or sharply curtails many forms of public assistance to noncitizen immigrants.

In the short run, two principal effects of reform will be noticeable. Some low-income people will lose eligibility for benefits. Most noncitizen immigrants will be deprived of SSI and food stamps, and nearly a quarter of disabled children who receive SSI could be removed from the rolls. Most new immigrants will be prohibited from coverage under medicaid. Cities and states where immigrants are concentrated must decide whether to use their own resources to replace the curtailed federal aid. For already fiscally hard-pressed cities like New York and Los Angeles, where poor legal immigrants are numerous, this will involve painful choices. Providing aid to indigent immigrants may not be affordable. On the other hand, many elderly and disabled immigrants have little capacity to support themselves and lack relatives and others to whom they can turn for support.

Second, the reform will also force the states to create new systems of child welfare and child protection. This process is already well under way in some states, including Florida and Wisconsin, which have used the federal waivers they were granted over the past half decade to establish work-oriented assistance programs that depart radically from the traditional income maintenance model. Other states, which have been reluctant to change their systems, will have to scramble to meet the new law's deadlines.

Although it is uncertain how states will respond in the long run to the incentives in the new law, it seems clear that all states will offer aid under more restrictive criteria than they imposed in the recent past. For most, assistance payments will be linked to adult recipients' ability to find and keep a job. In some states, benefits for able-bodied parents will be available only if they find a job or participate in a short-term training program. Even in states that adopt more liberal qualifying requirements, a larger percentage of adult aid recipients will be required to work in exchange for continued assistance. The new emphasis on work is a significant and welcome change in the orientation of aid programs, one that enjoys broad public approval.

This new emphasis will, however, impose serious hardship on some poor parents and their children. This will not be immediately apparent. It will be a few years before most welfare recipients become subject to a cutoff in cash aid. By the turn of the century, however, many families will have exhausted their eligibility for federally supported payments. Most long-term aid recipients have limited labor market skills and poor prospects for improving their skills. Many have behavioral and health problems that make steady work difficult. In a labor market where the real wages of the unskilled have declined steadily for two decades, there is little reason to expect that even half of today's long-term welfare recipients will find steady jobs that can support a family. Some states may be generous in supplementing the earnings or subsidizing the day care of parents with poor job opportunities. They will have the necessary resources in the short run because the new block grants will actually provide them with more federal aid for support payments than they would have received under the old law. If history is a guide, however, in the longer run many states will not be generous.

Although the work orientation of the reform represents a notable improvement over the previous program, at least three effects of the new law are likely to prove troubling. First, by abolishing the entitlement of needy children to an important form of federal assistance, the 1996 reform places a large and extremely vulnerable population at risk. The law's sponsors may be confident that states will devise new systems that ensure the well-being of poor children, but the actual record of many state governments makes this assumption questionable.

Second, the new law's weak maintenance-of-effort requirements will allow states to divert resources that they once spent on aid to other uses, including tax reductions. This will be a particularly strong temptation in states faced with other pressing public demands, such as surging school enrollment or soaring prison costs. States that are concerned that their generous levels of assistance might attract poor residents from nearby states will also be tempted to reduce their own spending on assistance. Under the new law, the federal government will no longer share in the cost of expanded caseloads or more generous benefits, sharply increasing the cost to a state of being generous.

Finally, the new law offers scant fiscal relief to states that are hit by an economic downturn. If the economy weakens and assistance rolls soar, the combination of sharply lower state revenue and increased need may force states to slash benefits or tighten eligibility rules. The old formula for calculating federal payments to states helped cushion the blow of recessions because the federal government picked up at least half the cost of extra aid when the welfare rolls grew. Although the old funding formula was far from perfect, it provided much better incentives for state governments to protect spending on the poor during recessions than does the new block grant formula.

Many of the policy choices made in the new welfare law are likely to be revisited over the next decade. Medicaid changes, however, are likely to come sooner. Efforts to reform medicaid will be driven by continued state dissatisfaction with federal program requirements and by the search for budget savings. Governors are likely to push for greater state flexibility in the management of the program. At the federal level, any serious plan to balance the budget is likely to seek significant savings from medicaid.

In considering potential medicaid reforms, Congress and the president should be cognizant of five simple facts. First, most medicaid spending is made on behalf of the elderly and people with disabilities. Large cuts in medicaid spending will almost inevitably result in reduced services for these populations, which could create significant problems for these individuals, their families, and their communities.

Second, the number of uninsured has been rising in recent years. This problem has been compounded because the cross-subsidies that have allowed hospitals and other providers to offer charity care have been disappearing as the health marketplace has become more price competitive and managed care has spread. Sensible reform should avoid increasing the ranks of the uninsured, as would happen if the poor's entitlement to health care were eliminated.

Third, no matter which set of reforms is adopted, the federal government will continue to provide most of the money spent on medicaid and therefore should continue to insist on certain essential requirements. While there are certainly areas where states should be given more flexibility, such as managed care, hospital and nursing home reimbursement, and long-term care services, there are others, such as national floors on eligibility and benefits, where federal requirements must be retained. Variation in state cultural values and political preferences means that the poor would have no assurance of adequate protection if there were no minimum national standards.

Fourth, open-ended funding is the only way to ensure adequate resources when needs are constantly changing and the costs of services are unpredictable. The decision to convert federal cash assistance for children into a block grant was a mistake for which both beneficiaries and states will eventually pay a price. If limits must be placed on the growth of medicaid spending, the most equitable approach would be to establish per capita caps for which levels are set according to a measure of each state's need rather than according to historic spending patterns.

Finally, very little is known about the potential of managed care and other innovations to save money when applied to the medicaid population. This is especially true for the elderly and disabled medicaid beneficiaries, on whom over two-thirds of the program's resources are spent. If efficiencies of this type cannot generate substantial savings, services will have to be reduced.

As further fundamental changes are made in cash assistance, medicaid, food stamps, and other safety net programs to help reduce the deficit, policymakers need to relate proposed budget savings to plausible and desirable actions by states and providers. This suggestion might seem obvious, but a striking feature of the recent debate over welfare and medicaid reform was the absence of detailed discussion of either the specific measures needed to achieve the proposed savings or the impact that these measures might have on the well-being of vulnerable populations. Careful evaluation of the consequences of policy changes could contribute to a more stable and efficient safety net.

References

Bloom, Dan, and David Butler. 1995. *Implementing Time-Limited Welfare: Early Experiences in Three States.* New York: Manpower Demonstration Research Corporation.

Congressional Budget Office. 1996a. *Reducing the Deficit: Spending and Revenue Options* (August).

———. 1996b. "Federal Budgetary Implications of H.R. 3734, The Personal Responsibility and Work Opportunity Act of 1996" (August).

Executive Office of the President. 1996. "President Clinton's Health Care Initiative" (February).

Farkas, Steve, and others. 1996. *The Values We Live By: What Americans Want from Welfare Reform.* New York: Public Agenda Foundation.

Friedlander, Daniel, and Gary Burtless, eds. 1995. *Five Years After: The Long-Term Effects of Welfare-to-Work Programs.* New York: Russell Sage Foundation.

Gold, Marsha, Hilary Frazer, and Cathy Schoen. 1995. "Managed Care and Low-Income Populations: A Case Study of Managed Care in Tennessee." Prepared by Mathematica Policy Research, Inc., for Kaiser Family Foundation and Commonwealth Fund.

Greenberg, Mark, and Steve Savner. 1996. *A Detailed Summary of Key Provisions of the Temporary Family Assistance for Needy Families Block Grant of H.R. 3734.* Washington: Center for Law and Social Policy.

Holahan, John, and David Liska. 1995. "The Impact of the 'Medigrant' Plan on Federal Payments to States." Washington: Kaiser Commission on the Future of Medicaid.

Holahan, John, and others. 1995. "Cutting Medicaid Spending in Response to Budget Caps." Washington: Urban Institute.

Holahan, John, and Len Nichols. 1996. "State Health Policy in the 1990s." Washington: Urban Institute.

Institute of Medicine. Committee on Nursing Home Regulation. 1986. *Improving the Quality of Care in Nursing Homes.* Washington: National Academy Press.

Kaiser-Harvard Program on the Public and Health/Social Policy. 1996. "Survey of Americans on Health Policy: Questionnaire and National Toplines, July 30, 1996." Menlo Park, Calif.: Kaiser Family Foundation.

Kane, Rosalie, and others. 1991. "Adult Foster Care for the Elderly in Oregon: A Mainstream Alternative to Nursing Homes?" *American Journal of Public Health* 81 (September): 113–20.

Kenyon, Daphne. Forthcoming. "Health Care Reform and Competition among the States." In *Health Policy, Federalism, and the American States*, edited by Robert F. Rich and William D. White. Washington: Urban Institute Press.

Liska, David, and others. 1995. "Medicaid Expenditures and Beneficiaries: National and State Profiles and Trends, 1984–1993." Washington: Kaiser Commission on the Future of Medicaid.

Maynard, Rebecca A., ed. 1996. *Kids Having Kids*. New York: Robin Hood Foundation.

Nightingale, Demetra, and Robert H. Haveman, eds. 1995. *The Work Alternative: Welfare Reform and the Realities of the Job Market*. Washington: Urban Institute Press.

Office of Management and Budget. 1996. *Mid-Session Review of the 1997 Budget*.

Pierson, Paul. 1995. "The Creeping Nationalization of Income Transfers in the United States, 1935–94." In *European Social Policy: Between Fragmentation and Integration*, edited by Stephan Leibfried and Paul Pierson, 301–28. Brookings.

Reischauer, Robert D., and R. Kent Weaver. 1995. "Financing Welfare: Are Block Grants the Answer?" In *Looking Before We Leap: Social Science and Welfare Reform*, edited by R. Kent Weaver and William T. Dickens, 13–26. Brookings Occasional Paper.

Rosenbaum, Sara, and Julie Darnell. 1996. "Medicaid Reform: A Comparison of Current Law, Medigrant and the National Governors' Association Medicaid Reform Proposal." Washington: George Washington University Medical Center, Center for Health Policy Research.

Rowland, Diane, and others. 1995. *Medicaid and Managed Care: Lessons from the Literature*. Washington: Kaiser Commission on the Future of Medicaid.

Sparer, Michael, Marsha Gold, and Lois Simon. 1996. "Managed Care and Low-Income Populations: A Case Study of Managed Care in California." Prepared by Mathematica Policy Research, Inc., for Kaiser Family Foundation and Commonwealth Fund.

Super, David A., and others. 1996. "The New Welfare Law." Washington: Center on Budget and Policy Priorities (August).

Urban Institute. 1996. *Potential Effects of Congressional Welfare Reform Legislation on Family Incomes*. Washington.

U.S. Department of Health and Human Services. Office of Disability, Aging and Long-Term Care Policy. 1994. *Cost Estimates for the Long-Term Care Provisions under the Health Security Act*.

U.S. General Accounting Office. 1993. *Alternatives for Improving the Distribution of Funds to States*. HRD-93-112FS.

———. 1995a. *Block Grants: Characteristics, Experience, and Lessons Learned*. HEHS-95-74.

———. 1995b. *Medicaid: Restructuring Approaches Leave Many Questions*. HEHS-95-103.

———. 1995c. *Medicaid: Spending Pressures Drive States toward Program Reinvention*. HEHS-95-122.

U.S. House of Representatives. Committee on Ways and Means. 1994. *Overview of Entitlement Programs: Background Material and Data on Programs within the Jurisdiction of the Committee on Ways and Means.* Committee Print. 103 Cong. 2 sess. Government Printing Office.

U.S. House of Representatives. 1994. *Proposed Legislation—Work and Responsibility Act of 1994.* H.Doc. 103-273. 103 Cong. 2 sess. Government Printing Office.

———. 1996. *Personal Responsibility and Work Opportunity Act of 1996: Conference Report to Accompany H.R. 3734.* H.Rept. 104-725. 104 Cong. 2 sess. Government Printing Office.

Weaver, R. Kent. 1996. "Deficits and Devolution and the 104th Congress." *Publius* 26 (Fall).

Weaver, R. Kent, and William T. Dickens. 1995. "Looking Before We Leap: An Introduction." In *Looking Before We Leap: Social Science and Welfare Reform*, edited by R. Kent Weaver and William T. Dickens, 1–12. Brookings Occasional Paper.

Weaver, R. Kent, Robert Y. Shapiro, and Lawrence R. Jacobs. 1995. "Public Opinion on Welfare Reform: A Mandate for What?" In *Looking Before We Leap: Social Science and Welfare Reform*, edited by R. Kent Weaver and William T. Dickens, 109–28. Brookings Occasional Paper.

Wiener, Joshua M. 1981. "A Sociological Analysis of Government Regulation: The Case of Nursing Homes." Harvard University, Department of Sociology.

———. Forthcoming. "Can Medicaid Long-Term Care Expenditures for the Elderly Be Reduced?" *Gerontologist* 36.

Wiener, Joshua M., and Raymond J. Hanley. 1992. "Caring for the Disabled Elderly: There's No Place Like Home." In *Improving Health Policy and Management: Nine Critical Research Issues for the 1990s*, edited by Stephen M. Shortell and Uwe E. Reinhardt, 75–110. Ann Arbor: Health Administration Press.

Wiener, Joshua M., Laurel Hixon Illston, and Raymond J. Hanley. 1994. *Sharing the Burden: Strategies for Public and Private Long-Term Care Insurance.* Brookings.

4

ROBERT D. REISCHAUER

The Unfulfillable Promise: Cutting Nondefense Discretionary Spending

IF PAST ACTIONS or current proposals are harbingers, discretionary spending will bear a major portion of the burden in future efforts to balance the federal budget. The two largest deficit reduction packages ever enacted, the Omnibus Reconciliation Acts of 1990 and 1993 (OBRA90 and OBRA93), relied heavily on restraining discretionary spending: they extracted 45 percent and 18 percent, respectively, of their savings from discretionary accounts.[1] All of the balanced budget plans proposed during the 1995 and 1996 budget debates called for disproportionate reductions in discretionary spending.

A bit over 40 percent of the federal government's program spending is devoted to "discretionary" activities. They have this designation because the levels of funding for them must be reconsidered each year when Congress and the president craft the thirteen annual appropriation bills. If Congress and the president decide to reduce or eliminate appropriations for a particular discretionary program, spending on that activity is scaled back or stops when previously provided resources run out. This contrasts with the procedure governing spending on entitlements—such as medicare, guaranteed student loans, food stamps, and veterans' pensions—and other mandatory programs. Their spending is determined by the payment rules and benefit eligibility criteria specified in authorizing legislation, which Congress does not have to act on each year.

The discretionary spending restraint that resulted from OBRA90 and OBRA93 largely affected defense accounts, which constitute just

---

1. Congressional Budget Office (1994, pp. 5, 7). These are percentages of the nondebt service deficit reduction over fiscal years 1991–95 and 1994–98.

under one-half of all discretionary spending. Although real, or inflation-adjusted, nondefense discretionary spending was reduced modestly between fiscal years 1995 and 1996 (and a bit further in 1997),
such spending in 1996 was still some 15 percent above 1990 levels.
Real defense spending, on the other hand, fell 28 percent over this
six-year period.

In contrast to this recent experience, the various balanced budget
plans debated during 1995 and 1996 called for extracting the vast
bulk of future discretionary savings from nondefense accounts. This
would represent a considerable challenge for the political system,
which has yet to prove that it can reduce nondefense discretionary
spending significantly over a sustained period. The implications of
substantial reductions in nondefense discretionary spending are not
fully appreciated by many policymakers nor by the public, which
generally has been presented with a caricature of this category of
federal spending, depicting it as a repository of waste, low-priority
activities, pork barrel programs, and funding for a bloated bureaucracy. This chapter examines the challenges and ramifications of sharp
cutbacks in nondefense discretionary spending. (Defense spending is
covered in chapter 5.)

What Is the Nondefense Discretionary Portion of the Budget?

The nondefense discretionary portion of the budget encompasses
a vast collection of federal activities, including international affairs,
environmental protection, space exploration, the federal court and
prison systems, health research, many categorical grants to states and
localities, the administrative expenses of many entitlement programs
such as social security and medicare, and the compensation for most
of the federal work force. In 1995 discretionary activities made up
over 90 percent of the budgets of the Departments of Defense, Commerce, Justice, Energy, Interior, Housing and Urban Development,
State, and Transportation and most independent agencies, such as the
Environmental Protection Agency (EPA), the National Aeronautical
and Space Administration (NASA), and the Small Business Administration (SBA).

It is difficult to provide a succinct or coherent description of nondefense discretionary spending because of its heterogeneity. Never-

FIGURE 4-1. Nondefense Discretionary Outlays, by Function, Fiscal Year 1996

Percent

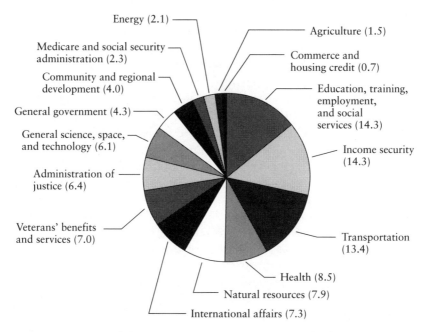

SOURCE: Congressional Budget Office.

theless, some understanding of this portion of the budget can be gained by examining the functional distribution of this spending and its composition from a variety of overlapping perspectives.

Unlike mandatory spending—virtually all of which is concentrated in the three superfunctions of income security (including social security), health (including medicare), and net interest—nondefense discretionary spending is spread out more evenly across the sixteen functional areas that are used to categorize federal spending (figure 4-1). Three functions—income security (mostly housing assistance), transportation, and education, training, employment, and social services—each accounted for roughly 14 percent of total nondefense discretionary spending in fiscal 1996. Six other functions—health, natural resources, international affairs, veterans' benefits, administration of justice, and general science, space, and technology—each constituted between 6 and 8 percent of the total.

A significant portion of nondefense discretionary spending—about one-third in fiscal 1995—is devoted to physical investment and research and development. Some examples of these activities are construction and rehabilitation of infrastructure (such as highways, airports, public housing, veterans' hospitals, and post offices), major acquisitions of equipment (such as new radar for the air traffic control system and new computers for the IRS), and research and development programs of the National Institutes of Health, NASA, the Department of Energy, the Department of Agriculture, and the EPA.

A bit over one-third of all nondefense discretionary spending is provided to state and local governments in the form of grants. The largest discretionary grant programs are for physical infrastructure (highways and mass transit), education (for the disadvantaged, disabled, and those with special needs), community development, low-income housing, and nutrition assistance (for low-income children and pregnant women).

Some federal grants represent relatively small additions to the state and local resources devoted to the activities for which they are provided. A reduction in or elimination of the federal grant would not cause significant disruption in such a circumstance. This would be true for the $155 million Department of Education grant for library services, which amounts to less than 3 percent of state and local library expenditures. Federal aid may be significant in some other areas, but it has largely substituted for state or local resources that have been freed up by the federal assistance for other public uses or tax relief. In such cases, recipient governments would increase their own commitments to offset a significant portion of any reduction of federal aid. There are still other areas, however, where states and localities devote almost none of their own resources to the particular activity supported by the federal grant program. Recipient governments are, in effect, agents administering a federal activity. They would not undertake similar activities without federal aid. Examples of this would be the Department of Agriculture's nutritional assistance grants for low-income pregnant women and infants (WIC) and Head Start. In such cases, termination of the federal grant program would probably mean an end to the provision of the affected service.

Most federal assistance for low-income individuals is provided through entitlement programs such as food stamps, medicaid, welfare, and supplemental security income. Nevertheless, a significant portion of the nondefense discretionary budget is aimed at helping vulnerable population groups. In fiscal year 1995, a bit over one-fifth of the nondefense discretionary budget was devoted to activities that assisted low-income persons.[2] The largest discretionary low-income programs are in the areas of housing, education (title I, Head Start, and Pell grants), nutrition (WIC), and community development.

A significant portion of the nondefense discretionary budget is devoted to employee compensation. Excluding the uniformed and civilian employees of the Department of Defense and Postal Service employees, the federal government employs some 1.2 million people.[3] Salaries and benefits for these workers amounted to 27 percent of all nondefense discretionary spending in fiscal year 1995.

Is All Discretionary Spending Really Discretionary?

The "discretionary" label is often interpreted as meaning that this spending is, in some sense, less essential than entitlement or mandatory spending and would therefore be less difficult to scale back. As a general rule, this is true. Certainly, some mandatory spending, such as interest payments on the federal debt, cannot be reduced directly; only actions that reduce the size of the national debt or lead to lower interest rates can ease the burden of debt service. Other mandatory spending programs, like social security and medicare, cannot be reduced significantly in the short run because they involve commitments made to the retired and disabled, many of whom have adjusted their saving during their working years based on the government's promises of future support. Current beneficiaries and those approaching retirement age have only a limited ability to compensate for any cutback that might be made in federal assistance. Furthermore, these programs, along with others such as unemployment compensation, veterans' pensions and compensation, and civil service and military retirement, are supported by large and powerful constituencies that vigorously resist efforts to reduce their benefits.

However, not all types of discretionary spending would be less difficult to reduce than mandatory program spending. At least four types have been and will continue to be difficult to scale back sub-

2. The Center on Budget and Policy Priorities (1996) estimated that 20.5 percent of nondefense discretionary appropriations were designated for low-income programs. This estimate excludes obligations for the Pell grant program.

3. This is the 1995 federal nondefense, non–Postal Service employment on a full-time equivalent basis.

TABLE 4-1. Nondefense Discretionary Spending That Would Be
Difficult to Cut[a]

Percent of fiscal 1995 nondefense discretionary outlays

Category	Percent
Administration of entitlement programs	4.1
Essential federal functions	19.0
Politically "sacrosanct"	24.2
Spending financed by offsetting receipts or trust fund revenues	14.1
Total[b]	46.7

SOURCE: Author's estimates from Office of Management and Budget data.
a. Because the detailed data needed to identify spending on certain activities are not available, the numbers here should be viewed as approximations.
b. Total is less than the sum of the categories because some programs are counted in more than one category.

stantially (see table 4-1). The first of these is the administrative spending associated with entitlement programs. Virtually all of the administrative costs of the social security and medicare programs are
categorized as discretionary spending, as are most of the federal-level
personnel and office expenditures associated with the administration
of welfare, guaranteed student loans, food stamps, and other entitlements.[4] Even if benefits in these programs were cut, administrative
costs would not necessarily decline. In fact, the opposite might be the
case. For example, medicare's administrative costs would probably
increase if an income-related part B premium were imposed or if a
more complex system allowing beneficiaries to choose among different health plans were adopted. It is, of course, possible to develop
more efficient administrative procedures, but such reforms often take
years to implement and require costly up-front investments in computers, software, and staff training. Moreover, they must be executed
carefully because indiscriminate cuts in program administration can
end up costing money if benefit error rates rise or the incidence of
fraud and abuse increases. In total, over $11 billion, or 4.1 percent,
of nondefense discretionary spending in fiscal year 1995 was associated with administering mandatory programs.

A second category of nondefense discretionary spending that will
be difficult to reduce substantially supports the conduct of certain
basic public activities that are necessary for the orderly functioning
of a heterogeneous society, a postindustrial economy, and a continental nation. Compared with most other advanced nations, the United

4. Federal payments to the states for their administrative costs are, for the most part,
mandatory spending.

States already delegates a great deal of the responsibility for public functions to subnational levels of government. Some minimal level of national effort is needed in areas where benefits or costs spill over state lines or where uniformity and coordination of policy are needed for efficiency or equity reasons. Included in this category would be the federal judicial system and the agencies that control immigration, protect the borders, keep the food supply safe, maintain public health, perform national police functions, forecast the weather, control air traffic, collect essential demographic and economic information, preserve the integrity of the financial system, and collect revenues for the federal government. The budgets of such entities constitute about 19 percent of nondefense discretionary spending.

Third are activities in the nondefense discretionary budget that have strong and enduring political support that transcends party differences. While any designation of the programs that might meet this criterion is necessarily subjective, spending on the National Institutes of Health, crime prevention, and veterans' programs would almost certainly be on any list of such activities. All told, about 24 percent of the nondefense discretionary spending might be considered politically mandatory and therefore difficult to scale back substantially to help balance the budget.

Finally, a handful of discretionary spending programs are financed, at least in part, by dedicated revenue sources. The most significant of these is the highway grant program, which is supported by the federal gasoline tax. If federal highway grants were reduced substantially, pressure would build to cut the federal gasoline tax commensurately, leading to little or no net deficit reduction. These types of programs constitute about 14 percent of discretionary spending.

For the balance of the discretionary accounts, where substantial cuts might be more feasible, spending would not fall immediately if decisions were made to scale back appropriations as part of the effort to balance the budget. This is because much of each year's discretionary outlays results from budget and contract authority provided in previous years. This is particularly true for activities that involve capital investment and forward-funded grants. Overall, some 52 percent of 1996 nondefense discretionary outlays resulted from spending authority granted before 1996. In some areas, the fraction is much higher. For example, 82 percent of fiscal 1996 spending on community and regional development was attributable to spending authority granted in previous fiscal years.

Trends in Nondefense Discretionary Spending

Before examining the extent to which the recent plans to balance the budget would reduce discretionary spending, it is instructive to look back over the past three decades to see how, where, and why nondefense discretionary spending has changed. Such an inquiry must start by selecting a sensible method of comparing discretionary spending in different years. A significant controversy has recently developed over the issue of how changes in federal discretionary spending should be characterized. Some have argued strongly that the focus of attention should be on nominal spending levels. They feel that the word "cut" should be used only when an activity is allocated fewer dollars in one year than it received before. Any increase in funds available to a program, no matter how small, should be characterized as an increase. After all, they reason, this comports with common usage, whether it be a change in one's pay or in the price of a gallon of gasoline bought at the pump.

Others think the focus should be on what the government can buy rather than on what it spends. Cognizant of the fact that inflation erodes the purchasing power of a dollar, they think that real or inflation-adjusted spending levels should be compared. In this framework, the term "cut" is applicable when a program is not provided sufficient funds to carry on the same level of activity from one year to the next. In other words, if prices rose 5 percent during a year, but a program's budget increased only 2 percent, they would argue that the program experienced a 3 percent cut. To illustrate their case, advocates of this position point to the defense budget, which was $282 billion in both 1987 and 1994. Those who are convinced that nominal spending levels represent the most appropriate comparisons would have to hold that the defense budget was not cut over this period. Why then did the Department of Defense scale back the number of active-duty Army divisions from 18 to 12, the number of Navy battle force ships from 546 to 373, and the number of active-duty uniformed personnel from 2.2 million to 1.6 million over this period? The answer, of course, was that the purchasing power of the dollar eroded significantly between 1987 and 1994; $282 billion did not buy as much in 1994 as it did seven years earlier.

Some would take this logic a step further by arguing that, since many government activities are intended to provide services to an ever-expanding population, the most appropriate way to measure whether there has been an expansion or contraction of a government activity is to examine what has happened to the per capita, inflation-adjusted value of the resources provided to the program. This, however, may represent an overstatement because the need for or value of some important discretionary services is little affected by the size of the nation's population. Defense would be an obvious example of this, as would spending on research and development, the weather service, and Coast Guard maintenance of navigational aids. For other federal activities, the size of the general population may be a poor proxy for the size of the specific group for whom the service is intended. For example, the need for educational grants is related to the size of the elementary and secondary school population, and the meals on wheels program to the number of low-income elderly.

It is clear that each of these measures has its merits as well as its limitations. However, for the purpose of comparing spending across long periods of time, the most useful overall yardstick is the level of real or inflation-adjusted spending. This measure provides a rough indication of whether a program can expand, can just hold its own, or must scale back its activities in the face of rising prices.

Using this metric, nondefense discretionary spending has gone through four distinct periods of expansion and contraction over the course of the past thirty-four years (see figure 4-2).[5] The expansions have occurred when Democrats have had majorities in both the Senate and the House of Representatives; the periods of restraint and retrenchment are broadly coincident with Republican control of at least one chamber.

From the early 1960s through 1980, inflation-adjusted nondefense discretionary spending grew at a robust 4.9 percent a year. International affairs was the only functional category of discretionary spending that declined (− 1.6 percent a year) during this period. The most rapid rates of growth were experienced by education, training, employment, and social services (12.8 percent a year), income security (11.9 percent), community development (11.3 percent), and transportation (8.9 percent). The growth of nondefense discretionary spending was primarily associated with the new programs that proliferated during Lyndon Johnson's Great Society and Richard Nixon's New Federalism eras. Title I educational assistance for the disadvan-

5. Data breaking federal spending into the discretionary and mandatory categories are available only for fiscal year 1962 and the years thereafter.

FIGURE 4-2. Growth of Real Nondefense Discretionary Spending, Fiscal Years 1962–96

1962 = 100[a]

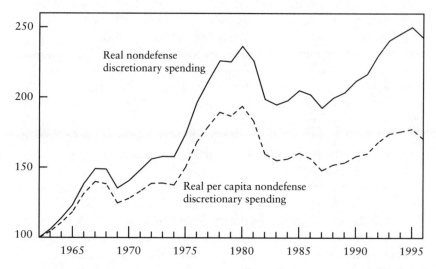

SOURCES: *Budget of the United States Government, Fiscal Year 1997, Historical Tables*; Congressional Budget Office; and Bureau of the Census.

a. In 1962 nondefense discretionary spending = $83.9 billion in fiscal 1987 dollars; per capita nondefense discretionary spending = $450 in fiscal 1987 dollars.

taged, Head Start, Pell grants, community development block grants, and section 8 rental housing assistance were just a few of the discretionary programs that were launched during this period.

Between 1980 and 1987, real nondefense discretionary spending declined by almost one-fifth (− 18.6 percent) or by 2.9 percent a year, even as real defense spending grew at 6 percent a year. This retrenchment was initiated by the Reagan administration and found support in the Republican-controlled Senate. The energy function, as well as the functions that had experienced the most rapid expansions during the previous era (with the exception of income security), suffered the greatest reductions during these years of retrenchment.[6] Those who remember the high inflation that characterized the beginning of the 1980s may assume that rapid and unexpected price increases helped

6. The annual average decline in commerce and housing was 14.5 percent; in community development, 11.6 percent; in education, training, and social services, 6.1 percent; and in energy, 7.3 percent.

to bring about the fall in inflation-adjusted nondefense discretionary spending. This was not the case, however. In fact, the rate of inflation, measured by the GDP deflator, was lower during 1980–87 than during 1962–80.[7]

The years 1987 to 1995 are generally considered a period of budget stringency. The Gramm-Rudman-Hollings budget restraints were in place, and the two largest deficit reduction packages in the nation's history (OBRA90 and OBRA93) were enacted. Nevertheless, while real defense discretionary spending shrank at 3.8 percent a year during these years, real nondefense discretionary spending grew at an annual rate of 3.3 percent. The functions experiencing the most rapid annual growth rates were administration of justice (7.0 percent), health (5.9 percent), income security (5.9 percent), and agriculture (5.0 percent).

All indications are that a new era of retrenchment in nondefense discretionary spending began in 1995, after Republicans won control of both the Senate and the House of Representatives. In the spring of 1995, they rescinded several billion dollars that the previous Congress had appropriated for fiscal 1995 and then cut real budget authority for 1996 by 7.1 percent. Real outlays on nondefense discretionary activities fell by about 2.2 percent between 1995 and 1996. The appropriations bills approved for fiscal 1997 imply a reduction in real nondefense discretionary budget authority and outlays from 1996 levels of 1.7 percent and 0.8 percent, respectively. As is discussed in more detail later in this chapter, the retrenchment will be longer and deeper than that experienced during 1980–87 if a plan similar to any of the balanced budget proposals debated during 1995 and 1996 is enacted into law and adhered to.

To summarize, real nondefense discretionary spending has increased by about two and one-half times over the past thirty-four years. This increase reflected the great expansion that took place in the scope of the government's discretionary activities. In 1962 the federal government did very little in the area of environmental protection, space science and exploration was in its infancy, grants to help school districts educate disadvantaged children did not exist, and federal assistance for low-income persons with high energy costs was

7. Using the implicit GDP deflator (chain-weighted), inflation was 4.7 percent a year between calendar years 1980 and 1987 and 5.3 percent a year between 1962 and 1980.

FIGURE 4-3. Nondefense Discretionary Spending as a Percentage of
Total Outlays and GDP, Fiscal Years 1962–96

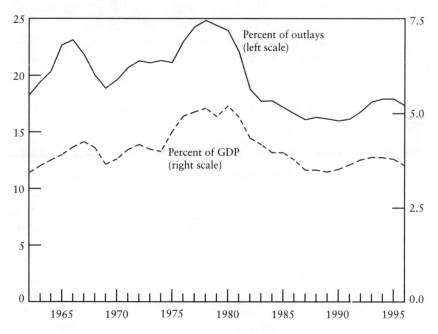

SOURCES: *Budget of the United States Government, Fiscal Year 1997, Historical Tables*; and Congressional Budget
Office.

unheard of. But over 90 percent of the increase occurred between
1962 and 1980. Since 1980 real nondefense discretionary spending
has increased only 6 percent.

As was mentioned previously, there are other ways to look at
discretionary spending trends. One of these is to examine changes in
real per capita spending. Using this measure, nondefense discretionary
spending increased by 94 percent between 1962 and 1980 (figure
4-2). Real per capita spending fell by about 24 percent from 1980
through 1987. Over the next eight years, it grew by 20 percent. In
1996 real per capita nondefense discretionary spending was 71 percent above the 1962 level but about 12 percent below the peak
reached in 1980.

Another way of looking at these trends is to examine the share of
total spending devoted to nondefense discretionary activities (figure
4-3). This share fluctuated a good deal over the past thirty-four years
but was not much different in 1996 from its level three decades earlier.

In 1962, 18.3 percent of all federal spending was devoted to nondefense discretionary programs. This share rose, although not steadily,
until the late 1970s, when over 24 percent of the budget was devoted
to nondefense discretionary programs. During the period of retrenchment, the share of the budget devoted to nondefense discretionary
activities receded to a low of 16.1 percent in 1987. It then inched
back up, reaching 17.9 percent by 1995 before falling back down to
17.3 percent in 1996.

Yet another way to examine nondefense discretionary spending
trends is to look at the changing share of the nation's resources—its
GDP—that is being devoted to these activities (figure 4-3). As a percentage of GDP, nondefense discretionary spending rose from 3.4
percent in 1962 to a peak of 5.2 percent in 1980. This ratio fell
gradually back to 3.4 percent in 1989, then rose to 3.8 percent in
1995, and edged down to 3.6 percent in 1996.

It is worth noting that much of the expansion in discretionary
spending has taken the form of increased grants to state and local
governments. Roughly one-third of the expansion in discretionary
spending was accounted for by increased grants to states and localities. Direct (nongrant) nondefense discretionary spending fell from
3.2 percent of GDP in 1962 to 2.5 percent in 1995.

This review of recent discretionary spending trends, viewed
through several different measures, puts into perspective the challenge
posed by the current effort to substantially reduce discretionary
spending to help balance the budget. It shows both that nondefense
discretionary spending has increased significantly over the past three
decades and that, during these years, this category of spending has
weathered one significant contraction. However, that retrenchment,
which occurred between 1980 and 1987, made cuts from historically
high spending levels.

The Appeal of Deficit Reduction through
Discretionary Spending Cuts

The budget-balancing plans that were proposed during the 1995
and 1996 debates derived between two-fifths and two-thirds of their
gross deficit reduction from cuts in total discretionary spending. These
contributions were disproportionate to either discretionary spending's
fraction of total spending or the contribution that such spending is

expected to make to the growth in total spending over the next decade. Why have policymakers chosen to rely so heavily on cuts in discretionary spending to balance the budget?

The primary explanation is straightforward: by relying on discretionary spending cuts, policymakers can claim credit for deficit reduction without having to identify the specific programs that would be affected. All that is required is that they impose overall limits on future aggregate discretionary spending. This situation arises because decisions about how much to spend on individual discretionary programs are made each year during the annual appropriation process and, therefore, there is no way to predetermine which programs would be cut to meet any limits that are placed on overall future discretionary spending. Deficit reduction derived from entitlement programs or tax increases, in contrast, involves immediate and identifiable changes in legislation spelling out how and when entitlement benefits would be cut or taxes would be hiked.

The political resistance to unspecified future discretionary spending cuts is limited because each claimant can imagine that, if it marshals its supporters effectively, it will not be harmed by restraints placed on this category of spending. Some also believe that the budget climate will change as the years go by and expect that any spending caps that are adopted now will be relaxed in the future.

The actual mechanism through which discretionary spending reductions are realized was established in the Budget Enforcement Act, which was title XIII of OBRA90, the deficit reduction measure President Bush and the Democratic Congress agreed to in October 1990. This legislation established annual limits or caps on the aggregate budget authority and outlays available for discretionary programs for fiscal years 1991–95. For 1991–93, separate limits (called fire walls) were set for defense, international, and domestic discretionary spending. After 1993, the division of the limited amount of discretionary resources among these three categories was left up to the regular appropriations process. The deficit reduction package put together by President Clinton and the Democratic Congress in 1993 (OBRA93) extended the overall discretionary spending limits to fiscal years 1996–98.

The limits established in 1990 and 1993 were set to allow only an 8.1 percent rise in nominal discretionary spending over the 1990–95 period and a 1.7 percent rise over 1995–98. Since inflation during these two periods was expected to be 20.3 percent and 7.7 percent, respectively, the limits implied a reduction in the real resources available for discretionary programs of about 18 percent over the 1990–98 period. (In real terms, actual discretionary outlays declined by a bit over 10 percent between 1990 and 1996.)

Under the Budget Enforcement Act, the limits are enforced by sequestration, a procedure that was created by the Balanced Budget and Emergency Deficit Control Act of 1985 (Gramm-Rudman-Hollings). If enacted appropriations cause the discretionary spending limits to be breached in any year, the Office of Management and Budget (OMB) is required to sequester, that is, reduce by an equal percentage, the spending authority of each discretionary activity to eliminate the excess.[8] This threat, along with House and Senate rules requiring that budget resolutions and appropriations bills stay within the Budget Enforcement Act caps, has been sufficient to restrain discretionary spending along the lines required by the caps.[9]

The Balanced Budget Proposals of 1995 and 1996

All of the plans to balance the budget that were proposed during the 1995 and 1996 debates called for reducing the existing discretionary spending caps through fiscal 1998 and establishing caps for 1999 through 2002.[10] The first of these plans to be debated, the fiscal 1996 congressional budget resolution, which was adopted in June 1995, relied on discretionary spending restraint for a bit over half of its gross deficit reduction (table 4-2).[11] Under this plan, overall real

8. The limits are adjusted to accommodate spending that both the president and Congress designate as for "emergency" purposes. With the exception of spending for the Gulf conflict (Desert Shield and Desert Storm), which was explicitly designated as an emergency in the law, the emergency escape hatch has been used sparingly, accounting for about $35.1 billion in nondefense outlays over the 1991–96 period. Most of this emergency spending was in response to natural disasters. The law also provides small special allowances for both budget authority and outlays. (P.L. 99-177, sec. 251(b)(2)(E) and (F).)

9. A technical drafting error in the foreign operations appropriation for fiscal 1991 caused an excess of $395 million, which was eliminated with a 1.9 percent across-the-board sequester of resources.

10. The Balanced Budget Act of 1995, the fiscal 1996 reconciliation bill, did not modify or extend the caps and OMB enforcement procedures because provisions to do this would have run afoul of the Senate rule (the Byrd rule) that precludes extraneous provisions in reconciliation bills. The caps were to be enforced, therefore, through the congressional budget resolutions and House and Senate rules.

11. The amounts of deficit reduction attributed to the various balanced budget plans are measured from the uncapped CBO baseline that was current at the time the proposal was made. They therefore include discretionary savings that are required by OBRA93.

TABLE 4-2. Discretionary Spending Reductions Required by Various Balanced Budget Plans[a]

	Percent of all noninterest deficit reduction						Percent reduction from uncapped baseline level					
	Total		Defense		Nondefense		Total		Defense		Nondefense	
Budget plan	1996–2002	2002	1996–2002	2002	1996–2002	2002	1996–2002	2002	1996–2002	2002	1996–2002	2002
Plans for the fiscal 1996 budget cycle												
Congressional budget resolution for fiscal 1996 (June 1995)	51.2	50.1	15.1	16.6	36.1	33.5	−15.4	−24.1	−9.5	−16.7	−20.9	−30.9
Balanced Budget Act (November 1995)	56.7	54.2	16.2	17.3	40.6	40.6	−14.7	−22.8	−8.8	−15.2	−20.3	−29.7
President's balanced budget plan (December 1995)[b]	67.5	67.2	26.6	18.1	40.8	49.1	−12.1	−22.9	−9.9	−13.1	−14.1	−32.6
Plans for the fiscal 1997 budget cycle												
Congressional budget resolution for fiscal 1997 (June 1996)	53.9	52.2	18.2	18.0	35.6	34.1	−9.8	−18.7	−7.8	−13.2	−14.7	−24.0
President's fiscal 1997 budget (March 1996)[c]	55.7	52.4	25.7	16.2	30.0	36.2	−9.4	−16.2	−8.8	−10.2	−9.9	−22.0
Senate Centrist Coalition (June 1996)[d]	46.1	45.3	23.3	21.9	22.8	23.5	−9.2	−16.6	−9.4	−16.3	−8.9	−16.9
House "Blue Dog" Coalition (June 1996)	46.8	49.6	18.5	19.8	28.4	29.8	−10.0	−16.0	−8.0	−13.0	−11.9	−18.9

a. Measured against the uncapped CBO baseline; includes discretionary spending reductions required by OBRA93.
b. Assumes the defense levels proposed in the president's 1997 budget.
c. Assumes that all of the contingent discretionary cuts would be in nondefense accounts.
d. Estimates are for the 1997–2003 period and for 2003.

discretionary spending in 2002 would have been reduced by 24 percent below 1995 levels; defense spending, by 17 percent, and nondefense spending, by 31 percent.

By November 1995, when Congress passed the Balanced Budget Act—the legislation embodying the budget resolution's tax and entitlement policies—the CBO had reduced its estimates of future baseline deficits and discretionary spending and increased its estimate of the fiscal dividend that would result from balancing the budget. These revisions meant that the spending cuts needed to both balance the budget and offset the revenue loss associated with the budget resolution's proposed tax cuts did not have to be as deep as those called for by the budget resolution. However, Congress chose to use this relief not to ease the restraint on discretionary spending but rather to scale back the resolution's proposed cuts in medicare, medicaid, and other entitlements. As a result, the discretionary spending cuts associated with the act were similar in severity to those called for in the budget resolution.

President Clinton vetoed the Balanced Budget Act in December 1995 and subsequently submitted the first administration deficit reduction plan that the CBO judged would achieve a balanced budget by 2002. Discretionary spending cuts constituted over two-thirds of the overall deficit reduction called for by the president's plan; this was an even greater share of the total than the Republicans had proposed. However, averaged over the entire 1996–2002 period, the president's plan required a bit less discretionary spending restraint than the Republican plan. A major reason why this was possible was that the president's plan called for substantially less in total spending reductions than the Balanced Budget Act. The president could achieve budget balance with smaller spending cuts in part because he proposed much smaller tax cuts. Moreover, the president's plan called for a more gradual reduction in the deficit between 1996 and 2000 and much sharper reductions during the final two years.[12]

Nevertheless, by 2002 the real discretionary spending cuts under the president's proposal would be every bit as deep—23 percent below 1995 levels—as those required by the Republican plan. The president did not specify how the discretionary cuts in his December 1995 plan would have been allocated between defense and nondefense pro-

12. Most of the resources made available from these decisions were devoted to protecting entitlement programs from severe cuts.

grams. However, if one assumes that defense spending in this plan would have been similar to that recommended in the fiscal 1997 budget proposal the administration released a few weeks later, the reduction in nondefense spending by 2002 would have been slightly larger than that called for by the Republican plan.

The fiscal 1996 appropriation bills were the first installment of the multiyear discretionary spending restraint called for in the fiscal 1996 budget resolution. As of the start of the fiscal year on October 1, 1995, Congress had sent to the president only two of the thirteen appropriation bills. The president vetoed one of these (legislative branch) and the House and Senate continued to wrangle with each other and with the administration over the eleven bills that had not yet cleared Congress. The president threatened to veto a number of these bills if Congress did not increase funding for domestic activities in general and add resources to some of the administration's priority programs in particular. A series of short-term appropriation measures, known as continuing resolutions, kept the government running. When the Congress and the president reached impasses on the terms under which these temporary funding measures would be extended, nonessential activities in departments and agencies whose appropriations had not been enacted were brought to a halt. The two partial government shutdowns that occurred, one lasting from November 14 though November 19 and the other from December 16 through January 5, 1996, were the longest budget shutdowns in the nation's history. It was not until April 26, 1996, over six and one-half months into the fiscal year, that the final appropriations measure was signed into law. The battles between Senate and House Republicans, between congressional Republicans and Democrats, and between the Congress and the administration over the 1996 appropriation bills only underscored the difficulties inherent in cutting nondefense discretionary spending significantly.

When the dust from the battle had settled, the Republican Congress had, for the most part, prevailed. Appropriations for 1996 were scaled back much along the lines laid out in the 1996 congressional budget resolution (table 4-3). Nondefense discretionary budget authority was cut about 7 percent in real terms, and nominal nondefense discretionary outlays increased by less than 1 percent, a reduction of about 2 percent in real terms. The allocation of discretionary spending between defense and nondefense activities was close to the division called for in the budget resolution, providing some $6.3 billion more

TABLE 4-3. Discretionary Budget Authority and Outlays,
Fiscal Years 1996 and 1997

Billions of dollars

Budget plan	1996			1997		
	Total	Defense	Non-defense	Total	Defense	Non-defense
1996 congressional budget resolution						
Budget authority	489.2	265.4	223.8	487.4	268.0	219.5
Outlays	534.0	264.0	269.9	524.1	265.7	258.4
President's 1996 budget (mid-session review)						
Budget authority	537.5	258.3	279.2	528.7	253.9	274.8
Outlays	544.9	261.5	283.3	548.7	257.1	291.6
Actual appropriations for 1996[a]						
Budget authority	497.5	264.6	232.9	...	...	...
Outlays	540.8	266.7	274.1	...	...	...
1997 congressional budget resolution						
Budget authority	...	...	...	497.4	266.4	231.0
Outlays	...	...	...	538.6	265.0	273.6
President's 1997 budget (mid-session review)						
Budget authority	...	...	...	501.5	255.0	246.5
Outlays	...	...	...	540.7	259.7	281.0
Actual appropriations for 1997[a]						
Budget authority	...	...	...	505.6	265.8	239.8
Outlays	...	...	...	541.6	264.9	278.4
Addendum: *Appropriations for 1995*[a]	*Before recissions*			*After recissions*		
Budget authority	510.4	262.3	248.1	504.9	267.8	237.1
Outlays	547.9	270.3	277.6	545.7	273.6	272.1

SOURCES: Author's estimates based on data from the Office of Management and Budget; *Mid-Session Review of the 1997 Budget; Mid-Session Review of the 1996 Budget*; Concurrent Resolution on the Budget for Fiscal Years 1996 and 1997; and Congressional Budget Office.

a. For 1995, includes $8.3 billion in budget authority and $8.8 billion in outlays for emergencies; for 1996 includes $5.0 billion in budget authority and $2.7 billion in outlays for emergencies; and for 1997 includes $1.9 billion in budget authority and $1.5 billion in outlays for emergencies.

budget authority for defense than the Clinton administration requested. In the battle over the spending bills, the president's only significant success was to force Congress to reallocate some of a shrunken nondefense pool of spending authority to some of the administration's priority programs.

The debate over the 1997 budget, which began before the final decisions had been made on the previous year's budget, centered on four plans: the president's fiscal 1997 budget proposal, the House Coalition ("Blue Dog") plan, the Senate Centrist Coalition (Chaffee-Breaux) plan, and the plan crafted by the Republican majorities of the Budget Committees, which became the fiscal 1997 congressional budget resolution. While all four had the same ultimate objective, they differed on several dimensions. With respect to taxes, the 1997 budget resolution accommodated $122 billion of net tax relief over the 1997–2002 period; the Senate Centrist Coalition budget allowed for a net revenue loss of $105 billion; the president's budget, including his contingent measures, reduced revenues by only $6 billion; and the House "Blue Dog" Coalition plan, which did not offer any tax cuts, called for a revenue increase of $90 billion.[13] Two of the plans, the Senate Centrist Coalition and the House "Blue Dog" proposals, recommended reducing the automatic annual inflation adjustments that are applied to many entitlement benefits and to certain parameters of the personal income tax code; they expected $91 billion and $51 billion of deficit reduction, respectively, from this reduced CPI indexing. The Senate Centrist Coalition plan achieved a balanced budget in 2003; the three other plans reached balance in 2002.

In spite of these differences, all four proposals, like the ones debated the year before, relied heavily on discretionary spending cuts to achieve the goal of a balanced budget (table 4-2). A bit over half of the gross deficit reduction called for by the budget resolution and the president's budget proposal (with contingencies) was derived from restraining discretionary spending. The two bipartisan proposals relied on discretionary spending restraint for over two-fifths of their needed deficit reduction.

The depth of the cuts in discretionary spending called for by the four plans appears to be a bit smaller than those proposed a year earlier. Rather than reductions from baseline levels of roughly 23 percent by 2002, the proposed cuts were in the range of 16 percent

13. The president's budget was designed to achieve balance under the administration's economic and technical assumptions. It also contained a set of contingent measures that would be employed if the administration's assumptions proved to be too optimistic. The CBO judged that these contingent measures, which included additional discretionary spending cuts, termination of his tax cuts after 2000, and other spending reductions, would be necessary to achieve balance by 2002 and so they are assumed in the subsequent analysis. For comparability purposes, the Senate Centrist Coalition tax cut figure is for 1997–2002, although this plan does not achieve balance until 2003.

to 19 percent. Much of this apparent moderation, however, is illusory. It reflects the fact that these cuts are measured from 1996 spending levels, which, as a result of the reductions adopted during the 1996 appropriation cycle, were below the 1995 spending levels against which the previous year's budget-balancing plans were measured. Together with a slight reduction in anticipated inflation over 1996–2002, the appropriation cuts of 1996 reduced the baseline level of discretionary outlays in 2002 by 5.1 percent.[14]

As was the case with the balanced budget plans of the previous years, the discretionary spending restraint proposed by all of the plans, except the Senate Centrist Coalition plan, was concentrated on the nondefense accounts. The budget resolution called for cutting nondefense accounts almost twice as deeply as the defense accounts by 2002. The administration did not detail how its contingent discretionary spending reductions would be allocated between defense and nondefense. Officials suggested, however, that all of this additional restraint would be exercised on nondefense activities. If this were the case, as the estimates in table 4-2 assume, the reductions in nondefense discretionary spending in 2002 associated with the president's plan were twice as deep as his proposed cuts in defense. Under the plans, real nondefense spending by 2002 would be down from 1996 levels by somewhere between 17 percent and 24 percent.

How Realistic Are the Nondefense Discretionary Cuts?

If real nondefense discretionary spending were to be reduced along the lines proposed in the four budget-balancing plans that were debated in 1996, the decline would be larger than any experienced in at least the last half century. During the 1980-87 period of retrenchment, real nondefense discretionary spending fell by 19 percent. The four balanced budget plans call for reductions in real nondefense spending by 2002 from the peak 1995 level of between 22 percent (Senate Centrist Coalition) and 29 percent (the congressional budget resolution).

As a percentage of GDP, nondefense discretionary spending would fall from 3.8 percent in 1995 to between 2.4 percent and 2.6 percent

14. In other words, the CBO's estimate of 1995 spending levels adjusted for inflation to 2002 was 5.1 percent higher than its estimate of 1996 spending levels adjusted for inflation to 2002.

when the budget was balanced.[15] Nondefense discretionary spending levels of about 2.5 percent of GDP would be considerably lower than any the nation has experienced in half a century. In the mid-1950s, the nation devoted about 3.3 percent of its GDP to nondefense discretionary activities.[16] Only two-thirds of this—or 2.1 percent of GDP—was spent on domestic activities; international affairs absorbed the balance. The balanced budget proposals anticipate devoting roughly the same fraction—2.3 percent of GDP—to domestic discretionary activities, suggesting that a range of government programs similar to that provided in the early 1950s might be sustainable. This would represent a far more limited set of federal activities than the public has come to expect.

In the mid-1950s, numerous government agencies did not exist. A partial list includes the Departments of Transportation, Education, Energy, and Housing and Urban Development and agencies such as NASA, EPA, the Nuclear Regulatory Commission, the National Endowments for the Arts and Humanities, the Federal Emergency Management Agency, and the Legal Services Corporation. Many activities now taken as routine were not viewed as part of the federal government's responsibilities in the early 1950s. For example, the National Institutes of Health did not engage in an extensive extramural research effort, there was no interstate highway program, no housing assistance other than public housing was provided for low-income families, and no grants were available for needy postsecondary students. The vast array of discretionary grant programs for states and localities, including grants for educating disadvantaged elementary and secondary school children, preschool programs, waste water treatment facilities, and nutrition assistance for pregnant women and children, did not exist. It follows to reason that, if nondefense discretionary spending were ratcheted back to 1950s levels, many of these activities would have to be scrapped, or others with even longer tenure would have to be terminated. It is doubtful that the political system has the fortitude to undertake such a retrenchment or that voters would accept the scaled-back government, increased state and local taxes, or interstate disparities in service levels that would result.

15. As a percentage of GDP, the 1980–87 retrenchment, which was from 5.2 percent to 3.5 percent of GDP, was larger than that called for by the balanced budget plans.

16. Official estimates of discretionary spending are not available for years before 1962. These figures were provided by John Cogan of the Hoover Institution, who has constructed discretionary spending estimates going back to 1955.

TABLE 4-4. Change in Discretionary Spending from Baseline Levels, Various Balanced Budget Plans

Percent

Function	President's plan (2002)[a]	Congressional budget resolution (2002)	Blue Dog Coalition (2002)	Senate Coalition (2003)
International affairs	−28.4	−32.8	−34.3	−19.7
General science, space, and technology	−31.1	−20.5	−16.8	−18.6
Energy	−18.9	−34.4	−16.7	−12.0
Natural resources	−19.7	−23.4	−18.6	−21.3
Agriculture	−38.1	−41.0	−23.8	−21.0
Commerce and housing credit	−21.0	−37.9	−24.2	−22.6
Transportation	−39.6	−23.5	−25.8	−17.5
Community and regional development	−62.6	−46.0	−38.5	−7.7
Education, training, employment, and social services	6.7	−21.2	−5.1	−13.5
Health	−23.4	−20.7	−17.3	−19.7
Income security	−17.2	−15.2	−13.5	−5.7
Medicare and social security administration	−41.4	−27.6	−23.2	−31.2
Veterans' benefits and services	−37.2	−19.2	−20.7	−22.4
Administration of justice	−1.9	−19.6	−14.4	−23.6
General government	−16.8	−24.7	−26.8	−21.8
Total discretionary outlays	−16.2	−18.7	−16.0	−16.6
Defense	−10.2	−13.2	−13.0	−16.3
Nondefense	−22.0	−24.0	−18.9	−16.9

a. Contingent reductions in discretionary spending are distributed proportionately to the specified reductions in the president's nondefense discretionary spending proposals.

Because the balanced budget plans do not list the specific activities and programs that would be reduced or eliminated to stay within their discretionary spending limits, it is not possible to show conclusively that these cuts are infeasible or to test the public's reaction to a spartan level of government. The decisions about which programs will be cut and by how much, as was noted earlier, would be made year by year in the appropriations process. Nevertheless, the plans do contain suggested functional allocations of the limited discretionary resources that each would make available. These provide a flavor of the challenges that would face policymakers in future years (table 4-4).

The 1997 congressional budget resolution calls for real spending reductions of at least 19 percent below 1996 levels in all functions by 2002. The deepest cuts would be made in community and regional development, agriculture, international affairs, and energy. The

House "Blue Dog" plan would cut international affairs and community and regional development by more than one-third while education, training, employment, and social services would be nicked and administration of justice and income security would experience relatively modest reductions. The Senate coalition plan would mete out restraint fairly evenly across the discretionary activities of government. Income security and community and regional development would experience the least restraint.

The president's plan did not allocate the $46 billion of contingent discretionary cuts that the CBO says would be needed to achieve balance in 2002. For illustrative purposes, these have been allocated in table 4-4 across the nondefense functions in a manner that reflects the administration's stated priorities.[17] In this exercise, community and regional development would be cut by almost two-thirds, and social security and medicare administration, transportation, veterans' benefits, and agriculture would be reduced by well over one-third. Deep cuts like these are required in this plan because real spending for the education, training, employment, and social services function grows by about 7 percent and spending in the administration of justice function is reduced only marginally.

The figures in table 4-4 should not be accorded a great deal of significance. Their main value is to illustrate the depth of the cuts that would be necessary in some functions if others were to be spared deep cuts and the discretionary spending caps were to be met. They clearly raise questions of practicality. Will the nation's political system undergo such a dramatic transformation that Congress will be willing to reduce spending on veterans' programs by a fifth or more? Will the United States be willing to substantially reduce its foreign commitments and see its influence abroad erode significantly, as would be implied if international affairs spending were scaled back by between one-fifth and one-third? Will the distribution of political power in the Senate shift sufficiently to permit discretionary agricultural and rural programs to be cut by somewhere between 20 and 40 percent? Will the structures of the medicare and social security programs be so radically transformed over the next six years that their administrative costs could be slashed by more than one-quarter?

17. Within the nondefense discretionary category, the contingency cuts have been distributed proportionately with the reductions specified in the administration's basic proposal, excluding the function of education, training, employment, and social services.

The pace at which the recommended cuts are to be phased in raises further skepticism about the feasibility of the nondefense discretionary reductions proposed by the president's and the Senate Coalition plans. Both call for disproportionately sharp reductions in the last few years before balance is achieved.[18] Moreover, all of the plans permit higher levels of nondefense discretionary spending in 1997 and 1998 than would be allowed if this spending were reduced at an even pace over the entire period.

Making Do with Less: Strategies and Consequences

Nondefense discretionary spending reductions of the magnitudes proposed by the various budget-balancing plans may prove to be unattainable, but there is little doubt that this portion of the budget will be cut significantly as the effort to reduce the deficit continues. It is therefore worth exploring some of the strategies that are available for realizing savings in this part of the budget. It is also worth discussing how squeezing nondefense discretionary spending may affect other segments of the budget and other levels of government.

Probably the least sensible way to go about reducing nondefense discretionary spending would be to reduce the budgets of all activities by approximately equal percentages. This would leave the program complexity of government unchanged, decrease efficiency as administrative costs gobbled up an even higher fraction of program budgets, and reduce many programs to levels that are below the minimums needed to operate an activity on a national scale. Instead, it would make more sense for the federal government to cease involvement in certain activities altogether. But which ones? Which represent low-priority federal activities? A heterogeneous society that lives in a continental nation across which values, conditions, and needs vary greatly has difficulty developing consensus on such questions. A liberal intellectual living in San Francisco may view subsidies for the arts, hu-

---

18. If nondefense discretionary spending cuts from the baseline level grew by an equal percentage each year, 71 percent of the total reduction for the six-year period would take place in the last three years, 2000–02. Under the president's budget, the 1997 budget resolution, and the Blue Dog plan the fractions are 86 percent, 73 percent, and 71 percent, respectively. The Senate Centrist Coalition plan achieves balance in 2003. If spending were cut by an equal percentage each year, 69 percent of the aggregate reduction would occur in 2001–03 rather than the 64 percent called for by that plan.

manrities, and public broadcasting as among the most essential discretionary activities of the federal government while placing little value on subsidies for rural business development. The conservative farmer living in Montana may have the opposite view. In the end, political forces will determine which programs are augmented, which are trimmed, which are slashed, and which are abolished. Nevertheless, as the political battles unfold it is worth remembering that there are certain general principles that can be used to guide cutbacks.

For years analysts have argued that the nation should sort out, that is, rationalize the division of responsibilities between the federal government and the states and localities.[19] Those activities that serve no strong national purpose and those whose benefits do not spill over state lines, it is maintained, should either be left to state and local governments or not done at all. Under this guidance, the federal government could terminate its various economic development programs for which benefits are local in nature and many of its industry-specific subsidies. The activities of the Economic Development Administration, the Appalachian Regional Commission, the Small Business Administration, the rural development agencies of the Agriculture Department, and the community development programs of the Department of Housing and Urban Development would be among the former. So too would most of EPA's waste water treatment grants and DOT's mass transit assistance and much of its highway construction spending.[20] Discretionary industry-oriented subsidies would include export promotion activities, tourism promotion, and much of the research supported by the Departments of Agriculture and Energy.[21]

Advocates of these programs argue that the nation's economy and employment would be harmed and regional economic disparities would widen if they were abolished. Economists, however, believe that these programs have little or no effect on the overall national levels of economic activity and employment and only a small effect on the geographic location of economic activity, that is, whether it takes place in rural Nebraska or in Ohio. To the extent that states are unwilling or unable to invest in the infrastructure and other activities supported by these programs, inter- and intrastate disparities in

19. A recent example of this literature is Rivlin (1992).

20. If the federal gasoline tax were reduced along with highway grants, discretionary spending would be reduced but the deficit would be unaffected.

21. Moore and Stansel (1996).

levels of economic activity might increase somewhat, but only to the extent that the terminated federal resources were distributed disproportionately to some states.

Another approach for reducing discretionary spending would be to eliminate a number of the federal grant programs for which the federal role is minor relative to that of states and localities. Such terminations would have little effect on the overall level of services received by the public. This approach would call for ending many education grants such as those for vocational education, library and museum grants, and anticrime grants. Although it would save little in the aggregate, individual grant programs that distribute small amounts of money could also be phased out. There are dozens of such programs—for example, rural community fire protection grants—that distribute less than $10 million a year. Even though some of these grants may support a substantial fraction of the affected state or local activity, the federal administrative overhead for such programs is often disproportionate to the money distributed, and the resources are insufficient to have much of an effect on a nation as large as the United States.

When deciding which grants to terminate, it probably makes the most sense to focus on project grants and formula grants that state and local governments are most likely to replace with their own resources. Recipient governments must apply for project grants, and many that seek this aid do not receive it. Therefore, few jurisdictions build the federal money into their budgets before they receive a federal commitment, and therefore few would have to scale back ongoing services if a project grant program were terminated. If recipient governments were to make up for the loss of federal formula aid, it would indicate that the main effect of the federal grant was to provide tax relief to the residents of the recipient government, which is a dubious federal purpose.

Another possible approach for dealing with the requirement to reduce nondefense discretionary spending would be an aggressive effort to raise (or impose) fees and charges on the business-type activities of the federal government. The federal government already collects receipts and fees for a wide range of activities for which discretionary expenditures are made. These include admissions to national parks, issuing passports, inspecting foods, testing pharmaceuticals, exploiting natural resources on federal lands, generating electricity, registering patents and trademarks, and regulating certain industries. Many of these collections are counted as mandatory negative outlays (offsetting collections); some are considered revenues (offsetting receipts). Notwithstanding the way they are classified for budget accounting purposes, these collections reduce the net public cost of providing specific services. Rarely, however, do they come anywhere near covering the government's full costs of providing the related service or equaling the value of the benefit the government is bestowing.

Especially in a period of extreme budget pressure, a good case can be made for raising these fees and charges substantially. Consumers of the electricity sold by the power-marketing authorities could be asked to pay for the full costs of generating this power. Similarly, air passengers, cargo shippers, and private aviation could be asked to pay the full, not just the partial, costs of operating the Federal Aviation Administration. The rights to exploit resources on public lands— grazing, mineral, and logging rights—could be sold for their market values. When this is less than the full costs incurred by the federal government—as has been the case with some timber sales—the federal government could curtail the money-losing activity. Entrance fees at national parks, which are well below those charged by commercial theme parks with attractions that pale next to those of Yellowstone, Yosemite, or Zion, could be raised significantly.

Such hikes would have to be phased in gradually to reduce the disruption that might otherwise be caused. But even such dislocation might be preferable to the alternative. For example, many Americans might regard higher entrance fees at national parks as preferable to closing the parks one day a week, keeping the public from vast unpatrolled areas, or allowing park facilities to deteriorate.

Whatever approach is taken to reduce discretionary spending, the consequences are likely to reverberate well beyond the confines of this portion of the budget. As pressure builds on domestic programs, it will spill over to the defense budget because the procedural limits that will be part of any future budget-balancing legislation will most likely apply to total discretionary spending, not just to nondefense discretionary spending.[22] As chapter 5 of this volume argues, a case can be made for reducing future defense spending more than has been proposed by the various balanced budget plans. If this were done, some

22. Section 301 of the 1997 congressional budget resolution establishes, for consideration by the Senate only, separate limits for defense and nondefense discretionary spending.

relief could be provided for the nondefense discretionary accounts while adhering to the overall discretionary spending limits.

The effort to reduce nondefense discretionary spending is also likely to spawn attempts to transform some discretionary programs into mandatory ones and to incorporate some services currently provided by discretionary programs into existing mandatory programs. For example, social security and medicare administrative costs could be recategorized as mandatory spending, as are state medicaid and food stamp administrative expenses. Medicare could be modified to pick up more of the costs now borne by discretionary veterans' health programs. WIC could be made into a supplement to the food stamp program. Complex procedural hurdles would have to be overcome if any of these suggestions were to provide true relief to the discretionary budget. Nevertheless, such transformations, if successful, would shift most of the budget battle onto the pay-as-you-go enforcement procedures used for entitlements, where more flexibility and creative gimmickry are possible.

With grants making up over one-third of nondefense discretionary spending, states and localities are likely to feel the brunt of the discretionary cutbacks. The primary reason to expect disproportionate reductions in federal discretionary grants is that the political costs of retrenchment would be shared. Unlike the case with direct federal programs, the political repercussion of a cut in a grant program will be borne partially by state and local officials. Federal grant funds are often mixed with state resources and then distributed to their ultimate recipient, the school district or citizen, as a state program. In some cases, recipient governments will be under pressure to maintain service levels, which will require increased taxes or a reduction in other services. Interstate disparities in service levels will increase, to the extent that states do not compensate for reductions in federal grants.

If states respond to federal spending cutbacks by reducing services considered vital by national policymakers, Congress may turn again to unfunded mandates—requirements placed on states and localities. Over the past two decades, a strong movement developed against such mandates. It culminated in the enactment of the Unfunded Mandate Act in March 1995. Although this legislation created several weak procedural hurdles that must be surmounted when Congress considers new unfunded mandates, it does not preclude new mandates on subnational levels of government or make the federal government pay for them.

Conclusion

Unless entitlement programs are cut more deeply, federal health care costs rise at unexpectedly slow rates, or taxes are raised, any balanced budget plan that is adopted over the next few years is likely to include very deep and probably unattainable discretionary spending reductions. The primary reason is that policymakers can claim credit for future deficit reduction without identifying the specific discretionary spending programs that would be cut. A secondary reason is the widespread public conviction that there are many wasteful or unnecessary programs buried in the nondefense discretionary portion of the budget. Undoubtedly, there are inefficient and wasteful activities within these accounts, just as there are in the other components of the federal budget and in the operations of any large private-sector organization. But it is doubtful that they absorb a great deal of resources; in other words, even if they were all removed from the budget, policymakers would still have a difficult time meeting the nondefense discretionary limits that have been proposed. However, it is not easy to identify, let alone ferret out, such activities. There may be no practical way to remove the unwanted elements without sacrificing desirable and valuable activities. While there is general agreement over what constitutes waste, abuse, or inefficiency, no consensus exists over which federal programs are unnecessary or low priority. What one person, group, or region regards as a nonessential federal activity, another regards as vital. But this does not mean that the nondefense discretionary budget cannot be cut substantially.

The effort to scale back the nondefense discretionary portion of the budget should provide an opportunity for a valuable national debate about the appropriate scope of federal activities; whether such a discussion will take place is another question. Rather than constantly accumulating new roles without reassessing the worth of old functions, policymakers should sort through the program clutter that has accumulated in the federal attic. Some programs, the ones that have already accomplished their objectives or failed, should be discarded. Others should be consolidated, streamlined, and restructured for the changed environment of the twenty-first century. There are still others that, even in a period of fiscal stringency, should be augmented. As programs are terminated, consolidated, and downsized, the public may come to better appreciate the importance of the remaining activities performed by the federal government.

The task of downsizing the discretionary portion of the budget will not be an easy one for Congress and the president. The way Congress makes appropriations decisions tends to emphasize parochial rather than national interests. In this environment, interest group pressures often cause weak claimants rather than weak claims to be sacrificed in times of fiscal austerity. The disproportionate cuts that the 104th Congress made in low-income discretionary programs and the enactment of welfare reform but not medicare reform attest to this.

While the structure of congressional decisionmaking may not augur well for rational retrenchment, the president could find himself with an important new power that could be used to inject national concerns and a bit of logic into the process of reducing discretionary spending. This is the authority provided by the Line Item Veto Act of 1996, which will go into effect in 1997.[23] If it is not declared unconstitutional, the president will be able to "cancel in whole any dollar amount of discretionary budget authority" provided in an appropriation law. This power will extend not just to amounts specified for individual appropriation accounts but also to the dollar amounts specified in the tables, charts, and explanatory text in committee reports. Congress can negate the president's cancellation by passing a disapproval bill within thirty days. Presumably, the president would use his constitutional authority to veto any disapproval bill approved by Congress, and his veto would stand unless it was overridden by a vote of two-thirds of both houses of Congress. Budget resources canceled by the president would not be available for reappropriation. Instead the discretionary spending caps would be reduced accordingly.

While the line item veto may appear to give the president a very strong hand in determining how much discretionary spending is appropriated each year and how these funds are allocated among federal activities, this may not be the case. With respect to overall funding levels, the item veto could, in theory, be used by a determined president to keep appropriations within the limits required by a balanced budget plan. However, the power would be somewhat redundant if the Budget Enforcement Act was extended. Already the act provides that, if Congress waives its own rules and appropriates more than is permitted, the OMB will sequester budget resources to stay within the discretionary spending limits. The item veto, however, would allow the president to select particular spending items to be cut rather

23. For a discussion of these issues, see Joyce and Reischauer (forthcoming).

than accepting the across-the-board reductions called for by the Budget Enforcement Act sequestration process.

With respect to the allocation of spending reductions, Congress has ways to protect its priorities from the item veto. It could decide to package spending in forms that offer the president few opportunities to exercise his new power. Set-asides and instructions that used to fill conference committee reports may disappear in favor of more subtle and informal communications from Congress to executive branch officials. Appropriation subcommittee chairmen may write letters with spending instructions to department secretaries. Congress may begin to adopt "sense of the Congress" resolutions that deal with spending matters. In the extreme, Congress may simply preempt the president's veto power by explicitly stating in a funding bill that the Line Item Veto Act does not apply.

Procedural innovations, like the line item veto or a constitutional amendment requiring a balanced budget, are not likely to reduce the political price of scaling back discretionary spending. At some level, probably well above those promised by the various balanced budget plans, the public will let their elected representatives know that they will not accept further retrenchment in nondefense discretionary spending. At that point policymakers will have to decide whether to raise taxes, cut defense and entitlement programs more, or live with larger deficits.

References

Center on Budget and Policy Priorities. 1996. "The House and Senate Omnibus Appropriation Bills: How Would They Affect Low-Income Programs?" Washington.

Congressional Budget Office. 1994. *Reducing the Deficit: Spending and Revenue Options* (March).

Joyce, Philip G., and Robert D. Reischauer. Forthcoming. "The Federal Line-Item Veto: It's Now the Law, but What Effect Will It Have?" *Public Administration Review*.

Moore, Stephen, and Dean Stansel. 1996. "How Corporate Welfare Won: Clinton and Congress Retreat from Cutting Business Subsidies." Cato Institute Policy Analysis 254 (May).

Rivlin, Alice M. 1992. *Reviving the American Dream: The Economy, the States, and the Federal Government*. Brookings.

5

JOHN D. STEINBRUNER
& WILLIAM W. KAUFMANN

International Security
Reconsidered

ONE OF THE most significant budgetary developments of
the last forty years has been the relative decline in the size of the
defense budget. In the years immediately following the Korean War
(1953–55), defense spending amounted to 13 percent of GDP and
67.1 percent of all federal spending. In 1993–95, by contrast, defense
spending amounted to only 4.1 percent of GDP and 19.3 percent of
all federal spending. The reduction in the relative importance of the
defense budget has allowed mandatory spending to increase substantially without a commensurate increase in overall government spending: spending on social entitlement programs that did not exist in the
early 1950s now amounts to 5.6 percent of GDP and 26.9 percent of
the budget.

The reduction in defense spending has also played a crucial role in
the effort to reduce the deficit. All of the reductions in real discretionary spending that have occurred in the 1990s have come out of the
defense budget function. While inflation-adjusted defense spending
fell by 28 percent between 1990 and 1996, nondefense discretionary
spending increased by 13.4 percent.

The extent to which defense cuts will contribute to further efforts
to reduce the deficit is an open question. Much will depend on the
international environment and the changing capabilities of our potential adversaries. But budgetary pressures will also play a role. The
administration's 1997 budget and the congressional budget resolution
for 1997, both of which strive to balance the budget by 2002, contemplate further modest reductions in defense spending. Under the

Research support for this chapter from the John D. and Catherine T. MacArthur
Foundation, The Carnegie Corporation of New York, and the W. Alton Jones Foundation
is gratefully acknowledged.

former, real defense spending by 2002 would be about 10 percent below 1996 levels; under the Republican plan, the cut would be about 13 percent. But the defense spending proposed by these broad plans is not sufficient to support the force structures and investment programs that either the administration or the Republicans have put forward. This problem only gets worse as one looks further into the future, when a major reinvestment program will be required. Additional pressure will be exerted by nondefense budgetary interests, which are slated to face cuts twice as deep as those on the defense side. Their proponents will look to the defense budget for relief.

And relief is definitely available. The United States has established a large and growing superiority over all potential adversaries, and the problems it can expect to encounter are changing substantially. The nation could make prudent adjustments of policy and forces to produce greater security at lower cost.

New Circumstances

During the cold war era (1950–90), the United States spent a total of $12.9 trillion in 1996 dollars on national defense, an annual average of $314.6 billion.[1] Some of that expenditure was consumed, that is, its effects were limited to immediate circumstances. But much of it represented a cumulative investment. The technology developed, the equipment purchased, the experience absorbed, and the overall competence acquired produced what is now universally recognized to be the world's most capable military establishment and the only one with global reach.

Beginning in 1990 with the dissolution of the opposing alliance that had inspired the cold war effort, the United States began a series of adjustments to its military forces and its underlying defense policy. In recognition that Russia would not constitute the same threat that the Soviet Union once posed and in reaction to the Persian Gulf War, the focus of preparation for conventional force engagements shifted away from central Europe and settled, somewhat more tentatively, on the possibility of fighting, perhaps at the same time, wars like those fought against Iraq or North Korea. Since these imaginable contingencies, even together, would not be as demanding as defending against a massive assault on western Europe, U.S. military forces were

---

1. *Budget of the United States Government, Fiscal Year 1996, Historical Tables*, table 6.1.

gradually reduced by some 30 percent and corresponding reductions were made in the defense budget. The $243 billion Defense Department budget President Clinton proposed for fiscal year 1997 is $95 billion less than would have been required to sustain the 1990 force levels.

The reduced forces, however, are still configured to perform the two basic missions that were the focus of the cold war defense effort: deterrence of nuclear attack and defense of allies against ground assault. Implicitly, it is assumed that the security problems associated with the new world environment will be variations of the traditional threats.

Despite the force reductions, the momentum of investment continues to generate substantial increases in the capacity to perform traditional missions. This has occurred in part because improved technologies have compensated for lower levels of deployment. Basically, the United States has uniquely exploited information technology to make the application of firepower more efficient, thereby increasing the absolute potential to conduct traditional military operations with fewer forces. But America's relative capability has also increased because other military establishments have not kept pace with U.S. military investment, as summarized in table 5-1.

The greater investment has been reinforced by alliances with most other industrial democracies. The major military establishments operating outside of these cooperative arrangements—most notably China and Russia—maintain large numbers of military personnel but have not been equipping or training them to the extent that would be required to make them competitive. As a result, they cannot generate a comparable capability for operations outside their own territories. The same is true to an even greater extent for Iraq and North Korea. Given these disparities in investment and in alliance collaboration, the U.S. advantage will continue to increase for at least another decade.

Military superiority was not the official aspiration of the American political system during the cold war effort. Nonetheless, the accomplishment has been broadly popular. The last force reduction decisions were made in 1993; since that time the defense budget has been exempted from making additional contributions to the new effort to balance the budget. The Clinton administration projects that the decade-long gradual decline in real defense budget authority will end in 1999 and that small increases will occur in subsequent years, as summarized in table

TABLE 5-1. Force Comparisons, United States and Selected Countries

Force component	United States	NATO, Japan, and South Korea	Russia	China	Iraq	North Korea
Military personnel (thousands)	1,482	3,491	1,270	2,930	382	1,054
National defense outlays in 1996 (billions of dollars)						
Total	266.3	222.7	40.0	40.0	2.7	2.4
Investment only	91.3	64.5	15.6	14.9	0.8	0.8
Nuclear weapons						
On long-range launchers	8,106[a]	544[b]	8,586[a]	7	0	0
Total inventory	9,255[c]	710[b]	11,900[c]	400[d]	0	0
Army brigades						
Number	36	297	144	264	81	112
Annual investment per brigade (millions of dollars)	435.9	50.3	23.2	26.4	6.4	4.6
Relative investments (percent)	100.0	11.5	5.3	6.1	1.5	1.1
Navy ships and submarines						
Major combatants	218	471	299	105	...	28
Annual investment per vessel (millions of dollars)	164.8	50.3	11.4	24.9	...	2.9
Relative investments (percent)	100.0	7.0	6.9	15.1	...	1.8
Air Force aircraft						
Combat aircraft	1,531	4,375	1,775	4,960	320	611
Annual investment per aircraft (millions of dollars)	25.9	4.1	4.7	1.1	0.35	0.11
Relative investments (percent)	100.0	15.8	18.2	4.3	1.4	0.4
Lift capacity						
Intertheater aircraft	364	...	595	...	...	...
Million-ton-miles/day	51	...	28.4	...	...	...
Intratheater aircraft	388	146	222	...	...	...
Million-ton-miles/day	11.2	4.0	2.0	...	...	...

SOURCES: Authors' estimates based on International Institute for Strategic Studies (1996, pp. 40, 49–74, 113–19, 133–34, 186–87); NATO (1995, pp. 3, 7, 8); Koziak (1996, pp. A-3, A-6, A-7, A-11, A-13); Arms Control Association (1996); Perry (1996, p. 190); and "British, French, and Chinese Nuclear Forces," *Bulletin of Atomic Scientists*, vol. 52 (July–August 1996), pp. 61–63; (September–October 1996), pp. 62–63; (November–December 1996), pp. 64–67.

a. START-accountable warheads; for Russia, includes those repatriated from Ukraine, Kazakhstan, and Belarus.
b. Britain and France only.
c. Current operational stockpile (not START-accountable numbers).
d. Approximate.

5-2. Congress added $7 billion to the administration's defense request in 1996 and $10.5 billion in 1997 and has promised further increases beyond 1997. Given the austerity that is being proposed for virtually all other segments of the federal budget, this represents relatively privileged treatment for the defense effort. So far the American electorate has not registered any major objection.

Eventually, however, this consensus can be expected to erode. In-

TABLE 5-2. Department of Defense Budget, Fiscal Years 1996–2001

Item	1996	1997	1998	1999	2000	2001
Budget authority						
FY 1997 topline total (billions of dollars)	251.8	242.6	248.1	254.3	261.7	269.6
Real growth (percent)	−3.7	−6.0	−0.2	0	0.5	0.6
Outlays						
FY 1997 topline total (billions of dollars)	254.3	247.5	243.9	246.5	253.9	256.6
Real growth (percent)	−4.1	−5.1	−3.8	−1.4	0.6	−1.3

SOURCE: Perry (1996, p. 251).

creasingly severe fiscal pressures will pit the national defense effort against the full array of domestic programs, and it is doubtful that the current logic of military planning can survive the scrutiny that will result. Quite apart from the wisdom of maintaining an unprecedented degree of military superiority at the expense of meeting domestic needs, there is a major question of design. Forces configured to deter or defeat classic forms of aggression are not well suited to deal with the more diffuse patterns of violence that are now emerging as the principal security problem. Even those who give absolute priority to national defense will be driven to contemplate a more substantial reconfiguration of the cold war military posture in response to dramatically altered international circumstances.

It does not seem likely that a new consensus about the nature of these circumstances will soon emerge to replace the cold war formulation. In a diverse democracy, a workable consensus of this sort is difficult to achieve and, once established, is also difficult to replace. Nonetheless, at least some of the elements of the new environment are apparent in broad outline. Whatever its other properties may prove to be, the emerging era is clearly one of global interactions where the central imperative of all nations is to connect productively to the information, product, technology, and investment flows of the international economy. Those that fail to do so will labor under tremendous disadvantage. It is reasonable, under these circumstances, to anticipate that domestic economic performance will be the central priority for all major nations and that, with a few limited but important exceptions, large-scale imperial adventures designed to seize and hold territory will be infeasible. Not only can the United States and its major allies readily defeat such aggression if they choose to do so, but even a success achieved by grace of their default could not be consolidated to advantage. Any exercise of aggression across international boundaries could be met with a lengthy period of economic isolation, and the inherent burdens of isolation would be compounded by the basic fact that political control of a large population imposed primarily by force is ruinously inefficient.

There are regional situations where military vigilance is clearly prudent: most notably, the Persian Gulf, the Korean peninsula, and the Taiwan straits. These are reasonably well defined situations, however, where vigilance is a natural product of previous experience. If competently handled, they do not pose problems of large magnitude. The greater difficulty has to do with less familiar situations—specifically, the internal coherence of economically burdened societies and the civil violence that emerges spontaneously from radical social disintegration. The widespread potential for social disintegration and the inexorable diffusion of advanced technology in the globalizing economy are the likely sources of the most demanding problems of international security.

Basic Strategic Policy

Most of the investment devoted to the two central missions of the cold war was designed to produce military forces available for use on very short notice. With Germany's Blitzkrieg assaults during World War II and Japan's attack on Pearl Harbor very much in mind, military planners assumed that massive aggression could be and would be effectively concealed until it actually began. In the case of nuclear weapons, the assumed notice was very short indeed. Nuclear forces were configured to be able to initiate comprehensive retaliation within twenty minutes of detecting and confirming the onset of attack, a time span set by the normal intercontinental flight time of a ballistic missile. Current nuclear forces still operate under this standard. In the case of conventional forces, the planning standard envisaged initial operations within a few weeks and full-scale combat within a few months. The advanced state of preparation for large combined arms engagements of the World War II variety continues to be the primary commitment for active conventional forces.

The resulting pattern of confrontation between large military forces configured for rapid reaction is not an inherently efficient or stable international security arrangement. It requires extensive preparations for activities that are not intended to be undertaken and is, in that sense, wasteful. It increases the risk of inadvertent engagements. It poses the problem of establishing an accepted apportionment of capability between states of different technical and economic potential and different degrees of geographic exposure. The costs and risks associated with this pattern were tolerated during the cold war because of the prevailing conviction that ideological rivalry precluded a more refined arrangement. Even so, a great deal of diplomatic effort was expended in working out agreements to regulate the force levels and operational practices of the two opposing alliances. By the latter stages of the cold war, comprehensive ceilings had been placed on nuclear weapons delivery systems and on the five main types of equipment used by conventional forces; agreements had been reached to completely eliminate several categories of weapons; and some operational rules had been devised to inhibit the ability to launch a surprise attack. These agreements document the fact that the two alliances engaged in confrontation recognized mutual interest in regulating its consequences.

With one of those two alliances now dissolved and its defining ideology largely abandoned, the central organizing principle of international security is open to question: Should the practice of deterrence through countervailing force be continued indefinitely despite the change of circumstance? Or should a serious attempt be made to transform it into a more inclusive pattern of collaboration? Either of these strategic policies would encounter practical impediments, but none so decisive that the issue can be summarily decided on that basis.

Citing general uncertainty and the need to hedge against the reemergence of a strategic opponent, U.S. military planners have so far chosen to sustain active deterrent practices, but without explicit reference to a designated enemy. That intention is embodied in the fiscal 1997 defense budget and in the associated six-year defense plan, both of which will provide for a nuclear retaliatory force as lethal as ever and a capacity for conventional force intervention admittedly larger than any contemporary situation is likely to require.[2] It is also reflected in current policy about NATO's future. A few central European states are deemed eligible in principle for imminent NATO membership, but Russia is explicitly excluded and the question is not even considered relevant for China or for India. These underlying policies

2. This underlying principle is expressed in the annual report of the secretary of defense: "More fundamentally, maintaining a two-MRC force helps ensure that the United States will have sufficient military capabilities to defend against a coalition of hostile powers or a larger, more capable adversary than is foreseen today." Perry (1996, p. 5).

are mitigated by more accommodating public dialogue with former opponents and by limited forms of collaboration with them. But in terms of greatest consequence—that is, relative military capability—the large advantage established by the United States and its allies imposes significant pressure on those nations that are not included, especially Russia and China, who are the principal historical opponents and potential future rivals.

This situation seems prudent to those who enjoy the advantage, as long as the classic forms of aggression are assumed to be the predominant security problem. The broader effects in an altered context promise to be quite troublesome, however, even for them. It is a serious question, for example, whether the Russian military establishment, with its limited resource base and extensive geographic exposure, can safely perform basic national security missions under conditions of implicit confrontation. If forced to operate from a position of irremediable and unmitigated disadvantage, the Russian military establishment can be expected to develop broad reliance on tactical uses of nuclear weapons and other dangerous means of offsetting threats from superior capabilities. That, in turn, would drive the general process of weapons proliferation and would also compound the already serious dangers of internal disintegration.

The United States has recognized these latter dangers well enough to initiate a collaborative effort with Russia to deactivate some nuclear weapons on both sides and to strengthen the managerial control practices that are used to handle weapons and fissionable materials. Congress appropriated $1.53 billion for this effort through the end of 1996, and annual increments of $300 million are being projected over a five-year period.[3] Russia has also been formally enlisted in NATO's Partnership for Peace Program, designed to prepare for joint peacekeeping exercises, and Russian forces have operated in Bosnia under U.S. command. A corresponding policy of engagement with China has also been articulated but is much less developed in practical terms.

These important but limited initiatives have been conceived as a supplement to the main deterrent policy rather than as a potential substitute. In principle, however, they could be developed into an alternative strategic policy that would systematically extend the security cooperation practiced within the U.S. alliance system to Russia,

---

3. U.S. General Accounting Office (1996c, p. 31); P.L. 104-201, sec. 1502.

China, and, ultimately, all of the major military establishments that still operate outside of it. Such a policy would basically subordinate the deterrent effect of implicit confrontation to the practice of positive reassurance. Utilizing the methods of reassurance, the very capable German and Japanese military establishments have been so successfully integrated into a pattern of international cooperation that they are not perceived to be either an immediate or a potential threat. Were a similar degree of integration to be achieved with the Russian, Chinese, and Indian militaries, the resulting dominant global pattern of cooperation would significantly reduce the costs and risks of hedging against the traditional forms of aggression and would provide a more effective response to the problems of diffuse violence. Rogue states could still emerge, but if effective cooperation were to be established among the major military powers and national economies, the threat from rogue states would be markedly reduced.

As a measure of how much the attitudes of the cold war still prevail, the cooperative security alternative is infrequently advanced in any forum and has, as yet, no prominent political advocates, even though it would appear to be a natural extension of what is commonly recognized as the outstanding achievement of the cold war period: the transformation of Germany and Japan into allied industrial democracies. Judging from the content of immediate political discussion, global cooperation does not appear likely to become the explicit central principle of U.S. security policy anytime soon. The idea is relevant, nonetheless. It indicates the direction in which the actual practice of security is evolving in response to unfolding events, and it provides a useful point of reference for the debate that is bound to occur over the size, configuration, and purpose of military forces. Moreover, it is useful to compare the defense budget needed to support the policy of implicit confrontation at currently projected levels of deployment with the budget that might plausibly result from systematic pursuit of a cooperative strategic policy. Since compromise is the normal outcome, it is also useful to compare the defense budget requirements of each of these options with an intermediate possibility.

Costs and Consequences

The word *security* implicitly refers to many different threats and is affected by so many different circumstances that the term does not admit to exact, comprehensive definition. That makes the identification of threat among the most difficult and most critical steps in developing an appropriate policy. As a reflection of the difficulty, there is no generally agreed listing of the principal security problems, let alone an ordering of their priorities. A commonsense approximation, however, might distinguish five categories in rough order of concern: full-scale nuclear attack; a conventional weapons assault; an explosion of a nuclear device or release of a mass casualty agent; sustained civil violence; and common terrorism. An adequate security policy should contain both preventive and reactive measures to deal with all five of these threat categories. It should be sensitive to unexpected interactions among them, which might be a greater problem than the categorical threats themselves.

The Current Defense Program

Current U.S. security policy includes measures directed to each of the five threat categories. Investment, however, is heavily concentrated on preparations for rapid reaction to nuclear attack and conventional war. Under the prevailing doctrine of deterrence, preparations for decisive reaction are considered to be the most effective means of prevention. Moreover, it is assumed that policies and activities directed to the more limited, more diffuse, and more clandestine forms of violence can be appropriately derived from the primary commitments; that is, that these concerns do not pose independent requirements sufficiently important to modify the main effort.

As can be appreciated from table 5-1, there is little reason to question the ability of U.S. forces to perform the central missions. Even after the reductions called for by the START II treaty have been fully implemented, the United States will deploy 3,500 strategic nuclear weapons on 921 launchers in its active forces and is intending to retain an additional 3,000 to 5,000 strategic weapons in reserve that would be available for deployment over the course of a year or so. Some 1,600 of these weapons are to be retained on immediately available alert status, and at least the submarine-based portion of those will be essentially invulnerable to preemptive attack. There are various judgments about the number of nuclear weapons that could be rationally used in any retaliatory attack, but the physical fact is that a few hundred nuclear weapons systematically distributed would so damage any nation that any further assault would be redundant. The large reductions that have been undertaken in the number of deployed nuclear weapons, therefore, have not diminished our underlying deterrent capability.

Assessments of conventional weapons capability—the combined effects of ground, naval, and air forces supported by information and supply flows and by command system direction—cannot be summarized as readily. Relative capabilities and many details of the context of application matter more in conventional engagements than they do for nuclear weapons. The comparisons presented in table 5-1 do suggest a very large American advantage, however. Although it is not often mentioned, it is a relevant fact that no country is in position to conduct a conventional assault on the United States and, therefore, all of our active capability is available, in principle, for application abroad. Two task forces of four to five ground force divisions, ten tactical air wings, and four to five aircraft carrier battle groups could be assembled in the unlikely event that we were called on to prevail, as current policy guidance requires, in two widely separated engagements in close sequence. Allied assets could also be employed. The limiting condition is lift capability, but in a situation serious enough to engage the full military capability of the United States, it is reasonable to presume that the very large pool of commercial transportation assets could be used.

Those countries that are currently identified with the official planning term "major regional conflicts"—Iraq and North Korea—simply do not have the potential to defeat this array of assets, particularly if they were applied at the initial stages of an aggressive mobilization. In order to relate all of the available forces to these contingencies, U.S. military planners have assumed that we would react only after initial assaults had actually seized territory we were committed to protecting, thus imposing the greater burden of conducting a liberating offensive. The planners have further assumed that we would conduct these offensives within a few weeks, with the help of only local allies, and with very modest casualties.[4] These assumptions are themselves testimony to the degree of superiority we have acquired. Efficient use of U.S. assets in such contingencies would conduct an

4. See Aspin (1993, pp. 8, 14, 15–17). The BUR explicitly states the "modest casualty" requirement on page 8. The scenario figures on page 14 indicate that only support from local allies is considered, while the phases of combat operations on pages 15–17 discuss the need to minimize territory captured (phase 1) and retake territory seized (phase 3). Thomas McNaugher of the RAND Corporation notes that we are much closer to having a "minimum risk force" today than we were during the cold war. See McNaugher (1996).

assertive defense against the initial assault using our decisive advantage in handling information and would not need the full measure of firepower that is actually available.

As for hedging against renewed belligerence from Russia or China, they are far from posing an immediate threat of aggression, despite the nominally large size of their military establishments (table 5-1). The investment component of their defense expenditures—a necessary accompaniment of technical quality—would have to be about $80 billion a year for Russia and $120 billion for China in order to match the U.S. rate of investment per person for their larger number of military personnel. In fact, their real rates of expenditure, though difficult to determine, do not appear to be anywhere near those levels. China's announced annual defense budget is only $7.5 billion, and the budget enacted by the Russian Duma is about $17 billion.[5] In both cases the real level of expenditure is considered to be higher, but most independent estimates of their overall defense budgets fall in the range of $40 billion to $50 billion with an investment component no greater than $20 billion a year. At that more plausible level, the investment rates of Russia and China for the main categories of military equipment are small fractions of those of the United States, as is their capacity to conduct conventional force operations beyond their own territory.

The problems with the current U.S. security posture, therefore, do not concern the traditional missions of deterring nuclear and conventional war. That much has been as reliably accomplished as it is ever likely to be. The very serious impending difficulty lies in the costs of

5. Determining the dollar value of the Russian defense budget in a way to make meaningful comparisons is a notoriously uncertain exercise. The Yeltsin government's draft 1996 budget included defense spending of 79 trillion rubles, which the Duma increased by 3.5 trillion in December. See "Draft Budget Released for 1996," *OMRI Daily Digest*, September 19, 1995; and "Duma Approves 1996 Budget," *OMRI Daily Digest*, December 7, 1995 (electronic versions). At the official exchange rate of about 5,200 rubles, this equals approximately $16 billion. Using a purchasing power parity rate of 4,300 rubles (75 percent), a preliminary estimate from the State Statistical Committee (Goskomstat), the dollar equivalent equals approximately $19 billion. An IMF purchasing power parity rate for GDP of 4,342 rubles also yields a dollar equivalent of $19 billion. (International Monetary Fund, World Economic Outlook database, 1996). These figures reflect only the official defense budget, which excludes such items as the cost of the Chechen war and the continuing subsidization of the army and the defense industry. See Vitaliy Shlykov, "Secrets of the Military Budget," *Nezavisimoye Voyennoye Obozreniye*, May 16, 1996, no. 9, pp. 1, 3 ("Russia: Shlykov Dismisses Military Fears of Budget Crunch," FBIS-UMA-96-123-S, May 16, 1996 [electronic version]).

sustaining the current effort and their expected effects on the ability to respond to the other categories of threat. Together, these factors make it apparent that implementation of the current defense plan will be subject to very serious question.

The cost problem is at root a procurement problem. Basic military equipment—tanks, aircraft, missiles, ships, helicopters—can be used for varying periods of time, ranging largely between twenty and forty years, after which it must be replaced. And, in the rolling process of replacement, equipment is also upgraded: a given piece of equipment is replaced with a more advanced and invariably more expensive model. For the major weapons systems, the full development cycle for the more advanced models used to replace existing equipment typically runs nearly twenty years, and this cycle has stubbornly resisted efforts to shorten it. The U.S. military planning system has never been able to set a stable pace for this basic cycle of replacing and upgrading its equipment, in part because it has also not been able to set a standard for force size that endures over the entire replacement cycle. Throughout the cold war period and right up to the present, fluctuations in the sense of threat have driven the annual rate of procurement either above or below the long-term rate of replacement, that is, the average annual rate required to reequip the existing force over a twenty-year period.

During the 1980s, procurement spending surged well above the stable replacement rate. As a result, the period between 1981 and 1985 marked the largest peacetime defense budget increase in U.S. history. The overall defense budget (inflation-adjusted budget authority) has declined since its 1985 peak, but it took a decade for the procurement surge to work its way through the system. While it did, force deployment levels were also reduced as the cold war ended. The combined effects of above-average replacement in the 1980s and force structure reductions in the 1990s have produced a relatively youthful current force. The average age of active military equipment is well below what it was in 1985. The combination of newer equipment and smaller forces has allowed procurement to fall well below the long-term replacement rate. That is a comfortable circumstance for the moment, but it portends another surge after 2000 that promises to be especially expensive since weapons development cycles after five decades of intense effort have been driven to extremely demanding technical frontiers. As detailed in table 5-3, it will require nearly $1.2 trillion to execute the current procurement plan for the programmed

TABLE 5-3. Estimated Cost of Proposed Upgrades and Replacements of Current Weapon Systems, Fiscal Years 1996–2016
Millions of 1996 dollars

Type of system	Cost
Upgrades	35,300
Replacements	
Combat aircraft	182,800
Support aircraft	44,182
Helicopters	41,774
Tracked and wheeled vehicles	18,114
Tactical missiles	69,100
Navy ships	110,970
Space systems	188,110
Ballistic missile defense	67,000
Other procurement	462,000
Total	1,219,350

SOURCES: See appendix table 5A-1.

forces by 2016—that is, to replace aging equipment with the advanced models being developed on the projected production schedules. (All of the figures in this discussion are constant 1996 dollars. For detailed estimates of the costs, see appendix table 5A-1.) At a stable annual rate, that would require $60 billion in procurement expenditures per year for the next twenty years. The amount actually appropriated for procurement in 1996 is $42 billion, and the president's 1997 budget projects that figure to decline to $38 billion in 1997 before increasing in stages to $54 billion by 2002. By 2002 the cumulative procurement shortfall will be nearly $71 billion. The procurement budget would have to be set at more than $65 billion for each of the thirteen years thereafter to compensate for this shortfall.

Table 5-4 displays what the financial consequences would be if U.S. military forces were continuously modernized and fully financed at the long-term replacement rate beginning in 1997 or, alternatively, if the annual defense budgets were increased after 2002 to compensate for the procurement shortfall up to that point. In either case, the process of replacing and upgrading equipment would ripple through the rest of the budget, producing annual budget authority requirements substantially higher than currently projected. Although it is sometimes claimed that more advanced military equipment is easier to maintain and operate, actual experience suggests that, in fact, it requires more effort from more highly trained personnel. If the defense budget is prudently reestimated on that basis, then full financing of the current forces would require an additional $140 billion over the period from 1997 to 2002 and a cumulative total of $810 billion more over a complete twenty-year replacement cycle.

If these additional resources were provided, the established nuclear and conventional force advantages would be increased, but this could induce dysfunctional reactions from the military establishments that are not part of the U.S. alliance and do not have the technical or economic resources to match its capabilities. For the large military forces attempting full-scale competition, the risk has to do with the consequences of their internal allocation of resources. For the smaller ones that cannot plausibly aspire to direct competition, the risk arises from the compensating strategies they might adopt, which could encourage the general process of weapons proliferation and lead to civil conflict and clandestine violence.

Internal balance is an especially serious question for the Russian military, supported by an economic base that is but a quarter of that of the United States and is caught up in a process of fundamental regeneration. For a decade or more to come, domestic investment will be an inescapable priority for Russia if social coherence is to be preserved. It is extremely unlikely that the allocation of resources provided for the military during the Soviet years could be restored, whatever the inclinations of the political leadership might be. Even an effort to do so would not make Russian forces competitive with the combined capabilities of the U.S. alliance system plus China. The stark implication is that Russia has no immediate prospect of overcoming the disadvantages indicated in table 5-1 and cannot sustain both a robust nuclear deterrent and a secure conventional defense of its large territory.

In fact, even the Russian deterrent force is questionable under cold war methods of assessment. If the United States were to initiate an optimally designed surprise attack on Russian nuclear forces in their normal daily posture, the number of weapons that could be expected to survive to undertake retaliation would be substantially less than the number the United States could count on under reverse circumstances—enough so that conservative Russian military planners are undoubtedly very uneasy with the situation. This basic inequity has serious consequences, however implausible an initial American attack might be. It certainly means that Russian deterrent policy will continue to rely on very rapid reaction to evidence of an impending attack in order to compensate for the physical vulnerability of its forces. This

TABLE 5-4. Financing Requirements of Current U.S. Forces, Fiscal Years 1996–2016
Billions of 1997 dollars

Fiscal year	Current defense program		Complete financing and modernization beginning in FY 1997			Complete financing and modernization beginning in FY 2003		
	Projected cost of replacing and modernizing military equipment	Annual budget authority (051)[a]	Projected cost of replacing and modernizing military equipment	Annual budget authority (051)[a]	Increase over current program	Projected cost of replacing and modernizing military equipment	Annual budget authority (051)[a]	Increase over current program
1996	1,201	242	1,201	242	0	1,201	242	0
1997	1,122	226	1,214	245	19	1,122	226	0
1998	1,123	226	1,227	247	21	1,123	226	0
1999	1,124	226	1,240	250	24	1,124	226	0
2000	1,133	228	1,253	252	24	1,133	228	0
2001	1,143	230	1,266	255	25	1,143	230	0
2002	1,147	231	1,279	258	27	1,147	231	0
2003[b]	1,147	231	1,293	260	29	1,363	267	36
2004	1,147	231	1,306	263	32	1,373	270	39

2005	1,147	231	1,320	266	35	1,384	274	43
2006	1,147	231	1,334	269	38	1,395	276	45
2007	1,147	231	1,348	271	40	1,405	281	50
2008	1,147	231	1,362	274	43	1,416	283	52
2009	1,147	231	1,376	277	46	1,427	287	56
2010	1,147	231	1,390	280	49	1,438	290	59
2011	1,147	231	1,405	284	53	1,450	294	63
2012	1,147	231	1,420	286	55	1,461	297	66
2013	1,147	231	1,435	289	58	1,472	301	70
2014	1,147	231	1,450	292	61	1,484	304	73
2015	1,147	231	1,465	295	64	1,496	308	77
2016	1,147	231	1,480	298	67	1,507	312	81
Total, 1997–2002	…	1,367	…	1,507	140	…	1,367	0
Total, 2003–2016	…	3,234	…	3,904	670	…	4,044	810
Total, 1997–2016	…	4,601	…	5,411	810	…	5,411	810

SOURCE: Authors' calculations.

a. For the purposes of this assessment, the $11 billion of the U.S. defense budget that is devoted to various purposes not associated with the financing of U.S. forces has been removed from the base budget. Assuming these expenditures continue, the 051 account would be $11 billion more than the base figures shown here, up to 2002.

b. Numbers shown for 2003 and beyond in first two columns are based on assumption that there will be no increase in defense budget after 2002.

operational configuration makes it inherently more difficult to pre-serve exacting standards of safety and control. It may also compro-mise the confidence that Russian commanders would have in their ability to limit any mobilization of nuclear weapons they might un-dertake in order to resist a major ground incursion in Asia. Their strategic exposure to the U.S. nuclear force serves to amplify any security problem that might arise between Russia and China and to entangle the United States indirectly in such a problem.

This underlying strategic sensitivity would be significantly intensi-fied if the United States undertakes an actual deployment of a ballistic missile defense system for protection of either forward-deployed thea-ter forces or its home territory. Actual deployment of such systems is not envisaged in the projected defense program of the Clinton admin-istration, but development efforts costing roughly $3 billion a year are designed to provide the basis for deployment decisions that might be made three years hence. Moreover, the Republican party has made a commitment to ballistic missile defense deployment a prominent part of its political agenda. Were this commitment to be added to the U.S. defense effort, it would be perceived by Russia and China as a significant threat to their nuclear forces, particularly if they had no ability to constrain the scale, area, and technical parameters of the American deployment. In that case, they would be virtually compelled to undertake some reaction against the deployment, since otherwise, in combination with the offensive superiority currently enjoyed, the United States would very nearly have a decisive disarming capability. The logical offsetting reactions involve elaborations of offensive mis-sile technology and the development of antisatellite operations, both of which would diminish the prospects for controlling general weap-ons proliferation.

Thus far, Russia has managed to preserve the integrity of its nuclear force operations while scaling down alert rates and implementing the schedule of deployment reductions mandated by the START I treaty. There are numerous signs of internal erosion of its conventional forces, however, painfully illustrated by the operations undertaken in Chechnya, and nuclear weapons operations are not immune from similar deterioration. Russian military planners do not believe they can match U.S. nuclear forces under the START II treaty provisions without constructing some 500 to 1,000 single-warhead missiles, and reluctance to finance that requirement threatens ratification of the treaty by the Russian Duma. Moreover, if the United States proceeded to deploy either a national ballistic missile defense or a broader area theater system without explicit agreement on terms, Russia would almost certainly stop implementing both treaties and take reactive measures.

Internal deterioration is virtually inevitable if Russian forces continue to be as underfinanced as they are today. The potential consequences of such underfinancing are quite serious, including loss of control over large weapons inventories and even over organized units. It would be extremely difficult under current circumstances for the Russian planning system to reduce its conventional force structure to levels that might be adequately financed. In part, this is because a socially tractable process of reduction would itself be expensive and, in part, it is because unilateral reductions, in the absence of any supportive international arrangement, would be an admission of indefinite weakness. In hedging against the return of a Russian capacity for aggression, the United States and its allies are running the greater risk of triggering perverse reactions and reinforcing a process of deterioration within the Russian establishment.

Internal deterioration is also a relevant concern for countries such as North Korea and Iraq, but fortunately most countries outside of the U.S. alliance system are not burdened with unmanageably large military establishments. Even so, it is important to be attentive to the longer-term incentives excluded countries have to develop some means of counteracting the offensive potential of the United States that they cannot directly balance. Some may be inclined to develop nuclear weapons or mass casualty agents for this purpose. And if smaller states begin to rely on capacities of this sort for what they consider to be defensive national security reasons, then it is prudent to assume that terrorist organizations would eventually emulate them for aggressive reasons. Others might well adapt advanced commercial technology to threaten the basing structure of U.S. forces, or even critical economic assets in the United States, with long-range precision attack by conventional munitions.

In general, the degree of advantage that the United States and its allies have achieved runs the risk of overburdening other military establishments and of touching off a dangerous set of reactions. The stimulus that might be given to the general process of weapons proliferation and to the more spontaneous forms of violence is potentially serious enough to override the benefits of preserving such a substantial margin of nuclear and conventional force superiority. Although the dangers of widespread proliferation and endemic civil violence are as yet less demonstrated than those of traditional aggression, they could prove to be quite serious. At any rate, these dangers provide strong reasons, on top of the cost, to question the currently projected course of U.S. security policy.

The More Cooperative Alternative

An alternative strategic policy, based on systematic cooperation, would be designed to reduce both the costs and the side effects of performing the traditional missions. Such a policy would set and enforce the principle that no military establishment will initiate an attack on any other. Force deployment standards and operational rules would be worked out to provide systematic reassurance that actual capability is consistent with that principle. By explicit agreement, active forces would be reduced to lower levels and preserved in a state of readiness that would essentially preclude an effective surprise attack. No nuclear weapons would be maintained on alert status. Intimidating concentrations and provocative activities of conventional forces would be prohibited. Any deployment of wide-area ballistic missile defense systems would be jointly determined in essential detail and might be jointly operated as well. A continuous exchange of information would be arranged to document compliance with the deployment standards and operational rules, to make violations more visible, and to stimulate timely reactions to detected violations.

The cooperative option would also include provisions for responding more directly to the other threats, in part by developing preventive measures and in part by tailoring military operations to deal with the diffuse forms of violence that the new international situation is most likely to generate. The continuous monitoring of force deployments by agreed exchanges of information would be extended to cover the use of potentially dangerous dual-use technologies. This task can be efficiently performed without an elaborate bureaucracy if there is a general scheme for indelible product labeling with automated reporting on the status of especially sensitive products. The information technology that generates the threat of high-precision attack can also be used to develop much more sophisticated protective monitoring, which will almost certainly be necessary to manage the consequences of technical diffusion. In instances when the failure of protective measures is imminently threatened or has actually occurred, preemptive and reactive actions would be jointly undertaken by members of the general security arrangement. The participating military establishments would develop common operational doctrine for controlling major instances of civil violence; the training of units designed for this task would be undertaken jointly; and actual operations of this sort would be jointly managed.

It is, of course, a significant question whether the detailed agreements required to implement these arrangements could actually be achieved. But the only way to answer the question is to formulate the policy and to make a serious attempt. As a practical matter neither Russia nor China is in a position to reject a comprehensive and genuinely equitable version of these provisions if the United States offered such an option. They could achieve a much higher standard of security and greater ease in preserving it through direct cooperation with the U.S. alliance system than by attempting direct competition. Both countries, at any rate, will have to reduce the size of their current military establishments substantially more than they have already done if they are to have any hope of equipping them adequately. It is one thing to pursue a traditional policy of great power rivalry from a position of substantial disadvantage if there appears to be no reasonable alternative. It is quite another to pursue this course if a decisively better option is available.

The United States is certainly capable of offering a decisively better option. It makes sense for the United States to diminish its large current advantage in exchange for reliable restraint on the future development of opposing forces. Since the basic investment and operational preparation required to develop a large-scale aggressive capability takes time and can be made visible, the current advantage translates into years, even decades, of warning before an effective threat of mass attack could be mounted against the U.S. alliance system. This advantage can be consolidated at lower levels of effort with little immediate risk. By being able to sustain lower levels of active deployment and operational readiness, the United States would be better prepared to respond to the threats that take longer to develop. That in turn would preserve a strong disincentive for any country to invest in those threats.[6] Moreover, with a formalized arrangement in place, the international capital markets could be expected to

6. Betts (1995).

reinforce the incentives for compliance by making it an element of creditworthiness.

Deriving appropriate force levels for a fully developed cooperative arrangement is more a matter of rough judgment than of exact calculation. Table 5-5 provides an illustration of what U.S. forces might look like under this notional arrangement. The United States would retain 1,060 nuclear warheads in active deployment and available within a few days for deterrent retaliation. At 3 brigades per division, there would be a total of 38 active and 9 reserve ground force brigades configured for standard conventional engagements. These would be supported by nearly 3,000 tactical aircraft operated by the Air Force and Marine Corps and organized into 11 active and 3.5 reserve wings available for major contingencies. The Navy would provide an additional 7 tactical air wings associated with its 7 carrier battle groups, 5 of which would be available for combat assignment in any standard contingency along with 2 Marine expeditionary brigades. An additional 30 combat ships, 19 submarines, and 7 support ships would provide continuing global surveillance, as well as logistical support for theater operations.

In addition to this traditionally configured force, four active and three reserve special operations groups would be formed, equipped, and trained for supporting international intervention in civil conflicts. These forces would be sufficient to permit simultaneous U.S. participation in four to six operations similar to those in Haiti and Bosnia should the need to do so arise. Although the public is currently wary of U.S. involvement in efforts to contain civil conflict, the potential seriousness of such problems suggests that some such preparations should be part of any prudent longer-term security policy.

The force structures of Russia and China that might appropriately correspond to this illustrative reduction of U.S. forces are even more difficult to determine. Both the Russian and Chinese military establishments have broader functions within their own societies and both, of course, have substantially greater geographic exposure. Nonetheless, some rough sense of an appropriate outcome can be derived by applying some practical and plausibly equitable principles. For example, mutually reassuring provisions might be made that would allow the Russian and Chinese military establishments to reduce their force deployments but increase their levels of investment over a ten-year period. Table 5-6 outlines how their total defense budgets and embedded investment programs might evolve in comparison with those of the United States if such an arrangement were initiated in 1998. The U.S. program would decline at a rate of 2.5 percent a year to arrive at the force structure illustrated in table 5-5. Russia and China could, if they chose to do so, increase their total defense expenditures and their investment component at the same 2.5 percent rate over this period, after which they would hold at a constant ceiling. By the end of this transition in 2008, Russia and China each could have improved their annual investment rates to 39 percent and 37 percent, respectively, of the U.S. standard, but the U.S. annual rate would still be larger than their combined total and would still provide a natural hedge against any subsequent breakdown of the arrangement. At the moment, even the idea of an arranged convergence of this sort would undoubtedly engender strong opposition from ardent nationalists in all three countries. Nonetheless, many practical observers would concede that current disparities are likely to be reduced.

In order to implement this illustrative agreement, Russia and China would have to scale back their military personnel substantially, and China would have to hold its defense investment increases below the 8 to 10 percent rate it appears to have maintained in recent years. The exact force reductions would depend on their future pay scales. Russia, for example, could sustain a volunteer armed force of 1.3 million personnel at an average pay scale of $15,000 per person but only about 665,000 military personnel at $30,000 per person.[7] Again, both countries should have strong incentives to make these reductions. Smaller but adequately financed Russian and Chinese forces would be more capable of performing the legitimate missions of national defense, and China's slower rate of investment would be more effective if relieved of the potential burden of triggering reactions from the United States and Japan.

In the context of a formally enacted arrangement constructed along these lines, the illustrative U.S. force structure could perform the traditional missions of nuclear deterrence and conventional defense just as confidently as the current force is able to do in the current context, but with less risk of triggering perverse reactions. It would provide the potential for prompt and decisive retaliation against any nuclear weapons attack but would not impose the burden and inherent danger of continuously maintaining an immediately available alert force. It would provide very explicit warning of a Russian or Chinese

7. The average pay scale for U.S. forces is $39,000 per person per year.

TABLE 5-5. Illustrative U.S. Forces under Cooperative and Intermediate Strategic Policies

	Cooperative policy		Intermediate strategic policy	
	Units in 2002	Annual cost in 2002 (billions of 1996 dollars)	Units in 2002	Annual cost in 2002 (billions of 1996 dollars)
Item	Active/Reserve	Active/Reserve	Active/Reserve	Active/Reserve
Force elements				
M/M III	100/0	0.6/0	300/0	1.8/0
T/C-4	0/0	0/0	96/0	2.2/0
T/D-5	240/0	5.1/0	240/0	5.1/0
B-2	0/0	0/0	16/0	5.2/0
KC-135	0/0	0/0	70/0	0/0.3
F-16	150/0	0/0.1	150/0	0/0.1
EW/C³	85/0	4.4/0	85/0	4.4/0
BMD	0/0	3.0/0	0/0	3.0/0
Total	...	13.1/0.1	...	21.7/0.4
Army				
Armor	1/0	4.3/0	1/0	4.2/0
Mechanized	2/2	6.9/2.2	2/2	6.9/2.2
Light infantry	3/0	9.1/0	3/0	9.1/0
Airborne	1/0	2.8/0	1/0	2.8/0
Air assault	1/0	3.3/0	1/0	3.3/0
ACR	5⅓/0	6.8/0	5⅓/0	6.8/0
Total	...	33.2/2.2	...	33.1/2.2
USMC				
Division	3/1	5.7/0.2	3/1	5.7/0.2
Wing	3/1	8.1/0.2	3/1	8.1/0.2
Total	...	13.8/0.4	...	13.8/0.4
Special operations forces				
Special units	4/3	11.5/2.4	4/3	11.5/2.4
Light infantry[a]	0/0	0/0	3/0	9.1/0
Total	...	11.5/2.4	...	11.5/2.4

AF tactical air				
Bombers	126/0	7.5/0	126/0	7.5/0
Fighter wings	8/3⅔	7.6/2.5	10/3⅔	10.5/2.5
Surveillance aircraft	62/0	3.4/0	62/0	3.4/0
Training aircraft	368/0	0.6/0	368/0	0.6/0
Support aircraft	375/0	0.8/0	375/0	0.8/0
Total	...	19.9/2.5	...	22.8/2.5
Navy				
CVBG	7/1CV	24.0/1.2	9/1CV	30.8/1.2
MEB lift	2/0	3.2/0.6	2/0	4.8/0.6
ASW by ocean	1/0	6.9/0	2/0	13.8/0
Total	...	34.1/1.8	...	49.4/1.8
Airlift				
Intertheater	364/0	12.3/0	364/0	12.3/0
Intratheater	158/284	1.0/0.9	158/284	1.0/0.9
Total	...	13.3/0.9	...	13.3/0.9
Pre-positioning				
MPS	13/0	0.6/0	13/0	0.6/0
AFPS	32/0	1.6/0	32/0	1.6/0
Total	...	2.2/0	...	2.2/0
Sealift				
Fast sealift	8/0	0.4/0	8/0	0.4/0
Tankers	20/0	0.9/0	20/0	0.9/0
Cargo	17/0	0.7/0	17/0	0.7/0
Total	...	2.0/0	...	2.0/0
National intelligence and communications				
Total	...	20.0/1.6	...	20.0/1.6
Total	...	163.1/11.9	...	189.8/12.2
Total	...	175.0	...	202.0

SOURCES: Authors' calculations.
a. See above (under Army).

TABLE 5-6. Illustrative Transition of U.S., Russian, and Chinese Defense Budgets and Investment Programs, Fiscal Years 1998–2008
Billions of 1996 dollars

	United States		Russia		China	
Fiscal year	Total base budget[a]	Total investment	Total budget	Total investment	Total budget	Total investment
1998	226.0	82.0	50.0	19.5	50.0	18.6
1999	220.3	80.0	51.3	20.0	51.3	19.1
2000	214.7	78.0	52.6	20.5	52.6	19.5
2001	209.3	76.1	54.0	21.0	54.0	20.0
2002	204.0	74.3	55.4	21.5	55.4	20.5
2003	198.9	72.4	56.8	22.1	56.8	21.1
2004	193.9	70.7	58.3	22.6	58.3	21.6
2005	189.0	68.9	59.8	23.2	59.8	22.1
2006	184.2	67.3	61.4	23.8	61.4	22.7
2007	179.5	65.6	63.0	24.4	63.0	23.2
2008	175.0	64.0	64.6	25.0	64.6	23.8
Total	2,194.8	799.3	627.2	243.6	627.2	232.2

SOURCE: Authors' calculations.

a. For the purposes of this assessment, the $11 billion of the U.S. defense budget that is devoted to various purposes not associated with the financing of U.S. forces has been removed from the base budget. Assuming these expenditures continue, the 051 account would be $11 billion more than the base figures shown here, up to 2002.

military investment program extending beyond the agreed standards and would give ample time to react to such a development. Even on short notice, it could handle any of the standard regional contingencies that might arise, and the chances of such contingencies actually arising would be more systematically constrained. In addition, it would provide a set of forces with fully integrated capabilities specifically designed for the instances of civil violence that are more likely to occur.

And all this would be substantially less expensive. If these arrangements were implemented over a ten-year period starting in 1998, the end-state U.S. force could be fully financed under the stable rate of replacement criterion with annual budgets of $175 billion (1996 dollars). This would be $67 billion less than the annual costs of the defense budgets proposed by President Clinton and $100 billion a year less than the budgets required to meet the full financing criterion for current forces.

The net savings, however, would not be as large. The logic of the cooperative security arrangement requires that greater preventive investment accompany the restrictions on standard military capability. For example, more extensive monitoring would be required, as would more deliberate efforts to control civil conflict at the very earliest stages. Such increases could cost significant amounts. Since direct intervention to preempt subsequent violence is not a very well developed or consciously practiced art, it is impossible to specify either the specific programs or the appropriate level of expenditure on direct measures of conflict prevention. Nonetheless, some rough judgment might be derived by considering the level of current activity.

As summarized in figure 5-1, the United States devoted approximately $7.3 billion in 1995 to official development assistance expenditures, the category of expenditure that might be considered most relevant for preventing or mitigating violent conflict even if the current programs have not been designed with that in mind. The corresponding program in 1990 was roughly twice as large. Unlike standard military preparation, the United States does not lead the world in this type of assistance. In 1995 the United States ranked fourth among the major donor countries in level of expenditure and last in effort relative to GDP. If the United States were to double its current level of expenditure to match that of Japan, its aid program would be restored to its 1990 level. If current expenditure were tripled, the U.S. effort would match the average level of effort (0.27 percent of GNP) of the major donor countries. These adjustments would commit only 7 percent or 15 percent, respectively, of the defense budget savings that might ultimately be derived from the cooperative security policy. A visible reallocation of effort in this range of an additional $7.5 billion to $15 billion and an appropriate redesign of the specific programs would certainly help to project the policy and might actually be necessary to secure the international agreement required to establish it.

There may be, then, an opportunity. A cooperative security policy engaging other major powers has the potential to provide better security that is more responsive to emerging circumstances at lower cost. The opportunity is not broadly recognized at the moment, and an initiative of the scope that would be required to respond to it has not yet been attempted. There are tentative policies of engagement that lead in this direction, however, and looming fiscal pressures, as well as core security interests, certainly encourage a more systematic effort. All of the major military establishments, including the United States, have a better chance of meeting their basic financial constraints by adopting a cooperative policy than they do by attempting to preserve the pattern of implicit confrontation. The illustrative budget

FIGURE 5-1. Overseas Development Assistance of Major Countries, 1995

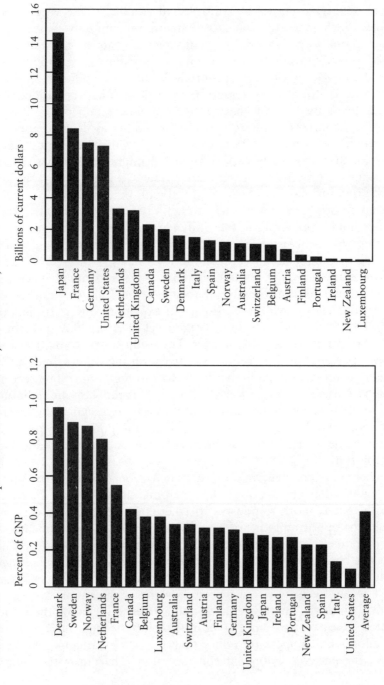

SOURCE: Organization for Economic Cooperation and Development (1996).

savings provide a rough measure of the incentive to evolve in this direction. For the United States it amounts to about $90 billion a year.

Intermediate Adaptation

It is likely that fiscal pressures will impose a budget limitation on the U.S. defense program long before there has been a systematic reformulation of strategic policy. Therefore the U.S. security posture is likely to fall somewhere between full preservation of advantage and the achievement of reliable cooperation. This intermediate position could be carried out badly. We might dissipate our absolute capability and relative advantage without achieving a general pattern of restraint on potentially opposing forces. But it need not be so. Fiscal constraint could drive a process of gradual adaptation to the new security circumstances, if there is some degree of consciousness about the main requirements.

Fiscal restraint. Budget reductions are a predictable result of impending fiscal austerity. Savings can be achieved without reformulating current policy. The current U.S. force advantage is sufficiently large that the defense budget could be reduced while preserving the capacity to perform the core missions of nuclear deterrence and conventional defense on short notice. Table 5-7 summarizes a number of constructive suggestions for translating the technological improvements and threat reductions that have already occurred into future savings.

Some of these proposals emphasize reliance on precision attack capability. They would capture the advantages of advanced information technology by reducing the amount of firepower that has to be purchased in order to conduct successful defense against conventional assault. Investment would be focused on the information service technologies—sensors, communications, and data integration capabilities—rather than on the introduction of increasingly more expensive versions of major combat systems like tactical aircraft.[8] The number of active ground force brigades and tactical air wings could be reduced as the new technologies increase their combat effectiveness. In addition, a smaller number of munitions could be purchased because the unit effectiveness of the advanced munitions would be

8. Krepinevich (1996a, 1996b); Nye and Owens (1996).

TABLE 5-7. Recent Proposals for Defense Budget Savings

Proposal category	Proponents	Potential annual savings	Logical basis
Force reduction proposals			
Force reductions based largely on revised assessment of Korean balance	Lawrence Korb (Brookings)	At least $40 billion	Reduced threat
Force reductions based on Lanchester models applied to Gulf War	William Kaufmann (Brookings)	At least $40 billion	Reduced threat
Greater reliance on airpower, decreased ground forces	Michael O'Hanlon (Brookings) Les Aspin (House Armed Services)	About $20 billion	Reduced threat, technological efficiency
Restructuring roles and missions: for example, consolidate light forces and close air support units	Congressional Budget Office Stimson Center	About $10 billion to $20 billion	Organizational efficiency
Decrease civilian work force, change HMO staffing, consolidate depots	Concord Coalition	$5 billion	Organizational efficiency
Force reductions based on analysis questioning logic of 2-war scenario	Carl Conetta (Project on Defense Alternatives)	Unspecified	Reduced threat
Proposals for internal reallocation[a]			
Forgo modernization of major combat systems	Thomas McNaugher (RAND) Charles Spinney (DOD)	Unspecified	Reduced threat, technological efficiency
Modernize munitions, sensors, C31, rather than advanced delivery platforms; potential over long term to reduce size of forces	Andrew Krepinevich (Center for Strategic and Budgetary Assessments) Former Vice-Chairman JCS Admiral William Owens Former Assistant Secretary of Defense Joseph Nye	At least $20 billion (estimate from Krepinevich)	Technological efficiency

Reduce reliance on marine and naval air	Former AF Chief Merrill McPeak	About $10 billion	Organizational efficiency
Reduce duplication of firepower support functions by Army artillery, Army helicopters and Air Force CAS, and other changes in roles and missions	Senator Sam Nunn	Unspecified	Organizational efficiency
Reduce alert levels and increase reliance on reserves; emphasis on using savings partially to fund ballistic missile defense	Senator John McCain	About $10 billion to $20 billion	Reduced near-term threat, yet possibly greater long-term threat

Proposals for longer-term restructuring

Reorganize tactical fighter wings and ground divisions through technological innovations in areas such as communications and precision standoff munitions	Eliot Cohen (SAIS)	Unspecified	Technological efficiency
Reliance on PGMs and B-2 aircraft; implied reductions in ground and tactical air forces	Glenn Buchan (RAND)	Unspecified	Technological efficiency
Reduce alert levels and increase reliance on reserves	Richard Betts (Columbia)	Unspecified	Reduced near-term threat, yet possibly greater long-term threat

SOURCES: Aspin (1992); Betts (1995); Blechman and others (1993); Buchan (1994); Cohen (1996); Concord Coalition (1995, p. 20); Conetta (1994); Congressional Budget Office (1992, 1994b); Kaufmann (1992); Krepinevich (1996a, 1996b), McCain (1996); McNaugher (1996); McPeak (1994); Nye and Owens (1996); O'Hanlon (1995); Spinney (1996).
a. These focus on using funds saved to ensure full funding of basic elements of the current plan; some would also modernize forces and build ballistic missile defense.

much greater than those they were replacing. Although the unit cost of the force components and of their munitions would be greater under this policy, the decline in the number of units required would actually reduce overall cost.

A somewhat overlapping set of adjustments has also been suggested as a means of achieving defense budget savings from the sharp reductions in immediate threat that have occurred with the dissolution of the Soviet Union.[9] The introduction of advanced models of major combat systems would be postponed because the potential regional opponents are not improving their capabilities at rates that require the United States to move to the next generation of basic weapons systems, such as tanks, aircraft, and helicopters. Similarly, active force deployments would be set at levels that more nearly reflect the actual requirements of the regional contingencies, even under the assumption that little warning would occur.

An intermediate force structure and associated defense budget that incorporate these suggestions are shown in table 5-5. The basic policy would hold the core capabilities for deterrent retaliation and conventional defense constant at levels adequate to perform these missions under the traditional supposition of surprise attack while extracting cost savings from efficiency gains and spontaneous (unnegotiated) threat reductions. As with the current defense program, the forces would be designed to support two regional conflicts independently, but with somewhat more restrictive assumptions about the degree of actual combat they would require. Current contingency planning, for example, assumes that tactical air assets (including bombers) would attack as many as 50,000 individual aimpoints in each of the two contingencies.[10] The forces presented in table 5-5 would be able to conduct sustained air campaigns at the same level as those of the Gulf War—about 35,000 individual aimpoints—in each assumed contingency, and standard methods of assessment indicate that the overall force available for each contingency should be able to stop an assault mounted by up to 126 attacking brigades within three weeks, assuming that the main capabilities of the United States and local allies are in

9. Aspin (1992); Betts (1995); Korb (1995); Conetta (1994); Kaufmann (1992); McNaugher (1996); O'Hanlon (1995); Spinney (1996).

10. According to the General Accounting Office, "during two major regional conflicts, U.S. military forces expect to encounter over 100,000 mobile or fixed targets." See U.S. General Accounting Office (1996b, p. 17).

position when the assault actually occurs.[11] An attack of this size is the outer edge of what either Iraq or North Korea would be able to mobilize, and their efforts to prepare such an attack would be visible.

Under the criterion of a stable cost of replacement, this intermediate force structure would cost $1.308 trillion (1996 dollars) over the six-year budget projection period; the annual budget in 2002 would be about $202 billion. Measured against President Clinton's defense budget proposal, the six-year savings would be nearly $125 billion, and the budget savings thereafter would be roughly $40 billion a year. Measured against the stable rate of replacement costs of the current defense program, the savings would be $198 billion over the 1997–2002 period and more than $55 billion a year thereafter. This contribution to fiscal relief can be made without any serious erosion of the traditional missions.

These cost reductions alone would not constitute an adaptive security policy, however, but simply a less expensive version of prevailing practice. The pressure imposed on Russia and China would not be intensified under this variant, but neither would it be reduced. The stimulus given to dangerous forms of weapons proliferation would also be unaffected. Progressive adaptation to new security circumstances requires force structure shifts that go beyond those designed to provide basic fiscal relief to ones that serve at least two additional purposes: mitigating the side effects of standard deterrent and conventional defense practices and responding directly to the problems of civil violence. The first of these purposes has to do with the overall safety of military deployments and the second with the stability of the societies they are intended to serve.

11. The results are derived from a U.S. bombing campaign with precision-guided munitions against a range of aimpoints, including enemy ground forces (taking a maximum of twenty-one days), followed by a ground attack by U.S. forces that eliminates residual enemy capabilities in eight days. The hypothetical campaign takes place on the Korean peninsula—the more demanding of the two current contingencies. The air campaign assumes a single-shot kill probability of 0.54 against soft aimpoints and 0.37 against hard targets. Enemy ground forces are reduced by 60 percent at a cost of twenty-one U.S. combat aircraft. In the ground attack on residual enemy forces, a U.S. division is assumed to be three times more powerful and twelve times more effective than a residual enemy division—a ratio that reflects the actual experience of the Gulf War. Lanchester equations were used to determine the length of the ground campaign and the casualties suffered by U.S. forces. For similar assessments, see Ochmanek and Bordeaux (1993, p. 4, fn. 4; p. 7, table 1; pp. 9–11; p. 13, fig. 4; p. 21; app. B); Bowie and others (1993, Summary, pp. xii–xix; p. 50, fn. 33).

Safety. Since conventional weapons are the most widely dispersed, absorb most of the money, and are the means used in virtually all of the aggression that actually occurs, they are the primary instruments of international security. Nonetheless, it is the disposition of nuclear weapons that sets the strategic pattern, simply because of their transcendent destructiveness. At the moment, international security is in a confrontational pattern regardless of how accommodating the political rhetoric might be. Russia and the United States are operating nuclear forces on continuous alert, ready to initiate mass attacks on each other within minutes, and are planning to do so indefinitely, even as they implement a schedule of substantial reductions and significant restructuring of their forces. That is the fundamental condition underlying all security relationships. An adaptive policy that is responsive to the new circumstances of international security would seek to alter this underlying condition as its first priority.

There are strong reasons for this priority. Preparations for executing massive retaliation in rapid reaction to evidence of a strategic attack put a tremendous load on the decisionmaking systems that must manage dispersed nuclear weapons and make it inherently more difficult to ensure that no accidental or unauthorized use of an individual weapon will occur and that no commitment to mass retaliation will be made that could be avoided. Although rarely heralded as such, these provisions of operational safety have always been and remain the most fundamental security requirement that must be preserved on a daily basis. Under the cold war supposition that the intricate and exceedingly dangerous maneuver of a calculated surprise attack might actually be attempted, the requirements of operational safety were subordinated to the perceived necessity to prepare for rapid retaliation, largely as a means of protecting against the chance that the entire command system would break down in the initial stages of the assault and that such a failure would prevent any retaliation. The many intricate provisions that were worked out to assure operational safety under the demanding requirements of rapid reaction were considered adequate during the cold war and were in fact successful. It was apparent, however, that the safety provisions were prone to failure under the pressures of a serious crisis, and there were numerous operational incidents that illustrated this concern.[12] As the cold war obsession with the possibility of a decisive surprise attack fades, the

12. Blair (1993); Sagan (1993).

underlying interest in operational safety becomes more prominent and an obvious opportunity for adjustment is presented. If preparations for retaliation are subordinated to considerations of operational safety rather than the other way around, much higher standards of safety can be achieved, and this can, in principle, be done while preserving a robust capacity for retaliation and its deterrent effect.[13]

This adjustment is a matter of some urgency, given the pressures on the Russian military establishment. The Russian military has to defend a new territorial configuration with a budget that does not allow adequate preparation under standard methods of assessment, which depend upon preserving an adequate balance in the number and quality of opposing units. Moreover, it has to do this while sustaining deterrent engagement with a nominally equal but technically superior U.S. force. In predictable reaction to these pressures, the Russians have intensified their reliance on rapid retaliation operations. In the overall context, that runs a significant risk of degrading the standards of operational safety they are able to maintain. Whether or not that effect is actually occurring, increased reliance on rapid reaction certainly prevents systematic improvements in operational safety and virtually assures that the current collaboration with the United States on this subject will have limited scope.

In order to achieve the highest standards of operational safety for deployed nuclear weapons, it would be necessary to terminate continuous alert operations and mass targeting practices completely and to devise means of ensuring that all the states that deploy nuclear weapons utilize the most advanced methods of accounting, monitoring, and physical security in managing them. Under a policy of gradual adaptation, there would be a continuing evolution toward those ends. At the final stages of that process, there would probably have to be a significant redesign of delivery system configurations and operational practices to ensure the invulnerability of the forces without relying on, or even allowing, rapid reaction procedures. These measures would impose some costs and yield some savings, but would probably not have a large net effect on the budget. They would be undertaken for reasons of safety rather than efficiency. They would provide a pervasive improvement in the fundamental conditions of security, and that effect makes them the single most important element of adaptation.

Stability. The calculations used to construct estimates of the con-

13. Blair (1995).

sequences of a full-scale nuclear war have no counterpart for the security problems associated with social instability. It is possible to imagine a massive breakdown of basic civil order, and there are reasons to fear that the combination of economic globalization and population dynamics might create the potential for such a development. There is virtually no accepted basis for measuring that potential, however, and there is a natural tendency to ignore that which cannot be reliably measured. Moreover, the difficulty of basic assessment is compounded by the fact that no practical measures for responding to the dangers of civil violence have been identified that promise anything like the pervasive, high-leverage effect on stability that improvements in the operational management of nuclear weapons would provide.

Nonetheless, it seems prudent to admit that endemic violence in a highly integrated world of over 8 billion people with undeniable access to destructive technology could readily become unmanageable for any and all of the existing military establishments. From that admission, it appears to follow that an adaptive security policy would have to devise some program for reacting to the potential danger of extensive civil violence well before that danger can be reliably assessed. There are two basic elements of such a program: preventive investment and rapid reaction to instances of impending breakdown.

Preventive investment, at the moment, is not much more than a phrase that has to be taken seriously despite the evident difficulties of doing so. The basic concept is that the combination of circumstances that have led to extended episodes of major civil violence within certain countries—Bosnia, Somalia, Rwanda, and Tajikistan, for example—must be prevented elsewhere by programs directed at the underlying causes. This overlaps the traditional agendas for economic development and humanitarian aid and suggests that parts of those agendas need to be understood conceptually and managed as a security investment. By nature, this is a broad multinational agenda. Developing it would require a basic shift in the relative allocation of effort by the United States along the lines suggested by the cooperative strategic policy. Under an adaptive strategic policy, this reallocation of effort should occur more gradually, but the basic principle would have to be established and the development of its specific implications would have to be seriously pursued.

The idea of organizing a rapid response to circumstances where preventive efforts are on the verge of failure emerges from assessments of the major recent instances of civil violence.[14] In all of these major cases, specific warnings of impending breakdown were issued by diplomats, scholars, and humanitarian aid officials who were observing the events. There was no effective response to these warnings, however, largely because appropriate reactions had not been prepared. The definition of national and international interest had not been developed. In particular, the general importance of protecting the basic elements of civil order had not been articulated. Moreover, the broad, inclusive international coalition that would be necessary to give legitimacy and credibility to such a determination of interest had not been organized, and the operational details of an effective intervention had not been worked out. The lessons drawn from these cases seem to suggest that, if the preconditions had been mastered and if appropriately designed operations had been rapidly undertaken in response to the initial warnings, much of the subsequent violence could have been prevented without large resource commitments.

An adaptive security policy will have to identify and develop more effective means for coping with future problems of this sort. Most likely, effective preparations for rapid reaction will eventually lead to a significant reconfiguration of the military forces that have been designed for the major regional contingencies. Adroit intervention to protect or restore basic civil order does not require massive firepower. It does require large flows of highly detailed information, rapid mobility, and, above all, effective command integration. In operations that may have to use specific forms of violence in order to prevent more widespread outbreaks, the actions of individual soldiers can have major strategic effects. This is not an art that can be improvised. It has to be pursued on its own terms at least as systematically as the traditional missions have been. The force structure and defense budget presented in table 5-5 presume that an adaptation of this sort would be undertaken.

Perspective

For the moment, what we choose is less important than what we debate. In the immediate future the United States will undoubtedly choose some variation of the intermediate policy—probably with a

14. See, for example, Lyons and Samatar (1995); Woodward (1995).

more modest fiscal adjustment and a less explicit adaptation than the one presented above. The political environment does not appear conducive to the more extensive alternatives. The pressures of budgets and events are likely to prove relentless, however. Eventually, the current strategic policy, which retains fundamental features of policy established during the cold war, will have to be substantially reformulated.

Unexpected events might affect the outcome in ways that we cannot conceive, let alone debate, today. Even that possibility, however, does not excuse neglecting basic and important questions, such as these: Is it wise to sustain indefinitely the particular military advantages that the United States has acquired? If so, is the United States prepared to pay the costs and absorb the reactions? If not, how should the country transform its current advantages into a better arrangement before a pattern of unfortunate reaction is locked into place? Valid answers to these questions require a more penetrating policy debate than has yet occurred.

TABLE 5A-1. Detailed Estimates of Proposed Upgrades and Replacements of Current Weapon Systems, Fiscal Years 1996–2016

Millions of 1996 dollars

Type of system	Estimated number	Estimated cost
Upgrades		
B-1 bomber	100	2,740
B-2 bomber	16	4,190
B-52H bomber	65	230
Minuteman III service life extension	500	4,000
AH-64 Army attack helicopter	788	8,400
OH-58D Army armed observation helicopter	225	3,400
M1 Abrams heavy tank	1,010	3,000
M2/3 Bradley armored infantry fighting vehicle	1,602	3,300
F/A-18C/D Navy multimission fighter/attack aircraft	72	1,500
E-2C Navy early warning aircraft	113	1,280
SH-60B Navy antisubmarine warfare helicopter	186	860
AV-8B Marine Corps V/STOL fighter-attack aircraft	72	2,000
E-3C/D AWACS, Air Force airborne warning and control system	10	400
Total	. . .	35,300
Replacements		
Combat aircraft		
F/A-18E/F multimission fighter/attack aircraft	700	63,000
Joint Strike Fighter (Navy and Air Force)	200	18,000
V-22 tilt-motor VTOL aircraft	425	35,560
F-22 stealth fighter	552	66,240
Total	. . .	182,800
Support aircraft		
JPATS joint primary trainer	288	5,134
T-45TS advanced trainer	176	5,456
C-17 airlift aircraft	88	24,200
E-8B Joint Stars aircraft	16	6,960
JTUAV unmanned aircraft (drone)	110	2,432
Total	. . .	44,182
Helicopters		
RAH-66 Comanche reconnaissance/attack	1,292	37,468
UH-60L Blackhawk Utility	470	3,046
AH-1W gunship	42	1,260
Total	. . .	41,774
Tracked and wheeled vehicles		
Advanced field artillery system (AFAS)	565	5,438
Future armored resupply vehicle—ammunition (FARV-A)	565	906
Family of medium tactical vehicles (FMTV)	61,000	10,112
High mobility multipurpose wheeled vehicles (HMMWV)	14,570	708
Light armored vehicles (LVT), Marine Corps	672	950
Total	. . .	18,114

TABLE 5A-1 (continued)

Type of system	Estimated number	Estimated cost
Tactical missiles		
Air-to-ground	262,000	44,100
Air-to-air	12,800	13,500
Ground-to-air	3,808	3,000
Ground-to-ground	32,465	8,500
Total	. . .	69,100
Navy ships		
CVN: nuclear-powered aircraft carrier	3	16,500
DDG-51: Aegis-equipped destroyer	35	31,500
SSN-21: nuclear-powered attack submarine	1	2,700
NSSN: new nuclear-powered attack submarine	17	30,600
Amphibious warfare ships	13	13,675
AAAV: advanced amphibious assault vehicle	1,013	6,700
Mine countermeasures ships	1	170
T-AGOS: ASW surveillance ships	1	225
Support ships and auxiliaries	20	8,900
Total	. . .	110,970
Space systems		
Titan IV	60	11,700
FLTSATCOM: fleet satellite communication system	12	2,271
DMSP: defense meteorological satellite program	8	1,748
DSCS: defense satellite communication system	12	1,216
DSP: defense support program (surveillance and warning of early missile attack)	12	12,853
MILSTAR: communication satellite system	6	6,975
NAVSTAR: global positioning satellite	84	5,847
NAVSTAR user equipment	102,000	3,500
Classified programs: photography and SIGINT satellites	. . .	142,000
Total	. . .	188,110
Ballistic missile defense		
Core theater missile defense (THAAD; PAC-3; Navy Lower and Upper Tier)	n.a.	34,781
Other theater defenses (Hawk; Corps SAM; Boost-phase intercept)	n.a.	11,068
National missile defense	n.a.	21,151
Total	. . .	67,000
Other procurement		
Aircraft spare parts	n.a.	86,000
Support equipment and vehicles	n.a.	132,000
Communications and electronics	n.a.	100,000
Ammunition	n.a.	76,000
Miscellaneous equipment	n.a.	68,000
Total	. . .	462,000

SOURCES: Congressional Budget Office (1994a, pp. 37, 38; 1994c, pp. xv, xx; 1994d, pp. 5, 6, 18, 19; 1994e, p. 8; 1995a, p. 50; 1995b, p. 40; 1995c, p. 28); Kaufmann (1990, table 17); U.S. General Accounting Office (1994a, p. 6; 1994b, p. 21; 1996a, pp. 8, 41, 49; 1996b, app. II, p. 50).
n.a. Not available.

References

Arms Control Association. 1996. "Latest START I Data for the United States"; "Latest START I Data for Russia and the States of the Former Soviet Union." Fact Sheet (October 7).

Aspin, Les. 1992. "An Approach to Sizing American Conventional Forces for the Post-Soviet Era." House Committee on Armed Services (January 24).

———. 1993. *Report on the Bottom-up Review.* Department of Defense (October).

Betts, Richard K. 1995. *Military Readiness: Concepts, Choices, Consequences.* Brookings.

Blair, Bruce G. 1993. *The Logic of Accidental Nuclear War.* Brookings.

———. 1995. *Global Zero Alert for Nuclear Forces.* Brookings.

Blechman, Barry M., and others. 1993. *Key West Revisited: Roles and Missions of the U.S. Armed Forces in the Twenty-First Century.* Report 8. Washington: Henry L. Stimson Center (March).

Bowie, Christopher, and others. 1993. *The New Calculus: Analyzing Airpower's Changing Role in Joint Theater Campaigns.* Santa Monica, Calif.: RAND.

Buchan, Glenn C. 1994. "The Use of Long-Range Bombers in a Changing World: A Classical Exercise in Systems Analysis." In *New Challenges for Defense Planning: Rethinking How Much Is Enough,* edited by Paul K. Davis, 393–450. Santa Monica: RAND.

Cohen, Eliot A. 1996. "A Revolution in Warfare." *Foreign Affairs* 75 (March–April): 37–54.

Concord Coalition. 1995. *The Zero Deficit Plan: A Plan for Eliminating the Federal Budget Deficit by the Year 2002.* Washington (May).

Conetta, Carl J. 1994. "Mismatch: 'The Bottom Up Review' and America's Security Requirements in the New Era." Testimony for the House Committee on Armed Services. (March 10).

Congressional Budget Office. 1992. *Structuring U.S. Forces after the Cold War: Costs and Effects of Increased Reliance on the Reserves* (September).

———. 1994a. "Planning for Defense: Affordability and Capability of the Administration's Program." CBO Memorandum (March).

———. 1994b. *Options for Reconfiguring Service Roles and Missions.* CBO Paper (March).

———. 1994c. *The Future of Theater Missile Defense* (June).

———. 1994d. "The Costs of the Administration's Plan for the Navy through the Year 2010." CBO Memorandum (November).

———. 1994e. "The Costs of the Administration's Plan for the Army through the Year 2010." CBO Memorandum (November)

———. 1995a. *Reducing the Deficit: Spending and Revenue Options* (February).

———. 1995b. *Options for Enhancing the Bomber Force* (July).

———. 1995c. *An Analysis of U.S. Army Helicopter Programs* (December).

International Institute for Strategic Studies. 1996. *The Military Balance, 1996–1997.* Oxford: Oxford University Press.

Kaufmann, William W. 1990. *Glasnost, Perestroika, and U.S. Defense Spending.* Brookings.

————. 1992. *Assessing the Base Force: How Much Is Too Much?* Brookings.

Korb, Lawrence J. 1995. "Our Overstuffed Armed Forces." *Foreign Affairs* 74 (November–December): 22–34.

Koziak, Steven M. 1996. *Analysis of the Fiscal 1997 Defense Budget Request.* Washington: Center for Strategic and Budgetary Assessments (April).

Krepinevich, Andrew F. Jr. 1996a. "Restructuring Defense for a New Era: The Value of Scenario-Based Planning." Center for Strategic and Budgetary Assessments (January).

————. 1996b. *A New Navy for a New Era.* Center for Strategic and Budgetary Assessments (May).

Lyons, Terrence, and Ahmed I. Samatar. 1995. *Somalia: State Collapse, Multilateral Intervention, and Strategies for Political Reconstruction.* Brookings.

McCain, John. 1996. "Ready Tomorrow: Defending American Interests in the 21st Century." Office of U.S. Senator John McCain (March).

McNaugher, Thomas L. 1996. "Planning Future Defense: Time to Confront the Cold War Mindset." *Brookings Review* 14 (Summer): 26–29.

McPeak, Merrill A. 1994. *Presentation to the Commission on Roles and Missions of the Armed Forces.* Government Printing Office (September 14).

NATO. 1995. "Defense Expenditures of NATO Countries, 1976–1995." Press release.

Nye, Joseph S. Jr., and William A. Owens. 1996. "America's Information Edge." *Foreign Affairs* 75 (March–April): 20–36.

Ochmanek, David, and John Bordeaux. 1993. "Comparing Air Power Projection Assets." RAND White Paper. Santa Monica, Calif.: RAND. (February).

O'Hanlon, Michael. 1995. *Defense Planning for the Late 1990s: Beyond the Desert Storm Framework.* Brookings.

Organization for Economic Cooperation and Development. Development Assistance Committee. 1996. "Financial Flows to Developing Countries in 1995: Sharp Decline in Official Aid; Private Flows Rise." News Release, June 11.

Perry, William J. 1996. *Annual Report to the President and the Congress.* Department of Defense. (March).

Sagan, Scott D. 1993. *The Limits of Safety: Organizations, Accidents and Nuclear Weapons.* Princeton University Press.

Spinney, Franklin C. 1996. "Defense Time Bomb: F-22/JSF Case Study Hypothetical Escape Option." *Challenge* (July–August): 23–33.

U.S. General Accounting Office. 1994a. *Navy Modernization: Alternatives for Achieving a More Affordble Force.* NSIAD-94-171 (April).

————. 1994b. *Attack Submarines: Alternatives for a More Affordable SSN Force Structure.* NSIAD-95-16 (October).

————. 1996a. *Marine Corps: Improving Amphibious Capability Would Require Larger Share of Budget Than Previously Provided.* NSIAD-96-47 (February).

————. 1996b. *U.S. Combat Air Power: Reassessing Plans to Modernize Interdiction Capabilities Could Save Billions.* NSIAD-96-72 (May).

————. 1996c. *Weapons of Mass Destruction: Status of the Cooperative Threat Reduction Program.* NSIAD-96-222 (September).

Woodward, Susan L. 1995. *Balkan Tragedy: Chaos and Dissolution after the Cold War.* Brookings.

DAVID M. CUTLER

6

Restructuring Medicare for the Future

MEDICARE is one of the nation's greatest public policy success stories and one of its most pressing problems. In the early 1960s, half the elderly were without health insurance and at risk for substantial medical expense. Today, nearly all of the elderly and disabled have coverage for acute medical needs, and the risk of impoverishment from uninsured medical costs has been greatly reduced. The enactment of medicare in 1965 and its subsequent expansion are largely responsible for this success. In an era when many government programs are denigrated, medicare is adored.

And yet the cost of medicare is placing the program in jeopardy. Medicare has been a major contributor to the sustained budget deficits of the past fifteen years, and without reform it will play a similar role in the future. If policymakers make good on their promise to balance the budget solely by reducing spending, medicare spending will have to be significantly cut.

But the link to short-run budget deficits is only one facet of the medicare problem. Medicare is as much a long-term fiscal concern as a short-term deficit problem. Costs are increasing so rapidly that even if medicare payments are scaled back by amounts envisioned in recent balanced-budget proposals, an unrestructured program would become unaffordable again early in the next century. This long-term problem must be addressed if the nation wants to have a sustainable health insurance program for future generations of elderly and disabled.

Independent of the budget, medicare represents an enormous commitment of social resources. No one who has examined medicare in detail believes that all its spending is worthwhile. Spending more than is needed on any program, particularly one as large as medicare, is a tremendous waste when other national needs remain unmet.

The author is grateful to Len Nichols and Kim Packard for many helpful discussions and to the National Institute on Aging for research support.

197

Medicare is in need of policy reform like few other public programs. There are three fundamental strategies for achieving reform: cutting payments to providers, shifting more of the costs of the program to beneficiaries, and redesigning the program to incorporate market-based incentives. In some fashion, reform along all three lines is needed. Short-run deficit reduction is best accomplished through mechanisms that have been used in the past: reductions in payments to providers and increases in the amount that beneficiaries pay for the program. But over the longer run, there is no escaping the need for structural reform. Medicare is increasingly an anachronism: it is a program that has changed little in the past thirty years, despite a sea change in the health system around it. If the program is to be solvent thirty years from now, changes must be made soon. Making this transition successfully is perhaps the key challenge facing policymakers over the next few years.

The Basics of Medicare

Medicare legislation was passed in 1965, and the system went into operation the following year.[1] For many years before passage of medicare, universal insurance coverage was the goal of social reformers. These reforms were opposed by provider groups (principally the American Medical Association) that did not want government provision of health care. The compromise was coverage for the elderly. The elderly were a natural group to insure since only about 50 percent of them had insurance coverage.

Medicare was expanded in 1972 to cover disabled people and people with end-stage renal disease. These two groups make up about 10 percent of medicare beneficiaries and costs. There has been no expansion of eligibility since then.

To ameliorate the concerns of provider groups that medicare would be used to restrict their incomes, the program was set up like prevailing Blue Cross insurance plans. Services were divided into part A (hospital insurance), covering inpatient services and some skilled nursing facilities, home health care, and hospice care; and part B (supplementary medical insurance), covering physician, outpatient, and laboratory services, and other ambulatory care. Part A accounts for

1. For a discussion of the history of medicare, see Davis and Schoen (1978); Moon (1996).

about two-thirds of program costs, part B for about one-third. People who are 65 or older are entitled to part A benefits if they or their spouses are eligible for social security or railroad retirement benefits. Insurance under part B requires participants to pay a premium equal to 25 percent of part B spending ($42.50 a month in 1996).

The distinction between part A and part B is less important medically than budgetarily. Part A expenses are paid out of the hospital insurance trust fund. The revenues to the trust fund come from a 2.9 percent payroll tax on all wage and salary income.[2] The fact that revenues to the trust fund are limited means the trust fund can go "bankrupt." Projections that medicare was headed toward bankruptcy early in the next century were a powerful rhetorical tool in the recent budget debate for those who wanted to reform the program. Indeed, the most recent projections are that the hospital insurance trust fund will be bankrupt in the year 2001.

In the context of an entire government budget, however, projections that one component will go bankrupt have little economic import. For example, the supplementary medical insurance trust fund, which pays for part B services, receives income from the premiums paid by beneficiaries and from general revenues. Because general revenue financing is uncapped, the supplementary medical insurance trust fund can not become bankrupt. And yet the part B program is no more financially sound than the part A program.

Indeed, the hospital insurance trust fund has been at or near the verge of bankruptcy for the past two decades.[3] Every few years, reforms—either increased taxes or reduced spending on services—have been adopted to bolster the trust fund. The recent "crisis" is no different from the previous ones, with the exception that it is more public. The imperative to reform medicare does not arise because the part A trust fund is going bankrupt, but rather because the program as a whole takes up too many resources. To the extent that the impending "bankruptcy" of the trust fund focuses attention on the important issue of the cost of medicare, that is good. But the temptation to make solvency of the trust fund *the* goal of reform is damaging. A

2. The tax is nominally levied 1.45 percent each on employers and employees. Most economists combine the two parts because they believe workers bear the burden of the employer share through lower cash compensation. The trust fund also receives a small amount attributable to the income tax levied on OASDI benefits of upper-income social security recipients and from other sources.

3. Aaron and Reischauer (1995).

reform that merely "saved" the hospital insurance trust fund for another five to ten years but did not address other important issues would not be a successful reform.

Medicare and Private Insurance

The medicare benefit package is substantially less generous than most private insurance policies. The most obvious difference is that medicare does not cover outpatient prescription drugs, which private policies generally do. Medicare also has very little coverage of long-term care services except for rehabilitative or transitional services related to an acute illness. In recent years, home health services have grown explosively and appear to be a backdoor way of providing more long-term care through medicare. Nevertheless, the vast majority of long-term-care services related to general aging or physical or cognitive deterioration are not covered. Long-term care is typically not covered by private insurance either, but medicare's omission is more important because the elderly are far more likely to need such care. Medicare is also less generous because it does not have a "stop-loss"—a maximum out-of-pocket liability that the insured is responsible for. Most private policies limit individual out-of-pocket spending to an annual maximum of $1,500 or $2,000. Because medicare does not have such a limitation, its beneficiaries can be responsible for substantial out-of-pocket expenses. Indeed, about one-half of 1 percent of medicare beneficiaries exhaust their part A benefits in any year.

The net effect is that medicare covers just under half of the medical costs of the aged. As a result, many elderly people obtain insurance to supplement the medicare package. Slightly over two-thirds of the elderly buy "medigap" policies or obtain supplemental insurance from a former employer. These policies typically cover the cost sharing required by medicare and outpatient prescription drugs,[4] but almost never long-term care. Another 15 percent of the elderly are sufficiently poor that their part B premium and cost sharing are paid for by medicaid. Only about 15 percent of the elderly have no coverage other than fee-for-service medicare.

From a fiscal perspective, supplemental coverage imposes a major

4. About 15 percent of purchased medigap insurance and most employer-provided supplemental insurance cover prescription drugs.

burden for the medicare system. People who have supplemental coverage use more medical services than people without it, since the effective price of medical care is lower for them. Although some of this additional use is paid for by the supplemental insurance policy, much of it is covered by medicare. Thus supplemental coverage raises overall medicare costs, one estimate being by $4 billion annually.[5]

It is politically important to keep this supplemental coverage in mind in designing medicare reform. When the Medicare Catastrophic Coverage Act was passed in 1988, many of the upper-income elderly rebelled because they already had catastrophic coverage through their supplemental policies and did not want to pay to subsidize such coverage for the lower-income elderly. The act was repealed a year later.

The linkage between medicare and medicaid is another important dimension that must be recognized in any reform effort. The distributional consequences of increased medicare premiums and cost sharing would be quite different if reforms were adopted that waived the current requirement that medicaid pick up medicare's premium, deductible, and coinsurance costs for poor aged and disabled people. Designing reform properly involves integrating the "wraparound" coverage of medicaid with medicare.

While medicare is, on average, a less generous package than private policies, it is more generous along some dimensions. Most important, medicare allows beneficiaries unrestricted choice of providers. There are no limits on whom beneficiaries can receive care from, provided the services are covered and the provider is licensed or certified. This type of coverage is increasingly rare in private policies. In 1993 less than half the privately insured population was covered by an unrestricted policy, and that number has been falling rapidly.

The coupling of generous access provisions with restricted overall benefits seems to present a natural policy option: allow medicare beneficiaries additional covered services in exchange for restricting their access to those providers who would accept discounted fees or manage their care.

Medicare Managed Care

The system described above is what nearly 90 percent of medicare beneficiaries participate in. The remainder are enrolled through medi-

5. Congressional Budget Office (1995).

care in health maintenance organizations (HMOs)—insurance plans that provide treatment using specified sets of providers. Medicare pays these plans 95 percent of the average fee-for-service medicare costs for similar individuals in the same area.

Costs in HMOs are limited by monitoring the services that are provided to patients and often by paying providers on a fixed, per enrollee ("capitated") basis, rather than a fee for service. Beneficiaries enrolling in HMOs agree to receive all or most of their care from providers the plan specifies, but in exchange they face little or no cost sharing. Because medicare does not allow plans to rebate to individuals any cost savings they generate, HMOs frequently attract medicare recipients by offering additional covered services such as outpatient prescription drugs.

Medicare allows enrollees to join an HMO but no other type of managed care. HMOs have very strict limits on whom beneficiaries can see, which many elderly people are reluctant to accept. Other types of plans have much broader networks of providers, which could appeal to more of the elderly. The combination of limited financial incentives to join managed care and a narrow choice of plans available helps to explain why HMO enrollment in medicare is only around 10 percent, despite managed care enrollment of over 50 percent in the private sector.

The medicare HMO program is particularly controversial because it appears that the program *adds* to medicare spending. Estimates suggest that the 95 percent of average fee-for-service costs that medicare pays for those who enroll in HMOs is an overpayment, because those who join HMOs would use less than 95 percent of average spending if they remained in fee-for-service medicare.[6] The important lesson to draw from this is that one needs to be careful how payments are made in any system where beneficiaries have their choice of health insurance plans.

Medicare Successes and Problems

Medicare has substantially improved access to health care among the elderly and disabled. Their use of medical care has increased greatly because of medicare, and impoverishment related to large medical bills for covered services has been virtually eliminated. Fur-

6. Brown and others (1993).

thermore, income from medicare has become the bedrock for many medical practices.

Indeed, the success of medicare shows up in the yardstick society cares most about: the health of the population. In the thirty years since medicare was implemented, life expectancy at age 65 has increased by more than it did in the sixty years before medicare. And while the United States does very poorly in international comparisons of life expectancy at virtually every age, it ranks much higher in life expectancy at age 80—the age at which medical care is likely to have a significant effect on longevity.[7] Medicare is one of the great successes of social policy.

But medicare has its problems as well. Although medicare has brought tremendous increases in living standards to its beneficiaries, it has come at a heavy price. In 1975 the nation spent 1 percent of GDP on medicare (see figure 6–1). Today, medicare accounts for about 2.5 percent of GDP, and if no action is taken it will be nearly 4 percent of GDP a decade from now. Indeed, the long-range projections are even more dramatic. Without reform, medicare is projected to account for over 4 percent of GDP in twenty years and 8 percent by the middle of the next century. To put this in perspective, note that public-sector (federal, state, and local) spending on education has remained constant at about 5 percent of GDP for over two decades, and federal spending on nondefense discretionary programs—such as education, infrastructure, and the environment—has been falling relative to the size of the economy for nearly two decades.

Any program accounting for as large a part of the national budget and growing as rapidly as medicare will necessarily draw public attention. This has happened, and restraining the growth of medicare costs is now implanted firmly on the public agenda. But there is not just one "medicare cost problem." There are really three problems, and it is important to understand all of them in designing effective policy.

Medicare and the Budget Deficit

The first problem is the one that has gathered the most attention: medicare is a large part of the deficit problem. In 1995 medicare spending was roughly $5,000 per beneficiary. In an era of tight budgets, medicare is one of the few programs that is still growing rapidly.

---

7. Manton and Vaupel (1995).

FIGURE 6-1. Medicare as a Share of GDP, 1965–2006

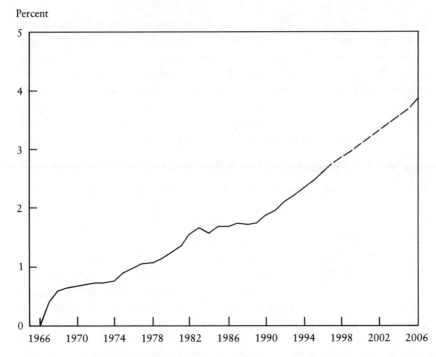

Percent

SOURCE: Congressional Budget Office (1996).

Between 1995 and 2002, real per capita medicare spending is projected to increase at over 5 percent annually. Nonmedicare outlays, in contrast, will increase by less than 1 percent annually. This growth rate is by no means unusual historically. Between 1975 and 1995, real per capita medicare spending grew by more than 6 percent annually.

Rising medicare costs are a substantial burden at a time when revenues are scarce and balancing the budget has become a national priority. Indeed, despite the large deficit reduction packages enacted in 1990 and 1993, the deficit is expected to worsen over the next several years, in large part because of the inexorable growth of medicare costs. Figure 6-2, which pictures the cyclically corrected federal deficit between 1989 and 1995 and projections for the deficit between 1996 and 2006, shows that the deficit has fallen substantially as a

FIGURE 6-2. Full-Employment Federal Deficit as a Share of GDP under Alternative Medicare Assumptions, 1989–2006

Percent

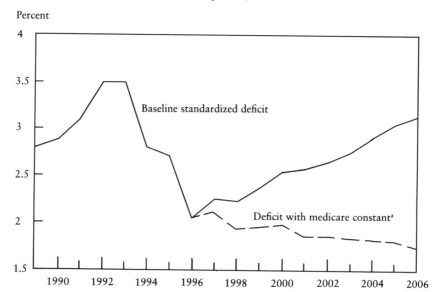

SOURCES: Author's calculations and Congressional Budget Office (1996).
a. Real per beneficiary terms.

share of GDP over the past several years. Without further spending cuts or tax increases, the deficit is expected to increase again beginning in fiscal year 1997. If instead medicare grew at the rate of inflation plus growth in the number of beneficiaries after 1996, rather than the much higher rate at which it is expected to grow, the deficit as a percentage of GDP would continue to decline.

Without large tax increases, balancing the budget is impossible unless sizable medicare savings are realized. Both Republicans and Democrats accept this fact, and all of the recent balanced budget proposals have called for large savings in the medicare program. Table 6-1 shows the magnitude of medicare savings in recent balanced budget proposals. The Balanced Budget Act of 1995, passed by Congress in November 1995 and vetoed by the president, called for $227 billion in medicare savings between 1996 and 2002, or about one-quarter of the noninterest outlay reductions required to reach a balanced budget. The administration's fiscal year 1997 budget, released

TABLE 6-1. Importance of Medicare Savings in Balanced Budget
Proposals

	Increase in medicare spending (percent)[a]	Savings		
Proposal		Total (billions of dollars)[b]	Medicare (billions of dollars)	Medicare (percent)
Baseline	4.8			
Balanced Budget Act of 1995[c]	2.0	889	227	26
Administration's fiscal year 1997 budget[d]	3.2	495	116	23
Congressional fiscal year 1997 budget[d]	2.6	640	158	25

SOURCE: Author's calculations based on Congressional Budget Office estimates.
a. Real per beneficiary terms.
b. Total savings are noninterest outlay reductions.
c. For 1996–2002.
d. For 1997–2002.

in February 1996, called for medicare reductions of about half that amount, or $116 billion between 1997 and 2002. This was again nearly one-quarter of the outlay reductions required for budget balance. The fiscal year 1997 congressional budget resolution specifies medicare savings of $158 billion through 2002.

These changes are substantial. The Omnibus Budget Reconciliation Act of 1990, by comparison, was projected to save about $69 billion from medicare over five years, through a combination of spending cuts and increases in the payroll tax base subject to the hospital insurance tax. The Omnibus Budget Reconciliation Act of 1993 was projected to save about $85 billion through similar mechanisms. The medicare savings in the recent balanced budget proposals are 50 to 200 percent larger than either of these. An alternative way of gauging the magnitude of these changes is to consider the rate of medicare spending growth under these policies. Without reform, real medicare spending per beneficiary would increase by about 5 percent annually. Under the balanced budget proposals, this falls to between 2.0 and 3.2 percent annually, a substantial 33 to 60 percent reduction in the growth rate.

Changes of this magnitude are large but feasible. The reductions and restructuring that have occurred in the private sector over the past few years have undoubtedly increased the ability to achieve substantial medicare savings. And the 1993 omnibus budget reconciliation package could have had much larger medicare savings, but some of these savings were held back for the administration's health reform effort. The Clinton administration's Health Security Act, for example, proposed $202 billion of medicare savings between 1996 and 2002. Although that proposal assumed universal insurance coverage, under which larger public-sector reductions are more feasible, savings on the order of those in the recent presidential and congressional proposals do not seem unduly large.

But it is a great mistake to focus on medicare savings for budget balance alone. There are two additional senses in which the costs of medicare are a public concern: the long-run projections for the federal budget, and the fact that many resources are wasted in the system. Excessive focus on the short-run deficit obscures these two issues.

Medicare and the Long-Run Budget

Balancing the budget is a short-run goal: savings are needed in the next few years to bring spending in line with receipts. The problem of medicare costs, however, is inherently a long-run issue. Medicare costs are growing at an unsustainable rate, and they will have to be restrained somehow over the longer run.

Figure 6-3, which shows the income accruing to the hospital insurance trust fund and expected outlays from the trust fund over the next seventy-five years, illustrates medicare's fundamental structural problem.[8] Currently, outlays from the trust fund roughly equal income to the fund. Twenty-five years from now, outlays are projected to exceed revenues by 3.5 percent of taxable payroll, and seventy-five years from now the differential will be over 8 percent. To get a sense of the magnitude of this problem, if the seventy-five-year trust fund deficit were to be solved by an increase in the hospital insurance tax, the payroll tax rate would have to rise from 2.9 percent to 7.42 percent immediately and remain at that level for the next seventy-five years. To close the deficit for just the next twenty-five years, tax rates would have to increase by nearly 2 percentage points. Even this smaller tax increase is politically unacceptable at the moment.

Two factors are important in explaining this long-run deficit. The first is the retirement of the baby boom generation and the aging of the population more generally. The baby boom generation will retire

---

8. While the projections are for the hospital insurance trust fund only, a similar relation would be true between the growth of overall medicare spending and projected tax revenues.

FIGURE 6-3. Projections of Costs and Income for the Hospital
Insurance Trust Fund, 1995–2070

Percent of taxable payroll

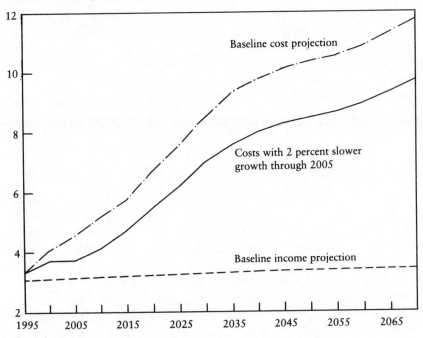

SOURCE: Hospital Insurance Trust Fund (1996, pp. 41–42).

between 2010 and 2030, and over that period, the number of beneficiaries is projected to grow by 2.5 percent a year, up from 1.5 percent
over 1995–2010. Of particular importance will be the growth in the
number of older elderly—those over 85—which is expected to be 2.4
percent a year from 2000 to 2030. Average expenditures on people
over 85 are about twice the expenditures on those aged 65 to 74.
Even beyond the baby boom generation, the low fertility rates the
United States has experienced since the late 1960s will increase the
ratio of beneficiaries to workers by the middle of the next century.

The second factor is the persistent growth of health costs. Over the
next twenty-five years, trust fund expenditures are expected to increase annually between 2 and 3 percentage points more rapidly than
taxable payroll, in substantial part because the growth rate of medical
costs exceeds the growth rate of the rest of the economy. Indeed,

figure 6-3 may understate the size of the long-run financing problem, since the medicare trustees' projections assume that after 2020 expenditures per enrollee will grow no more rapidly than hourly wages. If that optimistic assumption is not realized, the size of the seventy-five-year trust fund deficit would increase even further.

The spending cuts that have been proposed to balance the budget are insufficient to deal with the long-run problem. The middle line in figure 6-3 shows spending if the annual growth of medicare costs is held 2 percentage points below the pace expected for the next decade (roughly the requirement for a balanced budget) but resumes its projected rate after that. This policy makes only a small dent in the long-run medicare problem. Long-range trust fund spending still exceeds revenues by a substantial margin.

Extremely large spending cuts would be required to eliminate the trust fund deficit. Real spending per beneficiary is projected to increase by about 2.5 percent annually over the next twenty-five years. Real taxable payroll per beneficiary, in contrast, will be roughly constant or even falling as the number of workers per beneficiary drops from 3.9 in 1995 to 2.2 in 2030. Thus maintaining a twenty-five-year balance would require a 2.5 percentage point annual cut in spending growth. This would eliminate all of the growth in real services per beneficiary that would otherwise occur over the period. It is hard to imagine that private-sector cost reductions of that magnitude will be realized; therefore such a policy would almost certainly imply a growing gap between the coverage provided to medicare participants and that enjoyed by those with private insurance.

Neither politically realistic tax increases nor spending reductions alone seem capable of restoring the solvency of the trust fund for the next twenty-five years, let alone for seventy-five years or more. Some combination of these approaches—plus more—will almost certainly have to occur. The precise distribution of spending reductions and tax increases will depend crucially on the changes that occur in the private sector. But a reduction in cost growth of about 1.5 percentage points annually coupled with a 1 percentage point hospital insurance tax increase might be a reasonable expectation.

Medicare and Social Resources

Beyond the budgetary impact of medicare, there is another sense in which the program needs reform. Although medicare has provided enormous health and financial benefit to its participants and society at large, it also wastes substantial resources. Cost sharing under medicare is sufficiently low (particularly for those with supplemental insurance) that beneficiaries rarely have to decide if services are worth their cost. And providers have little incentive to pay attention to the cost of medical services because their payments are related to the number and type of services they provide and they know that insurance is picking up most of the bill. With little concern about costs on the part of either providers of care or beneficiaries, care is bound to be overprovided: some care will have little or no medical benefit, while other care will have some benefit but less than it costs.

Evidence abounds that there is a substantial amount of medicare spending that appears to have little value. Medicare spending in different parts of the country varies by a factor of four, but health outcomes are essentially unrelated to these spending differences.[9] Similarly, reductions in payments to providers reduce the care that is received by medicare beneficiaries but have no long-term health consequences.[10] And direct studies of how much patients benefit from particular services, although controversial, uniformly suggest that some medical care is of little or no value.[11] In each case, the inescapable conclusion is that money could be saved without substantially harming patient health.

The overprovision of health care is a waste of social resources. Clearly, it contributes to the budget problem posed by medicare. But it does much more than that. Even if the budget were balanced and medicare had no long-run financing problems, it would still be a waste to order medical treatments that did little or no good. Those medical resources could be used for other people (for example, the uninsured) or moved out of the health sector entirely. Thus, independent of any deficit problem, medicare should be reformed to make it more efficient.

Identifying and reducing the amount of low-value care, however, is not an easy task. Studies have shown that there is no strong correlation between spending levels and the amount of inappropriate care.[12] Crude efforts to scale back spending could, therefore, run the

9. Wennberg, Freeman, and Culp (1987).

10. Kahn and others (1990); Cutler (1995b).

11. Chassin and others (1987); Winslow and others (1988a, 1988b); Greenspan and others (1988); McClellan and Newhouse (1995).

12. Brook (1991).

risk of cutting valuable as well as low-value care, and thus reforms designed to limit wasteful services must be implemented carefully.

Why Do Medicare Costs Increase?

Before deciding what to do about medicare costs, it is important first to understand the reasons for the increase in spending. Appropriate policy actions are very different if the reason for rising costs is because medicare is overpaying for services rather than if the increase in costs is actually buying valuable care.

The basic fact about medicare costs—as it is about other health costs as well—is that they are rising because people are receiving more medical services than they used to. Services that were not even dreamed of three decades ago are now commonplace. Services that were available but rarely used a decade ago are now routine. Some of these new and more intensively used services are expensive and thus have pushed up medicare spending. Others are cheaper than previous treatments, but, because they are far less risky, utilization has risen enough to drive up total spending.

An example is instructive. In 1984, 90 percent of medicare beneficiaries with a heart attack were treated without invasive procedures. These patients received thrombolytic drugs and a variety of acute care treatments but did not receive intensive surgical interventions. By 1991, nearly half of medicare patients with a heart attack received an invasive procedure to detect the extent of artery blockage, and 30 percent went on to receive some intensive therapeutic care. What is striking about this example is that over this period, medicare payments to hospitals for each individual procedure were unchanged in real terms; the *entire* increase in costs for treating heart attacks, which was 4 percent in real terms annually over this period, was a result of the increase in the number of patients receiving these intensive services.[13]

This pattern is common throughout health care. Research has shown that 50 percent or more of the growth of medical spending is because of technological change in the practice of medicine.[14] This is true for both public and private health systems, each of which has

13. This example is discussed in more detail in Cutler and McClellan (1995).
14. Aaron (1991); Newhouse (1992).

increased in cost dramatically over the past thirty years. Ultimately, managing long-run cost growth must involve slowing down the development and spread of new medical services or increasing the development of new technologies that are capable of reducing costs for the medical system as a whole.

The emphasis on technological change need not be so extensive over a period of five or even ten years, during which payments per service can easily be reduced while more sophisticated and expensive treatments continue apace. But when spending growth is assessed over periods of longer than a decade, cutting payments continually is not a real option, and the debate must focus on just how much of an increase in medical technology society wishes to provide over time.

The Political Context for Medicare Reform

The political system places a variety of constraints on medicare reform, and these restrictions must be kept in mind as reform is contemplated. Medicare is enormously popular. Medicare is an oddity in these days of pessimism about government policy: it is a program that most of the public strongly supports. Polls continually show that the public is not in favor of a balanced budget if it means "cutting" medicare. The practical import of this popularity is that opportunities to reform medicare are rare. Therefore, when medicare is addressed, it is essential to deal with all of the problems of the system, not just its implications for short-run budget imbalance.

Part of the success of medicare is a result of its universality. All medicare beneficiaries are served by the same program, and thus all have a stake in preserving their access to high-quality care. A program that segregated rich from poor, or the elderly in Connecticut from those in Idaho, would probably not enjoy the popularity that the current medicare program does. The benefit of universality does not mean that all medicare beneficiaries must be treated exactly the same. Because of supplemental insurance, that is not even true today. What it does mean is that the program should be structured so that everyone feels he or she has a stake in its continuation and the same options are open to all.

Medicare also has to be considered in relation to health care for those not enrolled in the program. There are several parts to this relationship. The first is the relative generosity of the two systems. Medicare has worked well in part because its coverage is similar but a bit less generous than that provided by the average employer-sponsored policy. The working population pays for much of the costs of medicare through payroll taxes, and these workers could become upset if they thought they were paying for a type of care that was much better than that they received themselves. Medicare and the private sector are also related because the amount of savings each can realize depends on what is happening in the other system. The willingness of providers to see medicare and nonmedicare patients depends on the relative payments in the two systems. If medicare payments are cut substantially below payments made by private insurers, medicare beneficiaries are sure to have trouble gaining access. The same problem would face privately insured individuals if private payments fell substantially relative to medicare payments. Recent changes in the health care marketplace for the privately insured—the expansion of managed care, reductions in provider fees, and increased monitoring of physicians—have made medicare more attractive to providers and probably increased the amount by which medicare payments can be reduced without creating substantial access problems. This is fortunate as the government embarks on a new round of medicare reductions. If cost reductions are made in medicare, that would also enable the private sector to reduce costs further.

Medicare and the private sector are also related because of the systemwide benefits that medicare has promoted. Historically, generous reimbursement from medicare subsidized care for the uninsured and additional costs for services provided in teaching institutions. These cross-subsidies should be taken into account as reforms are designed. As the nation moves forward along one dimension of national health reform, it does not want to move backward on others.

The last political constraint is that raising taxes to pay for medicare does not appear to be a viable option at this time. This may change after the consequences of other reforms become apparent, but the first set of reforms has to concentrate on cost reductions rather than revenue increases.

Options for the Future

There are three fundamental strategies for restraining medicare's costs and reforming the system: reducing the payments that medicare makes for its current level of care, changing eligibility standards for the program, and changing the nature of the program's guarantee.

Payment Reductions

To understand the first option—cutting payments to providers—a little history is useful. Concern about the cost of medicare first came to the fore in the late 1970s. The consensus at the time was that the source of the rapid increase in costs was the fee-for-service nature of payments. Medicare paid providers on the basis of services performed. Each day in the hospital or additional test, for example, generated an additional fee. The result was an incentive to provide excessive medical care. This incentive had been recognized long ago. As George Bernard Shaw pointed out nearly a century ago, "That any sane nation, having observed that you could provide for the supply of bread by giving bakers a pecuniary interest in baking for you, should go on to give a surgeon a pecuniary interest in cutting off your leg, is enough to make one despair of political humanity."[15]

The solution was to "bundle" a set of services into one price. Rather than pay a hospital for each day of patient care, each test, each hour of operating room use, and countless other services, one price would be paid for the entire hospital admission. Then the services would be provided only when they were clinically valuable. Provided that the bundled payment was "reasonable," patients would not suffer reduced quality of care.

Thus was born the prospective payment system for hospitals in 1983. Prospective payment created roughly 470 diagnosis related groups (DRGs), into which each hospital admission has to be placed. Each DRG receives a weight reflecting the severity of problems afflicting patients in that group relative to the average medicare admission. Reimbursement for a patient is set at the product of the weight and the base payment per unit weight. The base payment is adjusted each year for rising input costs.

The prospective payment system created incentives for hospitals to be more efficient in their management of patients, and they have become so. Studies have shown that hospitals cut back on their use of inputs in response to prospective payment and that long-range patient outcomes did not suffer.[16]

The system also created a natural way to limit spending in the future. Because one base payment determines how much a hospital is

---

15. Shaw (1911).
16. Feder, Hadley, and Zuckerman (1987); Kahn and others (1990); Cutler (1995b).

TABLE 6-2. Sources of Medicare Savings, Balanced Budget Act of 1995[a]

Category	Savings (billions of dollars)[b]
Fee-for-service	142.4
Inpatient hospital	64.7
Outpatient hospital and ambulatory	19.1
Physicians	12.6
Home health	17.0
Skilled nursing	10.0
Other	19.0
Part B premiums	54.2
Choice-based system	18.6
Fail-safe mechanism	11.5
Total	226.7

SOURCE: Congressional Budget Office.
a. Passed by Congress in November 1995 and vetoed by President Clinton.
b. Savings are for a seven-year period from 1996 to 2002.

paid for a given patient, the growth rate of the base payment can be reduced to save money across the board. This is how medicare savings were realized in the deficit reduction efforts of 1990 and 1993. A substantial portion of the medicare savings in both the Republicans' and Democrats' plans to balance the budget by 2002 is also derived from reducing the growth rate of the base payment. Roughly one-third of the medicare savings in the Balanced Budget Act of 1995 were to have been from slowing payment increases to inpatient hospitals (see table 6-2). The prospective payment base payment was to increase 2.5 percentage points less rapidly than input costs in 1996 and 2 percentage points less rapidly than input costs from 1997 through 2002. Many of the other fee-for-service savings were to be from reduced provider payments as well. The Clinton administration's balanced budget proposal is similar in design but smaller in magnitude; the prospective payment base payment, for example, would increase 1.5 percentage points less rapidly than input costs from 1997 to 2002.

For several years, it looked as if prospective payment was the answer to medicare's long-run financing problems. Real per beneficiary spending grew quite rapidly from 1975 to 1982, at about 7 percent a year (figure 6-4). Spending growth, particularly inpatient hospital spending, then fell dramatically from 1982 to 1988, when prospective payment was implemented. Since then, spending growth

FIGURE 6-4. Growth of Medicare Spending, 1975–95

Annual growth (percent)[a]

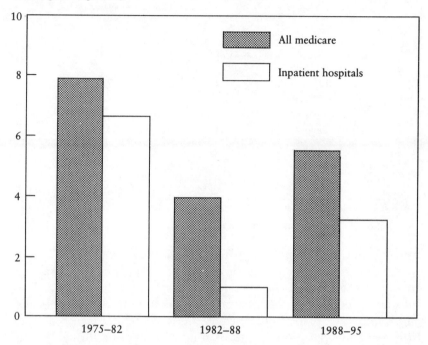

SOURCES: U.S. House of Representatives, (1994, pp. 188–89); Prospective Payment Assessment Commission (1996, pp. 117–19).
a. Real per beneficiary terms.

has again accelerated. Real per beneficiary medicare spending is increasing at nearly 6 percent annually, and inpatient spending is increasing at about 3 percent annually. The resurgent increase in inpatient spending growth between 1988 and 1995 is particularly surprising because over this period the base payment was increasingly less rapidly than inflation.

There are two reasons why these reforms failed to control medicare spending, even on the inpatient side. The first goes back to the distinction medicare makes between types of providers. Prospective payment applies only to inpatient hospital services. There are a variety of services that can be provided in different settings, however, such as rehabilitation services or skilled nursing services. When payments were reduced for inpatient services, some services were moved to an alternative site, where they were reimbursed more generously. The admission rate to inpatient hospitals, for example, fell by 10 percent between 1986 and 1993, but the admission rate to long-term-care hospitals rose by 75 percent and to rehabilitation hospitals by about 150 percent. The analogy, particularly apt in this case, is that medicare reform is like squeezing a balloon: as payments are compressed in one place, the services move to another. If medicare is to continue along its current path, it needs to move away from an approach focusing on the site of care and move to an approach focusing on treatment for a condition. This is the only way to limit large substitutions designed to avoid payment restrictions.

The second reason why these reforms failed to adequately control costs is that they targeted only one of the two determinants of total spending—price. Reducing the growth of the base payment would lower long-term medicare costs if the *price* of services alone was growing too rapidly. But as noted above, the primary reason for the rapid growth in medicare spending is that the *technological intensity* of services provided has been rising briskly. This increase in technological intensity has continued even as prices have been reduced, resulting in overall increases in medicare spending.

Even if price increases were the primary cause of the medicare cost problem, costs cannot be controlled over long periods of time by limiting reimbursement alone. Payments cannot fall indefinitely, particularly without reference to what is happening in the private sector. Furthermore, research has found that there is a particularly perverse effect of payment reductions on the provision of medical services. When provider payments are cut, providers respond by performing more services to offset some of their income loss.[17] Thus, as payments are cut further, ever more care is provided for reimbursement reasons, not because it is needed. This, of course, compounds the problem of overuse of low-value medical care. Thus payment reductions cannot be the long-run solution to the medicare cost problem.

The short-run situation is very different. In the short run, the easiest way to limit spending is simply to pay less for the services provided. Medicare payments are sufficiently high that few providers will refuse to see medicare patients if fees are cut modestly. And there is a great deal of experience with implementing such cuts. Thus the largest part of short-run cost savings will necessarily come from reductions in

17. Christensen (1992).

provider payments. But it is essential to remember that cutting fees is not a long-run solution to the medicare problem.

Increasing Beneficiary Payments

A second method of reducing public expenditures on medicare is to transfer some of the costs of the system to beneficiaries. There are a variety of options for doing this. One common proposal is to increase the cost sharing in medicare. The part B deductible is particularly low ($100 a year) when compared with similar deductibles in private plans, making a modest increase a reasonable option. Other services, such as clinical laboratories, skilled nursing facilities, and home health care, have little or no cost sharing, and out-of-pocket payments for these services could be increased.

Of course, for people with supplemental insurance, an increase in cost sharing would be just like an increase in the medicare premium, since supplemental policies would cover these additional out-of-pocket costs but would have to raise their premiums to do so. Thus a second approach is just to increase the part B premium directly. The increase could be across the board, age-related, income-related, or related to use of supplemental insurance (since such insurance already drives up medicare spending).

Increasing the part B premium was a part of the Balanced Budget Act of 1995. The act maintained the premium for all beneficiaries at 31.5 percent of program costs rather than letting it fall to 25 percent, as current law required. It also phased in a 100 percent premium for higher-income elderly people (the phase-in began at $60,000 a year for individuals and $90,000 a year for couples). The income-related premium was set at sufficiently high levels that few elderly people were substantially affected. Only about 10 percent of them would have had to pay above the 31.5 percent premium, and only about 2 percent would have paid a premium equal to the full per beneficiary cost of part B.[18]

An alternative approach to increasing beneficiary costs is to limit eligibility for medicare by increasing the age of eligibility. Medicare eligibility was set at age 65 because that was the age of eligibility for full retirement benefits under social security when medicare was im-

18. A premium set at 100 percent of average costs would still be considered favorably compared with private individual policies because the medicare policy would be automatically renewable and community-rated.

plemented. Social security, in turn, set the retirement age at 65 because when it was established in 1935 life expectancy at age 65 was about ten years, and a decade was thought to be a reasonable period for retirement. Life expectancy at age 65 is now about twenty years, however. The public sector is financing a much longer retirement much more generously than it used to, even as the ability to work and be productive at older ages may be increasing. Thus it seems natural to refocus eligibility on the older elderly. Indeed, the age for full retirement benefits for social security is scheduled to increase gradually from 65 to 67 in the first quarter of the next century. The legislation calling for this was enacted in 1983, when the social security trust fund was nearly bankrupt. Once again, social security has a long-run financing problem, as does medicare. Coupling a further increase or a more rapid phase-in of the scheduled increase in the social security normal retirement age with an increase in the age of medicare eligibility is a natural solution to both problems.

Increasing the age of medicare eligibility was discussed in 1995. The reconciliation recommendations reported from the Senate Finance Committee called for an increase in the age of medicare eligibility to match that of social security, beginning in 2003. That proposal was not part of the Balanced Budget Act of 1995, however.

The biggest difficulty with increasing retirement ages in the short run is that it may increase the ranks of the uninsured if retirees lose access to their employer-sponsored health insurance before they are eligible for medicare. Many workers already retire at or before age 65. In 1994, 55 percent of males and 66 percent of females aged 62 to 64 were not in the labor force. Of those aged 65 and 66, only 33 percent of males and 21 percent of females were in the labor force. An alternative to excluding younger retirees from medicare would be to raise the "normal" eligibility age to 67 (or higher) and allow younger retirees to buy into medicare at a higher price. For example, retirees between ages 62 and 66 could be charged a premium equal to expected program costs, while those aged 67 or older would pay what they currently do.

Making beneficiaries pay more for medicare has a natural appeal. The increase in medicare costs over time is like a "tax" on society: more has to be paid than was previously required to support a desired set of benefits. As with any tax, someone has to pay it. It makes sense to impose at least part of the burden on medicare beneficiaries, since they are the ones receiving the benefits.

In evaluating cost-sharing proposals it is important to keep in mind their distributional implications. Increasing beneficiary costs is more tolerable for elderly people with high incomes than for those with low incomes. The desirability of these reforms, therefore, depends on whether or not medicaid or its successor program will pay the additional costs imposed on low-income elderly. Indeed, if increased beneficiary cost sharing is a large part of medicare reform, it makes sense to wrap the part of medicaid paying for medicare supplemental coverage into the medicare program and design the two parts jointly.

It is also important to note that most of the proposals for increased cost sharing do *not* affect the underlying level of medicare costs. Rather, they change the *distribution* of those costs between beneficiaries and taxpayers. When part B premiums are increased, for example, beneficiaries pay more and taxpayers pay less, but the total bill remains the same. In that sense, most of these proposals do nothing to affect the determinant of long-run medicare costs—the growing use of medical services.[19] And most will do little to limit the provision of unnecessary medical care. Thus, as reasonable as these proposals may be, they do not represent a complete solution to the medicare cost problem.

Restructuring the Medicare Program

The third option for medicare reform is to redesign the system in a way that can both control costs and improve efficiency. One approach to this would be to convert medicare into a "choice-based" system—one that would give participants a broad range of health insurance arrangements to choose from and create financial incentives for efficient choice.[20]

The basis for this approach is twofold. The first is the belief that alternative forms of health insurance—particularly managed care—can limit unnecessary spending on medical services. HMOs and a

19. The one potential exception is increasing deductibles or coinsurance rates. For those without supplemental insurance, this would be an increase in the price of medical care, decreasing its use. Such a small share of the population is without medigap coverage, however, that the overall incentives generated by this are small.

20. In other contexts, this is termed a voucher system, but the system described here involves more regulation than a voucher system traditionally has. A more appropriate terminology is therefore a choice-based system. Cutler (1995a) and Aaron and Reischauer (1995) describe choice-based medicare systems in more detail.

range of related plans have become extremely popular in the private sector. In 1987 about three-quarters of the privately insured population was in traditional, unmanaged health insurance. By 1993 that share was below 50 percent. Evidence suggests that these kinds of provider limitations result in less spending on medical care without adversely affecting health.[21]

The second tenet of choice-based structural reform is the belief that people can, if given the ability and financial incentives to do so, make informed choices about which insurance plan they want to join. Unlike the decision about which medical treatment to receive—which is often made on an emergency basis and under a great deal of stress—the decision about insurance can be made when people have time to think about their options and compare policies.

A move to consumer choice and alternative insurance arrangements would have profound implications for medicare. Medicare currently guarantees people a particular insurance plan (the medicare package). A consumer choice system would instead guarantee people a particular amount of money with which to purchase health insurance, but would not specify which policy they are to receive.

To understand this system, it is easiest to think about it in its purest form. In a pure choice-based system, fee-for-service medicare would not be offered by the government. Instead, private insurers would offer medicare beneficiaries a range of plans, differing in the degree of management, the amount of cost sharing, the services covered, and the price. The government would give every beneficiary a coupon equal to a fixed amount, for example, the cost of the average policy. Once a year, beneficiaries would choose which of the competing plans they wished to enroll in. Plans would have to accept everyone who wanted to enroll. Plans would also be required to charge one price for all enrollees. If the price was greater than the coupon amount, enrollees would have to pay the additional amount themselves. If the price was less than the coupon amount, enrollees could keep the savings.

The potential advantages of this system are twofold. The first is that shopping for insurance plans would encourage plans to be efficient. A high-cost plan that did not provide commensurately high-quality service would need to reduce its premiums to attract cus-

21. Miller and Luft (1994).

tomers; one proven way of doing this would be to monitor excessive charges by providers and eliminate care of low value. Thus a choice-based system could make the medicare system more efficient.

Second, structural reform might contribute to a less rapid increase in medicare spending. Just as having a choice over insurance creates incentives for plans to cut out care that is high cost but low value, it may also create incentives for plans to invest in technology that reduces cost growth over time. If cost-reducing technology is developed to a sufficient extent, some of the long-run financing problems of medicare will ease. The potential for long-run reductions in cost growth is a subject of great debate. Some technologies will certainly come along that improve health but at substantial cost; the genetic revolution is a prime example. Many of these technologies will be valuable, and society will choose to buy them—in the process raising medicare spending. Choice-based reform should not prevent this cost-increasing investment. But it is also true that there is no real incentive now to develop or acquire cost-reducing technology. A choice-based system would help create these incentives. Thus, although choice-based reform will not guarantee that medicare will be affordable over the long term, it will make the medicare system more rational.

However, choice in practice is more difficult than choice in principle. The discussion above of the current medicare HMO program suggests as much. The pure system described above would confront a number of problems, four of which are particularly important.

Choices offered. Health plans eligible for medicare coupons would almost certainly be required to provide coverage for some minimum package of services. After all, the public is not concerned with whether elderly and disabled people are officially "insured" but with whether they receive medical care that society regards as adequate. The minimum covered services would almost certainly be more generous than the current medicare package. It makes little sense to design a new system that does not cover outpatient prescription drugs or that does not cover catastrophic costs, for example. A choice-based system is, therefore, a way to include some of the services that are most glaringly absent from the current medicare package.

Providing some additional services will cost more than the current medicare system if the guarantee is kept at the current medicare level along other dimensions. Some increase in spending might be appropriate in the short run, however, if the elderly are being asked to pay more or accept more restrictions on their receipt of medical care in the long run.

Beyond ensuring that certain services are covered, the government would also need to ensure that plans met quality standards. Health insurance is a very complex product, and people do not know the implications of all its provisions (how many check the fine print of their plan's bone marrow transplant coverage?). Even if coverage is promised, that does not necessarily mean that quality care is actually available (how many patients who do not have cancer know the number of oncologists affiliated with their insurance plan?). Plans would also have to disclose outcome data to the government or other sources, since making sensible insurance choices requires knowledge of quality as well as price. In the private sector, these monitoring and information roles are performed by employers; in the public sector, the government would have to oversee these roles.

Even for plans that meet all of these requirements, there might be reasons to limit their availability to the medicare population. Some plans by their very nature will disproportionately attract the healthiest beneficiaries. If the coupon payment to these plans cannot be reduced sufficiently to account for their favorable enrollment profile, medicare will overcompensate these plans for the services they provide and total spending will rise. This concern has been raised most strongly about medical savings accounts (MSAs)—plans with a high-deductible insurance policy and a nontaxable account out of which individuals would pay for noncatastrophic medical expenses. The high deductible seems likely to attract disproportionate numbers of the healthiest in the medicare pool. If coupon payments were not adjusted to reflect this, medicare might overpay for those choosing MSAs. The question of whether MSAs should be in or out of a choice-based system has attracted a great deal of attention.[22]

There is a further question about the status of traditional fee-for-service medicare under a choice-based system. In a pure choice-based system, fee-for-service medicare would not be guaranteed; it would be available only if private insurers chose to offer it and enrollees chose to participate. Because the medicare package is so familiar to and popular with beneficiaries, however, the fee-for-service option

22. There are also tax concerns associated with the establishment of MSAs. If MSA balances accumulate interest that is untaxed, MSA plans would be a tax shield for those with substantial interest income.

might be run in tandem with the choice-based system. That is, enrollees could continue under the current medicare system, with the same premium and cost-sharing requirements, or could opt into the choice-based system, where a different menu of choices would be offered. This arrangement could be permanent or transitional.

Eligibility. A tenet of the choice-based system is that enrollees are capable of making appropriate decisions about the plan they wish to join. For the cognitively impaired, this is clearly not the case, and some alternative mechanism would be needed. Even among the non-impaired population, many of the oldest old could have difficulty evaluating alternative health insurance plans. People who joined medicare before employer-sponsored insurance adopted managed care, for example, may not have the experience to equip them to make informed insurance decisions. Thus, if fee-for-service medicare were not continued as an option, people above a certain age (perhaps 75) should probably be grandfathered into the current system, while the younger population should be enrolled in the choice-based system. If fee-for-service medicare is continued as an option, choice could easily be extended to all beneficiaries with much less fear about the consequences of poor decisionmaking.

Minimizing redistribution. A choice-based system has the potential to harm poorer medicare beneficiaries. If the coupon amount is set too low, the poor elderly may not be able to afford plans above the least expensive. If low-cost plans provide low-quality care, the poor may be relegated to significantly worse medical care than the rich. This would overturn one of medicare's greatest achievements—the fact that poor and rich alike are both on the same system.

The amount of redistribution will depend on the level of the coupon payment. If the coupon is sufficient to pay for an average cost policy or higher, redistribution concerns would not be particularly important. If the coupon is set at a lower level, however—for example, the cost of the least expensive plan—this would be more of a concern. In such a situation, it would be desirable to supplement the coupon payment to the poor elderly. By varying the coupon payment with income, meaningful choice could be guaranteed to rich and poor alike. This type of supplement might replace the medicaid coverage currently offered to the low-income elderly for those who opt into managed care.

Pricing restrictions. The most difficult issues in choice-based systems revolve around pricing. Saying people have a choice of insurance policies begs the question: at what price? This is a particular concern about health insurance markets. People naturally have different tastes for insurance policies, and these tastes will be correlated with health status. The older and sicker will want few restrictions on their choice of providers; the younger and healthier will be more willing to enter managed care, with its attendant restrictions on provider choice. If there is complete choice of insurance with no other rules or regulations, healthier people will disproportionately enroll in some plans and sicker people will disproportionately enroll in others. Premiums will reflect these differences; more generous plans will charge substantially more than less generous plans, in part because the people in more generous plans will be less healthy.

Although plans that offer more generous benefits or are less efficient should cost more, it is not beneficial if a plan's premiums are higher because the people it covers are sicker. This penalizes the less healthy simply because they are less healthy. It also discourages the healthy from joining these plans, since they would face above-average premiums to subsidize the less healthy. And it provides incentives for plans to encourage the less healthy not to enroll, so that they can attract healthier people.

Choice-based insurance will not work well without some mechanism to offset the tendency of people to chose plans based on their health status. There is a natural solution: pay more to plans that enroll a less healthy mix of people and less to plans that enroll a more healthy mix. Plans that are compensated more for less healthy enrollees will find they can care for them and not have to charge more to everyone else. The task of designing an appropriate set of adjusted payments is difficult and will take some time to resolve. To fashion such a payment system, the government will have to know how people sort themselves across plans and the extent to which plans can affect these choices. At least in the short run, the adjustments will not work perfectly, and some doubt that a workable system is feasible at all.[23]

This discussion makes clear that a choice-based system is neither perfect nor easy to implement. Regulation is a necessary part of choice-based health insurance—to limit the practices of insurers, guarantee that services promised are actually delivered, and reduce the importance of nonrandom enrollment. And even the regulation that can be implemented may not make the system work perfectly.

23. For a more detailed discussion of selection issues, see Newhouse (1994).

Coupled with this is the fact that choice-based systems are unlikely to save a large amount of money in the short run. Most analyses find substantial savings only if the guarantee of the fee-for-service medicare system is eliminated as a part of reform and the growth of the coupon payment is set very low relative to the growth of baseline medicare costs. Effectively what this does is to increase substantially the price to beneficiaries of keeping the current generosity of benefits. If the fee-for-service option is preserved at no additional beneficiary cost or the coupon amount grows at the rate of overall medicare costs, near-term budget savings from a choice-based system are generally projected to be small.[24]

Thus a choice-based system is not the best single alternative if the goal is short-run budget savings. In such an environment, reductions in provider payments or increases in costs to beneficiaries make a good deal more sense. Both can be done quickly; neither has substantial implementation problems; and the savings can be much larger.

The virtue of the choice-based system is not its effect on short-term costs but instead its potential to change the long-run dynamics of medicare. The clear conclusion from the past decade of medicare is that the traditional methods for saving money are not sufficient. The choice-based system is the only option on the table that may help medicare substantially in the long run. Thus a choice-based approach almost certainly needs to be a part of long-run medicare reform.

Proposals for Choice-Based Reform

Some form of choice-based reform has been a feature of many recent health reform proposals. Choice was encouraged under the Bush administration health plan (through the creation of "health insurance networks") and the Clinton administration health plan (through "health alliances"). Increased choice is also a component of both the Republican and Democratic medicare reform proposals. Table 6-3 provides a comparison of the choice-based reform proposals in the Balanced Budget Act of 1995 and the administration's fiscal year 1997 budget proposal. Both of the plans would expand the choices available to medicare beneficiaries, including a much larger set of managed care plans than is currently available. Both would also preserve medicare's traditional fee-for-service system at no additional

---

24. Urban Institute (1995).

TABLE 6-3. Choice-Based Provisions of Medicare Reform Proposals

Feature	Balanced Budget Act of 1995	Administration's fiscal year 1997 budget proposal
Choices offered		
Non-fee-for-service	All	No MSAs
Fee-for-service medicare	Preserved	Preserved
Beneficiary cost or saving from choice	75% of savings; all of additional costs	No cost or saving
Eligibility	All	All
Pricing	Risk adjustment	Risk adjustment

cost to the beneficiary as an option outside the choice-based system. A major substantive difference between the two proposals was whether beneficiaries would be allowed to enroll in MSAs. These plans were allowed under the Balanced Budget Act but not under the administration's budget proposal.

The plans also differ with respect to the financial consequences associated with the choice-based reform. In the Republican proposal, beneficiaries could receive a cash rebate of up to 75 percent of any cost savings resulting from choosing an insurance plan with costs below the federal coupon contribution. The balance would be retained by the hospital insurance trust fund. Beneficiaries would be able to select plans that charged more than the federal contribution under this proposal, but they would have to pay all of the additional premium. The financial consequences associated with plan choice under the administration's proposal would remain unchanged from what they are under the current medicare HMO option. In other words, if a plan's costs for providing the required medicare services were less than the federal coupon, the plan could devote the savings to enriched services but not to cash rebates to beneficiaries.

In both proposals all beneficiaries would be free to join the choice-based system. With the fee-for-service medicare option available in both cases, allowing all beneficiaries access to the choice-based system is not particularly worrisome. Finally, medicare's payments to plans would be adjusted for health status when methods for doing this were developed.

The administration and the Republicans differed on the amount of overall medicare savings they thought necessary, but these differences were comparatively minor and a compromise between them could have been reached. In contrast, the differences in the proposals for fundamental reform, which involved the types of plans that would be offered and the ability to realize savings from lower premiums, were much greater and in the end proved unbridgeable. This was one important reason why the 1995–96 budget negotiations never reached a reconciliation.

In part, the failure to reach agreement on choice-based reform may be a consequence of the fact that medicare reform was considered in the context of deficit reduction. As noted above, with a horizon of only a few years, choice-based reform is not necessary. It is only in the longer-term context that structural reform becomes important. Moving the debate about medicare reform out of the budget context and into a broader discussion of the long-run fiscal dilemma facing the nation might facilitate agreement that was not possible during the 1995–96 debate.

Capping Medicare Spending

None of the three options for medicare reform—cutting provider payments, increasing beneficiary costs, or restructuring—would guarantee savings to the government, in either the short run or the long run. In each case, changes in utilization or the insurance plans people choose would affect the savings realized. This uncertainty has been a source of concern for those who want to guarantee budget balance by a date certain or protect medicare's long-term affordability. In response to this dilemma, some have proposed that maximum spending levels for medicare be set in law, thus "locking in" a given level of spending.

There are two approaches to capping spending. The first is represented by the "fail-safe" provisions of the Balanced Budget Act of 1995. That proposal set annual limits on total medicare benefit spending and on the annual average value of the coupon for the choice-based system. Limiting the coupon value is easy; limiting spending in the fee-for-service sector to meet an overall target is harder, since the government controls only the price paid for services, not total spending. To resolve this problem the fail-safe required automatic reductions in payments for categories of services (inpatient hospital services, physicians' services, diagnostic tests) whose growth exceeded acceptable rates that were specified in the law. Although these controls were billed as a backup, the Congressional Budget Office projected that they would be required to reduce spending by $11.5 billion over 1996 to 2002 (see table 6-2).

"Global budgets" represent the second approach for capping spending. Under this approach various sectors, such as hospitals, would be paid a fixed amount for the entire year rather than receive separate payments for each service or admission. Many countries rely on this type of budgeting as the basis of their national health insurance systems.

Although proposals to "lock in" savings seem sensible, they raise some very difficult problems. As noted above, the degree to which medicare cost growth can be restrained is limited by what is happening for nonmedicare patients. If an automatic adjustment mechanism holds medicare cost growth substantially below that in the private sector, access problems could develop for medicare recipients. This is particularly true for the mechanisms that enforce spending reductions by reducing fees paid to providers.

In addition, overall budgets typically fail to account for interactions in the different parts of the medicare system. Consider the Republican fail-safe system as an example. Suppose that as choice is introduced into medicare, healthier people leave the fee-for-service sector and coupon payments are not adjusted to reflect this. The remaining fee-for-service pool will be more expensive than initially anticipated and its spending limit will be exceeded, triggering reductions in fee-for-service payments. But the payment reductions would be unwarranted. Indeed, the long-run dynamics of this type of response may be particularly pernicious if providers are induced to leave the fee-for-service sector and join the choice-based sector because of the reduced payment rates in the fee-for-service sector.

The converse situation could also occur. The fail-safe in the Balanced Budget Act establishes a fixed annual medicare benefit budget. The coupon payments for participants in choice plans are subtracted from this amount, leaving a residual fixed budget for the fee-for-service system. Because the average coupon grows more slowly than the overall medicare budget, the residual limit on the fee-for-service budget could grow increasingly lax over time. If large numbers of beneficiaries enrolled in choice plans, this could significantly relax the restraints on spending in the fee-for-service sector when that would not be warranted.

Clearly, it will be extremely difficult to enforce any overall budget limit, and yet such constraints are useful to have. Budget limits would force policymakers to reexamine medicare when spending exceeded expectations in the same way that the periodic threat of "bankruptcy" of the hospital insurance trust fund has forced medicare reforms in the past. There are less severe alternatives to a system of mandatory budget limits with an enforcement mechanism that might be valuable. For example, Congress could set "targets" for total medicare spending five to ten years in advance. If spending exceeded these targets, Congress could be required to evaluate the causes of the excess spending and consider program changes, possibly under expedited legislative procedures. Ideally, continual reevaluation of the program would provide most of the benefits of a fixed spending limit.

The Social Role of Medicare

In deciding on medicare reforms, it is important to consider the effects that these changes could have on the rest of the health system. Historically, medicare was a quite generous system, and the implications of this generosity extended well beyond medicare beneficiaries. Generous payments made it easier for providers to take care of the uninsured and supported the broad range of activities provided by teaching hospitals.

An unrestrained focus on cost savings would adversely affect both of these social goals. Private markets in general do a poor job of redistributing to those who cannot afford goods and services, and health care is no exception. Similarly, the additional costs of supporting teaching institutions will not be easily absorbed by insurers looking predominantly for cost savings. Thus, as medicare is reformed, both of these services are at some risk.

It would be appropriate to direct some of the money saved by medicare reform to institutions that provide clinical training to medical professionals and facilities that care for the uninsured. Providing direct subsidies as indirect ones are eliminated can help prevent the harm that cost containment might otherwise bring.

Conclusion

As the costs of medicare continue to increase, medicare reform becomes more and more important. The desire for a balanced budget brought medicare to the table; the need to structure a system that can ensure adequate health care for the baby boomers and subsequent generations will keep it there.

As policymakers craft their proposals to reform medicare, they must keep three basic facts in mind. First, medicare costs are a concern for reasons far beyond the federal budget. Medicare has been, is, and will continue to be a substantial contributor to the deficit problem. But beyond the deficit, medicare costs are increasing far faster than society's ability to pay for them. And virtually every analyst who has studied medicare believes that the program could spend less than it does now without sacrificing the quality of care. It is a great mistake to focus on medicare only in the narrow issue of budget balance and ignore the other concerns about the system.

Second, the appropriate policy steps almost surely differ in the short run and the long run. Budget balance is best achieved in a way that is easy and can be implemented quickly. Reducing payments to providers or increasing beneficiary costs are natural steps. Both have been done in the past, and both can be implemented without significant redistribution. These steps together can easily generate medicare's share of the savings needed to balance the budget in the next several years.

But together these steps are not capable of providing a complete solution to the longer-run challenge. Payment reductions do not address the underlying source of cost increases and cannot be repeated indefinitely. Increased cost sharing shifts some of the medicare burden to beneficiaries but does not affect overall spending. To encourage long-run reductions in program costs, the best alternative is to restructure the program into a choice-based system. By using consumer choice, it may be possible to rationalize a system that is not now performing in the appropriate way.

Finally, it is important to recognize medicare's interconnections with the rest of the health system. Focusing medicare on containing costs will reduce the implicit subsidies the program has made to the uninsured and to teaching hospitals. These services are important, and as the market eliminates them, the government has to step forward to make up for their demise.

Medicare reform is one of the most difficult tasks on the public agenda. Medicare has been enormously successful in providing for the health and welfare of the elderly and disabled and, as a result, the program is immensely popular. Medicare reform is also difficult because the crises in the system will not be particularly severe for a decade or more. In the political world, there is always a temptation to plan for the next few years but not beyond. Medicare reform will be a test of whether the nation's political system has the capacity to think and act in the long term, or whether it is destined to lurch from crisis to crisis.

References

Aaron, Henry J. 1991. *Serious and Unstable Condition: Financing America's Health Care*. Brookings.

Aaron, Henry J., and Robert Reischauer. 1995. "The Medicare Reform Debate: What Is the Next Step?" *Health Affairs* 14 (Winter): 8–30.

Brook, Robert H. 1991. "Health, Health Insurance, and the Uninsured." *Journal of the American Medical Association*, June 12, 2998–3002.

Brown, Randall, and others. 1993. "The Medicare Risk Program for HMOs: Final Summary Report on Findings from the Evaluation." Princeton: Mathematica Policy Research.

Chassin, Mark R., and others. 1987. "Does Appropriate Use Explain Geographic Variables in the Use of Health Care Services?" *Journal of the American Medical Association*, November 13, 2533–37.

Christensen, Sandra. 1992. "Volume Responses to Exogenous Changes in Medicare's Payment Policies." *Health Services Research* 27 (April): 65–79.

Congressional Budget Office. 1995. *Reducing the Deficit: Spending and Revenue Options* (February).

———. 1996. *The Economic and Budget Outlook* (May).

Cutler, David M. 1995a. "Cutting Costs and Improving Health: Making Reform Work." *Health Affairs* 14 (Spring): 161–72.

Cutler, David M. 1995b. "The Incidence of Adverse Medical Outcomes under Prospective Payment." *Econometrica* 63 (January): 29–50.

Cutler, David M., and Mark McClellan. 1995. "What Determines Technological Change?" Paper prepared for conference on "Economics of Aging."

Davis, Karen, and Cathy Schoen. 1978. *Health and the War on Poverty: A Ten-Year Appraisal*. Brookings.

Feder, Judith, Jack Hadley, and Stephen Zuckerman. 1987. "How Did Medicare's Prospective Payment System Affect Hospitals?" *New England Journal of Medicine*, October 1, 867–73.

Greenspan, Allan M., and others. 1988. "Incidence of Unwarranted Implantation of Permanent Cardiac Pacemakers in a Large Medical Population." *New England Journal of Medicine*, January 21, 158–63.

Hospital Insurance Trust Fund. 1996. *Annual Report of the Board of Trustees of the Federal Hospital Insurance Trust Fund*. Washington.

Kahn, Katherine L., and others. 1990. "Comparing Outcomes of Care before and after Implementation of the DRG-Based Prospective Payment System." *Journal of the American Medical Association*, October 17, 1984–88.

McClellan, Mark, and Joseph P. Newhouse. 1995. "The Marginal Benefits of Medical Technology." Harvard University Medical School.

Manton, Kenneth, and James Vaupel. 1995. "Survival after the Age of 80 in the United States, Sweden, France, England, and Japan." *New England Journal of Medicine*, November 2, 1232–35.

Miller, Robert, and Harold Luft. 1994. "Managed Care Plan Performance since 1980; A Literature Analysis." *Journal of the American Medical Association*, May 18, 1512–19.

Moon, Marilyn. 1996. *Medicare Now and in the Future*, 2d ed. Washington: Urban Institute.

Newhouse, Joseph P. 1992. "Medical Care Costs: How Much Welfare Loss?" *Journal of Economic Perspectives* 6 (Summer): 3–21.

Newhouse, Joseph P. 1994. "Patients at Risk." *Health Affairs* 13 (Spring): 132–46.

Prospective Payment Assessment Commission. 1996. *Medicare and the American Health Care System*. Washington.

Shaw, George Bernard. 1911. *The Doctor's Dilemma*. New York: Garland.

U.S. House of Representatives. Committee on Ways and Means. 1994. *Overview of Entitlement Programs: Background Material and Data on Programs within the Jurisdiction of the Committee on Ways and Means*. Committee Print. Government Printing Office.

Wennberg, John E., J. L. Freeman, and W. J. Culp. 1987. "Are Hospital Services Rationed in New Haven or Over-Utilized in Boston?" *Lancet*, May 23, 1185–88.

Urban Institute. 1995. "Searching for Savings in Medicare." Washington.

Winslow, Constance M., and others. 1988a. "The Appropriateness of Carotid Endarterectomy." *New England Journal of Medicine*, March 24, 721–27.

Winslow, Constance M., and others. 1988b. "The Appropriateness of Performing Coronary Artery Bypass Surgery." *Journal of the American Medical Association*, July 22, 505–09.

7

HENRY J. AARON
& WILLIAM G. GALE

Fundamental Tax Reform:
Miracle or Mirage?

TAX REFORM has reappeared on the nation's policy
agenda. During 1996, senior members of Congress from both parties
and several candidates for the Republican presidential nomination
advanced proposals to replace the personal and corporation income
taxes with some form of consumption tax or to radically restructure
the personal income tax.[1] These proposals come only a decade after
President Ronald Reagan signed the Tax Reform Act of 1986, which
was the culmination of a decades-long effort to broaden the bases
and cut the rates of the personal and corporation income taxes. At
the time, many hoped that the act would be the reform to end reforms,
that after enacting this landmark legislation the nation could move
on to other issues. But it has not turned out that way.

While the reformers of 1986 sought to broaden the base and lower
the rates of the existing tax system, most of the reformers of 1996
seek to replace the income taxes with some form of consumption

1. Most notably, the Freedom and Fairness Restoration Act (H.R. 2060 and S. 1050),
sponsored by House Majority Leader Richard Armey (Republican of Texas) and Senator
Richard Shelby (Republican of Alabama); the USA Tax Act of 1995 (S. 722), sponsored
by Senators Sam Nunn (Democrat of Georgia) and Pete Domenici (Republican of New
Mexico); and the National Retail Sales Tax of 1996 (H.R. 3039), sponsored by Representatives Dan Schaefer (Republican of Colorado), Billy Tauzin (Republican of Louisiana),
and Dick Chrysler (Republican of Michigan). In addition, flat tax proposals by the Kemp
commission and 1996 presidential candidate Steve Forbes and the 10 percent plan proposed
by House Minority Leader Richard Gephardt (Democrat of Missouri) have gained considerable attention. Other flat tax proposals include H.R. 1780, sponsored by Representative
Mark Souder (Republican of Indiana), S. 488, sponsored by Senator Arlen Specter (Republican of Pennsylvania), and the Crane Tithe Act of 1995 (H.R. 214), sponsored by Representative Phillip Crane (Republican of Illinois). Proposals by Representatives Sam Gibbons
(Democrat of Florida) and Bill Archer (Republican of Texas) and Senator Richard Lugar
(Republican of Indiana) exist only in the form of speeches and statements.

taxation. In 1986 the Treasury Department examined various replacements for the income tax, including consumption taxation. In the end, however, it concluded that the potential gains were not large enough to justify the uncertainties associated with such a far-reaching move and the possibilities for error in legislation and implementation. Although current consumption tax plans have not been subject to the intense analysis that the Treasury Department devoted to planning for the Tax Reform Act of 1986, it is clear that many advocates now believe that the potential benefits of moving to a consumption tax are worth the risks.

There are several reasons for the renewed interest in fundamental tax reform. First, nearly everyone finds the current tax system too complicated. Complexity assumes many guises, such as lengthy personal forms for individuals with capital income and itemized deductions, detailed recordkeeping requirements for small businesses, and mountains of paperwork for large corporations. Perhaps the most telling indicator of angst is that in recent years almost one-half of all individual filers have hired others to prepare their returns.

Second, some believe that tax reform can spur economic growth. Since 1973 output per capita has grown at an annual rate of only 1.5 percent, much below the 2.5 percent growth achieved in the preceding quarter century. Some advocates of tax reform think that the current tax system has depressed saving and entrepreneurship, thereby contributing to the problem of slow growth.

Finally, many claim that the current tax system collects either too little or too much revenue. Some deficit hawks believe tax increases will be a necessary, if unpleasant, component of any successful plan to balance the budget. For them, a reformed tax system might make the task of raising additional revenues more politically palatable and less distortionary. On the other side are some conservatives who see tax reform combined with tax cuts not just as a way to spur growth but also as a means to curb what they think is excessive government.

The major reforms now on the table present the American people and their representatives with some wrenching choices. A simpler tax system with lower rates is possible, but moving to such a system may put vital American institutions in jeopardy, particularly during the transition to a new system. The current tax system is embedded in myriad and complex ways in the nation's economic, social, and institutional structures. Fundamental changes in the tax system would shift tax burdens, alter asset values, disrupt state and local government finance, and affect the viability of for-profit and not-for-profit entities. The purpose of the remainder of this chapter is not to recommend a particular tax system but to make clear the nature of the choices that must be faced.

The Reform Proposals

Five different approaches to reform are being discussed (see table 7-1). Four would replace the current system with some variant of a tax on consumption, that is, on the portion of income that a family does not save. Such taxes can be levied directly on the goods and services people consume or can be imposed at the household level on the difference between income and saving. The remaining approach involves major reform of the current income tax. The following descriptions illustrate these approaches to reform and some of the difficulties inherent in the transition to any new system.

The Retail Sales Tax

All but five of the fifty United States levy retail sales taxes. Representative Bill Archer and Senator Richard Lugar have proposed replacing the personal and corporation income taxes and the estate tax with a national retail sales tax. If all consumption were taxed, a 15 percent national retail sales tax rate would be required to generate the same revenue as the current income tax system. In practice, all state retail sales taxes contain large exemptions—as would any federal retail sales tax—because some consumption is difficult or unpalatable to tax. Such exempt consumption includes spending on education, medical care, professional and financial services, food consumed at home, and housing. If all of these categories of consumption were exempted, the tax base would be reduced by more than half and the retail sales tax rate necessary to replace current personal and corporate income tax revenue would exceed 30 percent.

The total sales tax rate that faced consumers would be even higher because it would include current state retail sales taxes. But these state sales tax rates would probably rise substantially if the federal government abandoned its income tax. States now depend heavily on the recordkeeping required for the federal income tax in administering their own income taxes and, without this information, many might jettison their own income taxes and increase their sales taxes com-

TABLE 7-1. Comparing the Tax Plans

Tax provision	Current law	Retail sales tax	Value-added tax	Armey-Shelby flat tax	USA tax	Gephardt
Change in system	None	Replaces individual and corporate income tax and estate tax	Replaces individual and corporate income tax	Replaces individual and corporate income tax and estate tax	Replaces individual and corporate income tax; offsets payroll taxes	Modifies current system
Individual-level tax Summary	Imposes graduated-rate tax on wage and capital income with exemptions and deductions	Eliminates individual-level income tax	Eliminates individual-level income tax	Imposes single-rate tax on wages and pension distributions with large exemptions and no deductions	Imposes graduated-rate tax on wage and capital income less saving and other deductions, with a credit for employee payroll taxes	Broadens base and reduces rates relative to current system
Tax base						
Wages and salaries	Yes	…	…	Yes	Yes	Yes
State and local bond interest	No	…	…	No	No	Yes
Other interest, dividends, rent, royalties	Yes	…	…	No	Yes	Yes
Realized capital gains	Yes (at preferred rates)	…	…	No	Yes	Yes
Health insurance	No	…	…	No	No	Yes

Employer pension contribution	No	...	No	No	Yes
Employee pension contribution	No	...	No[a]	No	Yes
Accumulation in pensions	No	...	No	No	No
Pension receipts	Yes	...	Yes	Yes	Yes
Social security	Yes	...	No	Yes	Yes
Deductions					
Nonpension saving	No	...	No	Yes	No
Mortgage interest	Yes	...	No[b]	Yes	Yes
Charitable contributions	Yes	...	No[b]	Yes	No
Property taxes	Yes	...	No	No	No
State and local taxes	Yes	...	No	No	No
Tax rates (percent)	15, 28, 31, 36, and 39.6[c]	...	20 in 1996–97, 17 thereafter	After 1999, rates are 8, 19, and 40[d]	10, 20, 26, 32, and 34[c]
Exempt range (dollars)[f]	...	...	...	...	...
Single person	6,400	...	10,700	6,950	7,750
Married couple	11,550	...	21,400	12,500	13,850
Family of four	16,550	...	31,400	17,600	19,350
EITC	Yes	...	No	Yes	Yes
Payroll tax credit	No	...	No	Yes	No
Child care credit	Yes	...	No	No	No

TABLE 7-1 (continued)

Tax provision	Current law	Retail sales tax	Value-added tax	Armey-Shelby flat tax	USA tax	Gephardt
Business-level tax						
Summary	Corporations pay essentially flat-rate tax on net income; other businesses pay taxes under individual income tax	Imposes flat-rate tax on sales to consumers by all businesses	Imposes flat-rate tax on all business sales to consumers and other businesses less costs of inputs and capital goods	Imposes flat-rate tax on value-added base less wages and employer pension contributions	Imposes flat-rate tax on value-added base with export exemptions plus refundable credit for payroll taxes paid by employer	Retains current tax and cuts "corporate welfare" by $50 billion (no details specified)
Tax base						
Sales of goods and services[g]	Yes	Yes	Yes	Yes	Yes	Yes
Financial income	Yes	No	No	No	No	Yes
Foreign-source income	Yes	No	No	No	No	Yes

Deductions	In general, taxes export sales	Taxes imports; exempts exports	Taxes imports; exempts exports	Taxes exports; exempts imports	Taxes imports; exempts exports	Same as current law
Wages and salaries	Yes	No	No	Yes	No	Yes
Employer pension contribution	Yes	No	No	Yes	No	Yes
Investment	Depreciated	Expensed	Expensed	Expensed	Expensed	Depreciated
Payroll taxes	Yes	No	No	No	Credit	Yes
Other taxes	Yes	No	No	No	No	Yes
Interest paid	Yes	No	No	No	No	Yes
Health insurance	Yes	No	No	No	No	Yes
Tax rates (percent)	35[h]	17[i]	17[i]	20 in 1996–97, 17 thereafter[i]	11	Same as current law
Foreign trade	In general, taxes export sales	Taxes imports; exempts exports	Taxes imports; exempts exports	Taxes exports; exempts imports	Taxes imports; exempts exports	Same as current law

a. The legislation is unclear, but if all pension receipts are taxed, all pension contributions should be untaxed.

b. A flat-tax plan submitted by Senator Arlen Specter (Republican of Pennsylvania) would retain this deduction.

c. In 1995 taxable income brackets were $0–$23,350, $23,350–$56,550, $56,550–$117,950, $117,950–$256,500, and over $256,500 for single filers; $0–$39,000, $39,000–$94,250, $94,250–$143,60, $143,600–$256,500, and over $256,500 for married filers; and $0–$31,250, $31,250–$80,750, $80,750–$130,800, $130,800–$256,500, and over $256,500 for heads of household.

d. The rates would originally be set at 19, 27, and 40 percent but would fall over time. After 1999 rates would be set at 8, 19, and 40 percent. For years 2000 and beyond, taxable income brackets are $0–$3,200, $3,200–$14,400, and over $14,400 for single filers; $0–$5,400, $5,400–$24,000, and over $24,000 for married filers; and $0–$4,750, $4,750–$21,110, and over $21,100 for heads of household.

e. Taxable income brackets are $0–$24,050, $24,050–$58,300, $58,300–$121,600, $121,600–$264,450, and over $264,450 for single filers; $0–$40,200, $40,200–$97,150, $97,150–$148,150, $148,150–$264,450, and over $264,450 for married filers; $0–$32,250, $32,250–$83,250, $83,250–$134,850, $134,850–$264,450, and over $264,450 for heads of household.

f. This range ignores the EITC and payroll tax credit and is the sum of personal and dependent exemptions and the standard deduction in the income tax; personal and dependent exemptions in the flat tax; personal and dependent exemptions plus a "family living allowance" in the USA tax; and personal and dependent exemptions in the Gephardt plan.

g. For the retail sales tax, only goods and services sold to consumers would be taxed. For other plans, all sales are included in the tax base.

h. Taxable income brackets are $0–$50,000, $50,000–$75,000, $75,000–$100,000, $100,000–$335,000, $335,000–$10,000,000, $10,000,000–$15,000,000, $15,000,000–$18,333,333, and over $18,333,333. The respective tax rates are 15 percent, 25 percent, 34 percent, 39 percent, 35 percent, 38 percent, 35 percent, and 35 percent. Almost all corporate income is taxed at the 34 percent rate or higher.

i. At this rate, the new system would raise less revenue than the current system.

mensurately. Increasing retail sales tax rates enough to replace state income tax would boost rates about one-fifth. A retail sales tax with such high rates could prove to be unadministrable because incentives to evade the tax would all be focused at one point, the retail sale.[2] No jurisdiction has successfully levied a retail sales tax at rates above about 10 percent.[3]

A retail sales tax with very high rates suffers from two problems in addition to its questionable administrability. Businesses—particularly small businesses—often pay retail sales taxes on their purchases because they buy products from stores that deal principally with households. When sales among businesses are taxed, the retail sales tax cascades, capriciously generating higher cumulative tax on certain goods and services, which then distorts prices and consumption. It is possible to exempt intrabusiness sales by giving businesses registered tax exemptions, but doing so is administratively cumbersome and creates the risk of evasion by business employees who are tempted to use the exemption for purchases of their own. The second problem concerns distribution. Low-income households consume a higher proportion of their annual income than high-income households do. The retail sales tax, therefore, claims a larger share of the incomes of the poor than of the rich. This pattern is the reverse of the income tax, for which rates rise with taxable income and low-income households are entirely exempt.

The Value-Added Tax

More than fifty countries around the world levy taxes on value added—that is, on gross revenues less purchases from other businesses at each stage of production, distribution, and sales. In some countries, value-added taxes collect about as large a share of national product as the U.S. personal and corporation income taxes yield. The value-added tax base is the same, in principle, as the retail sales tax base, but the revenue is collected differently. Instead of being collected only at the retail stage, the VAT is collected from all businesses on the difference between sales proceeds and purchases from other busi-

---

2. Slemrod (1996).

3. "The general view among experts, a view obviously shared by most governments, is that 10 percent may well be the maximum rate feasible under a retail sales tax" (Tanzi, 1995, pp. 50–51).

nesses. That difference equals the sum of payments to workers and to owners of capital. The value of a good sold to a household is the sum of successive additions to value that took place as that good proceeded through the production cycle.

The VAT solves some of the problems that afflict the retail sales tax. Because the revenue is collected from all businesses rather than just the minority of businesses that sell to households, the incentives to evade the tax have proven controllable. The tax does not cascade, because sales from one business to another are implicitly excluded as each such sale creates taxable income for the seller and an exactly offsetting deduction for the buyer. But the VAT shifts tax burdens from the rich to the poor just as the retail sales tax does. It is possible to apply reduced rates to "necessities," but this method of protecting low-income families works poorly, cutting revenues far more than it helps the intended beneficiaries of relief. This occurs because families at all income levels buy necessities, and even those with low incomes spend a sizable fraction of income on other items.

Many people favor the value-added tax because they believe it will improve the U.S. trade balance. Countries in the European Union rebate the VAT on exports and impose the tax on imports. This practice is unlike rules governing the corporation income tax, which falls on profits generated by exports as well as imports and does not fall on profits of foreign companies generated by sales in the United States. VAT advocates claim that replacing the corporation income tax with a value-added tax (or a retail sales tax) will improve the international competitive position of U.S. businesses.

This argument is seductively plausible, but wrong. It ignores a fundamental constraint governing the trade balance of any country. The trade balance (exports less imports) is simply the difference between national output and the sum of consumption and investment, both public and private. Tax policy can affect the trade balance only if it changes national product, consumption, or investment. Available evidence, presented below, suggests that the reforms now under discussion will not materially change output, consumption, or investment. If these quantities do not change, the trade balance cannot change. Instead, the major consequence of replacing the corporation income tax with a value-added tax would be to push up the value of the U.S. dollar enough to offset the effects of tax policy on export and import prices, leaving the trade balance unchanged. While overall U.S. competitiveness would be little changed, some companies that now pay particularly large corporation income taxes might experience some competitive gains. To the extent that these companies gained, however, other companies that now pay little corporation income tax would lose competitiveness.[4]

The Flat Tax

The flat tax is a consumption tax collected from businesses and households. Under the flat tax, businesses may take all the deductions allowed under the VAT, plus deductions for wage payments and pension contributions for workers. Families are subject to a separate tax on their cash wages and pension income above an exempt earnings level. This exemption spares families with low earnings any direct tax, relieving them of much of the burden they bear under a retail sales tax or value-added tax. Earnings above the threshold are subject to tax at the same rate businesses face.

The flat tax rate that would be needed to replace the corporation and personal income tax depends on the size of the family earnings exemption and the number of itemized deductions that are retained. The flat tax proposed by Representative Richard Armey and Senator Richard Shelby would exempt $31,400 for a family of four. It taxes employer-financed health insurance; eliminates all itemized deductions, including those for mortgage interest, charitable contributions, and state and local taxes; and repeals the earned income tax credit (EITC)—a refundable wage subsidy for low-income workers. This plan would require a rate of about 21 percent to replace the corporation and personal income taxes. We will examine later some of the problems that would arise in trying to implement the flat tax.

The USA Tax

The USA tax, which has been proposed by Senators Pete Domenici and Sam Nunn, combines two distinct elements: a personal consumption tax on families and a value-added tax on businesses. Families would calculate their income and subtract certain itemized deductions and exclusions, much as they do under current law. They would be entitled to exemptions based on family size, and every homeowner

---

4. In calculating the burdens a company faces, one must include not only the taxes the company pays directly but also the taxes paid by suppliers. A full analysis requires an input-output table.

would be able to deduct mortgage interest payments. Families would also be entitled to deductions for charitable contributions, alimony, and a limited amount of tuition. In addition, families would be able to deduct all of their net saving, thereby receiving an *unlimited savings allowance* (hence the name of the proposal). While net additions to savings would be deductible, net reductions in savings would be taxable. An exception would be made for a portion of wealth already in existence when the new tax takes effect. Consumption financed by old wealth above $50,000 would be included in the tax base.

The USA tax would be levied on income less exemptions and deductions (including the unlimited savings deduction) at three graduated rates. The rates would originally be set at 19, 27, and 40 percent, but would fall over time. After 1999 rates would be set at 8, 19, and 40 percent. These rates are not as high as they seem because families would be given a refundable credit for the portion of payroll taxes that is deducted from workers' wages. Businesses would face a separate 11 percent value-added tax and would receive a credit for the employer portion of payroll taxes.

The USA tax raises administrative problems not present in the current system or other proposed reforms.[5] The most notable of these relates to the need to keep track of assets in existence when the new tax takes effect and to distinguish these assets from those created later. For example, taxpayers with assets of more than $50,000 would have powerful incentives to conceal their old wealth, perhaps by moving it abroad and then bringing it back disguised as saving after the new tax takes effect. To the extent that those with wealth succeed in concealing their old accumulations of assets, they would be able to shield current consumption from tax with the unlimited savings allowance. Policing such evasion would be extremely difficult, if not impossible.

Income Tax Reform

The Tax Reform Act of 1986 broadened the income tax base by terminating or limiting many deductions, exclusions, allowances, and credits and used the additional revenue to cut rates. Representative Richard Gephardt proposes a reprise of that approach to tax reform. His proposal would end deductions for state and local taxes and

---

5. Some critics of the USA tax point out that it also contains provisions that would encourage avoidance behavior that is hard to rationalize. See Ginsburg (1995).

charitable contributions, various deductions for pension contributions, and the exemption of interest paid on municipal bonds, but
would retain the EITC. This plan would treat employer-financed
health insurance as part of the employee's taxable income. This base
broadening would allow a bottom rate of 10 percent (rather than 15
percent under current law) above an exempt income level, with rates
rising to a maximum of 34 percent (rather than 39.6 percent under
current law). As under current law, the personal exemption would be
phased out for high-income families. The plan would make few
changes in the corporation income tax other than in the treatment of
pension contributions. This plan entails smaller changes in tax structure than the consumption tax proposals, apart from the vexing administrative task of calculating the value of health insurance to impute
to each worker with employer-sponsored health insurance.

Elements of Tax Reform

Tax reform revolves around three sorts of issues: what base to tax,
what deductions to permit, and what rates to levy.

Tax Base

The tax base of the current system is a hybrid between that of an
income tax, which falls on both income and saving, and that of a
consumption tax. A pure income tax base would include all labor
compensation and income from capital, whether realized or not. The
current personal income tax base deviates from this principle in important ways. Some employee compensation and capital income is
untaxed. For example, employee fringe benefits, such as health insurance financed by employers and parking and term life insurance below
certain amounts, are not taxed. The appreciation of assets that are
not sold adds to net worth but is usually not taxed until the assets
are sold;[6] and if the owner holds the assets until death, appreciation
is never taxed under the income tax. Contributions to approved pension plans, by employers or by individuals, add to their ultimate
beneficiary's net worth, but are not included in current taxable income. This exclusion also applies to the investment earnings of pen-

6. There are some important exceptions. Accruing value on zero-coupon bonds is
imputed and taxed annually. Futures contracts are "marked to market" and the change in
value is subject to tax each year.

sion funds and the buildup in the cash value of life insurance. Instead, individuals must pay tax on pensions only when received.

The various consumption tax plans would abandon the taxation of all new saving. Under the USA tax, all saving would be treated much like "sheltered" saving is now handled: deposits would be untaxed, while withdrawals from these assets would be taxed. Under the retail sales tax, the value-added tax, and the flat tax, only consumption would be taxed.

Deductions, Credits, and Allowances

Current tax law permits dozens of allowances, credits, exclusions, and deductions for purposes that Congress and the president thought meritorious at the time of enactment. Each provides tax relief that supporters believe improves tax equity (such as the ability to deduct medical expenses above 7.5 percent of income) or encourages some worthwhile activity (such as the charitable contributions deduction). Taken together, they reduced the personal tax base by an estimated $1.3 trillion in 1993, or about 50 percent of the actual base. If these provisions were all eliminated, tax rates could be reduced across the board, or the same amount of revenue could be raised with a flat rate of 13.5 percent. The deductions require higher rates to raise a given amount of revenue, which increases the distortions and inefficiencies of the tax system, since distortions rise with the tax rate. They also complicate compliance and enforcement, because higher rates boost the gains from tax avoidance.

These provisions also have other effects. For example, the current system's deductibility of mortgage interest and property taxes encourages people to invest in owner-occupied housing, thereby increasing demand and raising house prices. Removing this tax advantage would lower the price of owner-occupied housing relative to prices of other assets. Capitalization of tax advantages into asset values means that their repeal may redistribute income or wealth in unacceptable ways, thus hindering the removal of even ill-considered provisions.

Tax Rates

Tax rates raise two important issues. First, the higher the tax rate, the greater the effect of a deduction or exclusion on economic behavior and the greater the disincentive effects of the tax system. A deduction that would matter little if the tax rate were 10 percent becomes powerful when the rate is 40 percent. Second, tax rates influence the distribution of tax burdens across families with different incomes. The current personal income tax has six rates—0, 15, 28, 31, 36, and 39.6 percent—which are imposed at successively higher taxable incomes. For certain high-income filers, the top two rates may be increased by nearly 2 percentage points by provisions of the tax code that gradually "phase out" personal exemptions and certain itemized deductions.

Multiple rates in personal taxes are the primary means used to achieve a desired distribution of tax burdens among individuals and families. Exempting those with little income or consumption also simplifies administration and compliance, by excusing families with few resources and little potential tax liability from the need to file returns or maintain records. Multiple rates help generate progressivity but raise compliance and administrative costs. Contrary to popular lore, the computational burden posed by multiple rates is trivial. Most people look up their income tax liability from a tax table. The major problem with multiple rates is that they foster transactional complexity. Multiple rates make it profitable to split capital transactions into separate components. Allocating deductions to high-rate taxpayers and income to low-rate taxpayers can reduce or defer taxes, sometimes dramatically. In the extreme case, reductions in tax from deductions can exceed the tax levied on income flows, turning the tax system into a subsidy system.

Dilemmas of Tax Reform

A tax reform that raises the same amount of revenue in a new way will inevitably redistribute tax burdens among taxpayers.[7] It is also likely to change asset values. Those who stand to lose often seek to modify the reform or to secure "transition relief" in order to avoid or delay the full brunt of the new law. Although such changes may

7. Some advocates of a consumption tax link their proposals to large tax cuts, perhaps to reduce the number of losers from tax reform and the size of their losses, but also to promote a general contraction of government. These plans link two distinct initiatives—structural tax reform and tax reductions. Although it may be politically attractive to link these two initiatives, the issues raised by structural tax reform can be understood best by examining them without the confounding effects of quite separate initiatives.

make the reform more palatable, they can also undermine the desired improvements in simplicity, equity, or increased economic growth. The critical question is whether proposals for fundamental reform can withstand pressures to restore deductions or to introduce transition relief that would change the fundamental character of the reform. Although the following examination of these dilemmas is framed with reference to the Armey-Shelby flat tax, similar problems would arise if the corporation and personal income taxes were replaced with a value-added, retail sales, or USA-type tax.

Transition

A switch to a consumption tax from an income tax creates a major transition problem that appears under different guises with the various reform plans. It involves the treatment of existing assets. Under the flat tax, the problem shows up at the business level.[8] Businesses may now deduct depreciation—the loss of value of capital assets over their useful lives—when computing taxable business income. The flat tax would permit businesses to "expense" new investments, deducting the full value of the asset in the year the asset is purchased. The practical problem involves deciding how to treat existing assets that have not been fully depreciated when the new tax takes effect. Companies with such "old" capital will have to compete with companies equipped with "new" capital purchased after the consumption tax takes effect. Those that lost depreciation deductions will argue that they have been put at an unfair competitive disadvantage relative to businesses that can expense new investments.

The stakes are high. In 1993 corporations claimed $363 billion in depreciation deductions. For unincorporated businesses, depreciation was about one-third as large. In addition, many businesses now have net operating losses that they can carry forward to offset any future profits they may earn. The status of existing depreciation deductions and loss carryforwards under a new tax system remains an open

---

8. The problem also shows up at the business level under the value-added tax. Under the retail sales tax and the personal component of the USA tax, the problem shows up at the household level. Households with assets accumulated from previously taxed income can consume those assets without further tax under the personal income tax. Under the consumption taxes, additional tax would be due on this consumption. The USA tax contains a provision explicitly exempting $50,000 in consumption financed from assets in existence when the new tax takes effect. Additional consumption from preexisting assets would be taxed. There is no obvious way to provide such transition relief under the retail sales tax.

TABLE 7-2. Required Tax Rates under Alternative Versions of the Flat Tax

Alternative	If only one adjustment is made	If all adjustments up to this are made
Armey-Shelby flat tax (no adjustments)[a]	20.8	20.8
Allow transition relief[b]	23.1	23.1
Retain mortgage interest deduction[b]	21.8	24.4
Retain health insurance deduction (businesses)[c]	22.3	26.5
Retain charitable contribution deduction (households)[b]	21.1	27.0
Retain earned income tax credit[d]	21.1	27.5
Retain state and local income and property tax deductions[b]	21.6	29.0
Retain payroll tax deduction (businesses)[b]	22.3	31.9
Add payroll tax deduction for workers[b]	21.9	34.0

a. Based on U.S. Department of Treasury (1996).
b. Authors' calculations, as described in Gale (1996).
c. Authors' calculations, based on approximately $250 billion of employer health insurance payments in 1996.
d. Authors' calculations, based on estimated program cost of $10 billion in reduced revenue plus $10 billion in government expenditures in 1996.

question. If Congress allowed companies to continue to take deductions for undepreciated existing assets and unused loss carryovers after tax reform takes effect, the flat tax rate would have to be increased 2 to 3 percentage points to maintain revenue neutrality (see table 7-2).[9]

Housing

Under current tax law, owner-occupied housing enjoys major advantages over other investments. Homeowners may deduct mortgage interest and property taxes, but they are not required to report the imputed rental income they receive as owners. These provisions increase demand for and the price of owner-occupied housing, as well as the land on which it sits, relative to the price of other assets. The flat tax would treat owner-occupied housing the same as other assets, thereby reducing the price of housing relative to other assets. A recent

9. Gale (1996). For a similar estimate, see Auerbach (1996).

analysis, based on 1990 data, estimates that the average price of owner-occupied housing nationwide would fall by an average of 29 percent if the flat tax replaced the income tax and interest rates did not change.[10] The drop in price would vary, depending on average state and local personal income tax and property tax rates. Across the sixty-three metropolitan areas examined in the study, the average price reductions ranged from 19 to 52 percent. These effects would be reduced if, as some of its advocates predict, the flat tax causes a large fall in interest rates. For example, if interest rates fell by 2 percentage points, the average decline in housing prices would be 9 percent rather than 29 percent. However, not all analysts agree that enactment of the flat tax would lower interest rates. Some think that interest rates might rise because investment demand would increase. Others note that U.S. interest rates are constrained by interest rates abroad, which U.S. tax reform would not directly affect.

Even a price decline of 10 to 15 percent, as other studies have predicted, would cause large losses that substantially reduce family net worth. Housing equity is most families' largest single asset, accounting for over one-quarter of household wealth. Housing wealth is often of crucial importance in retirement. Sharp declines in housing prices would also increase mortgage defaults and could jeopardize the financial viability of some lending institutions. In light of these possibilities, public pressure to retain the tax advantages of owner-occupied housing would be powerful. But retaining the mortgage interest deduction within the flat tax would create two major problems. First, the flat tax rate would have to be increased by 1.3 percentage points to replace revenue lost by adding the mortgage interest deduction (see table 7-2).[11] Second, not taxing interest income while allowing deductions for interest payments would encourage precisely the type of tax-induced, debt-financed investment activity that a well-designed tax reform should discourage rather than encourage.

10. Capozza, Green, and Hendershott (1996). If interest rates fall 1 percentage point, prices will fall 19 percentage points. For roughly similar estimates of the effect of the flat tax on housing prices, see Brinner, Lasky, and Wyss (1995). For much lower estimates, see Holtz-Eakin (1996); Sullivan (1996); or Foster (1996).

11. This estimate is based on the assumed provision of transition relief. If continuation of the mortgage interest deduction is the only deviation from the Armey-Shelby proposal, the tax rate increase is 1 percentage point (table 7-2).

Employer-Financed Health Insurance

Current tax law encourages employers to provide health insurance to their employees. If employees (other than the self-employed) buy their own insurance, they must first pay income and payroll taxes on the earnings they use to pay insurance premiums. If employers buy the insurance, this element of compensation, unlike cash wages, is exempt from personal income and payroll taxes. Under the flat tax, employers may deduct cash wages and pension contributions in computing company income, and families must pay tax on cash wages and pension benefits. The cost of fringe benefits—other than pension contributions—is not deductible at the company level. Thus health insurance, which is currently deductible at the business level, would become taxable at the flat tax rate.

A recent study has calculated that this tax change would boost the price of health insurance by an average of 21 percent.[12] A price increase of this size would lead to a reduction in both the number of people covered by employer-sponsored insurance and the amount of insurance offered to those who remain insured. Available evidence does not permit firm judgments on the relative sizes of these two responses, but the previously mentioned study estimates that the number of uninsured, currently 40 million, would increase by as many as 5.5 million to 14.3 million persons (by 14 to 36 percent) if employer expenditures on health insurance were no longer tax deductible.

There are several ways to deal with this problem. The exclusion of health insurance could be retained but capped at a level high enough to purchase a basic health insurance plan. This approach suffers from some serious administrative and equity problems. In setting the cap on the cost of a "basic" health plan, Congress would be forced to define the benefits such a plan should provide, something that it has been reluctant to do in the past. Whatever the definition, the cost of such a plan would vary by region and by such worker characteristics as age, gender, disability status, and (for family benefits) marital status and family size, and Congress would have to adjust the cap periodically as the price of health care and the menu of health care services changed.

---

12. Gruber and Poterba (1996). The price increase under the retail sales tax and the value-added tax is the same. The USA tax would push up the price of health insurance by about 38 percent, since it would end the tax advantage of exclusion from the payroll tax as well as the exclusion from income tax.

Any equitable set of caps would be very complex. These difficulties might cause Congress to retain the exclusion of all company-financed health insurance from tax at the company level. Retaining the exclusion would buy administrative simplicity and avoid the loss of health insurance coverage, but at a price: the flat tax rate would have to be increased another 2.1 percentage points (see table 7-2).[13]

Charitable Contributions

The Armey-Shelby flat tax would terminate the charitable contributions deduction currently allowed under the individual and corporation income taxes and would repeal the estate and gift tax. These provisions promote giving because they reduce the amount of consumption or bequests that donors must forgo when they make a contribution. A recent study estimated that the Armey-Shelby flat tax would reduce individuals' charitable gifts by 10 to 22 percent and charitable bequests by 24 to 45 percent.[14] The ranges reflect uncertainty about the sensitivity of giving to the current deduction.

Even the lower estimates, which imply that donors are relatively insensitive to tax effects, would fuel intense concern among the public and members of Congress that tax reform would cripple charitable organizations and would doubtlessly lead to a parade of highly sympathetic witnesses before congressional committees, pleading for retention of the charitable contributions deduction. Such pressures would be particularly hard to resist for two reasons. First, retaining this deduction does no violence to the underlying principles of the flat tax. Indeed, the flat tax proposal of Senator Arlen Specter allows a limited deduction for charitable contributions. Second, removing the deduction seems particularly hard to rationalize at a time when reductions in government spending on behalf of low-income people and other beneficiaries of charitable contributions are being justified on the grounds that private philanthropy should pick up the slack. If Congress decided to retain the deduction, along with the other adjustments described above, it would have to raise the flat tax rate by 0.5 percentage points to make up the lost revenue (see table 7-2).

13. This estimate assumes that the plan provides transition relief and retains the mortgage interest deduction. If exclusion of employer-financed health insurance were the only deviation from the Armey-Shelby plan, the increase would be 1.5 percentage points.

14. Clotfelter and Schmalbeck (1996).

Distribution of Income

Tax reform proposals are being debated against a backdrop of increasing inequality of before- and after-tax incomes.[15] Over the past two decades, incomes of those at the top of the income pyramid have risen while incomes of those at the bottom have fallen. Although tax policy has not been a major cause of these changes, it does not follow that the nation should adopt tax policies that reinforce these changes. But replacing the existing progressive income tax with a flat tax system would do just that. It would reduce taxes for high-income families and raise them for low-income families. The exempt earnings range under the flat tax attenuates this effect.[16] In addition, the flat tax would repeal the EITC, which in 1996 provided a subsidy of 40 percent on earnings up to $8,890, a maximum credit of $3,556, for a family with two or more children. The subsidy was reduced by 21.06 percent of income above $11,610. Families whose income tax is less than their earned income tax credit would lose this subsidy under the flat tax.

A recent study estimated that replacing the personal and corporation income taxes with the Armey-Shelby flat tax would redistribute tax burdens as shown in figure 7-1. In general, low-income households would lose from the swap, very high-income households would gain, and moderate-income households would experience little change in tax liability. Even within income groups that would experience little average change in tax burden, there would be considerable redistribution among families. Those with significant itemized deductions would see their tax burdens rise. Retaining the EITC reduces the burden on low-income families but necessitates an increase in the flat tax rate of 0.5 percentage points, if the previous adjustments are made (see table 7-2). A VAT or retail sales tax would result in an even more pronounced redistribution of the tax burden.

Paying Taxes on Taxes

Currently businesses receive deductions for state and local income, property, and payroll tax payments. Families that itemize can deduct

---

15. Weinberg (1996).

16. The current income tax imposes no net tax on tax units of a single person, a couple filing a joint return, and a couple with two children filing a joint return with earnings of $7,546, $11,800, and $23,672 or less, respectively. The corresponding tax entry points under the flat tax would be $10,700, $21,400, and $31,400, respectively.

FIGURE 7-1. Average Effective Tax Rates under Current Law and the Flat Tax[a]

Percent

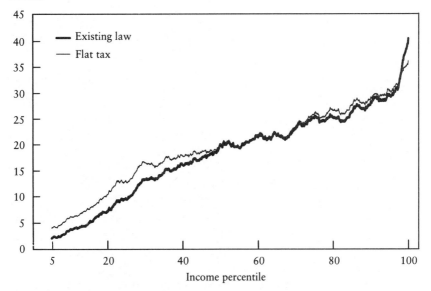

Income percentile

SOURCE: Gale, Houser, and Scholz (1996).
   a. Includes the effects of the personal and corporate income taxes, payroll taxes, and state income taxes.

state and local income and property taxes. The Armey-Shelby flat tax would eliminate all of these deductions. However, there is broad support, even among flat tax advocates, for the notion that people should not have to pay taxes on other taxes they have already paid.[17] Whether this view is justified depends on whether taxes serve as prices citizens pay for public services or for other benefits they receive directly. In the cases of local taxes for schools or garbage collection and national payroll taxes to finance pensions (for retirees, survivors, and the disabled) and health benefits, the taxes paid bear some resemblance to prices paid for ordinary goods and services, which are not deductible. The case for deductibility grows stronger if benefits are taxed.[18]

If the deductions for state and local income taxes were retained in

   17. National Commission on Economic Growth and Tax Reform (1996).
   18. Unemployment compensation is subject to income tax when received. Medicare benefits are not. A portion of social security benefits are for recipients with incomes above certain thresholds.

the Armey-Shelby flat tax, the tax rate needed to generate the same revenues as the current system's would have to be raised by 1.5 percentage points, given the other adjustments. Retaining the business payroll tax deduction would require an additional 2.9 percentage point increase. Adding a payroll tax deduction for workers, as advocated by the Kemp commission on tax policy and economic growth, would require an additional 2.7 percentage point increase.

No Free Lunch

By now, the pattern should be clear. The flat tax is a simple tax with a relatively low 21 percent rate in large part because it ends deductions and exclusions that retain widespread popular support and that no Congress has yet dared touch. The removal of these provisions would produce important effects that the majority of Americans are thought to deplore. But, as more deductions and exclusions are reinstated or retained, the required tax rate rises, and the increased rates would reduce, and perhaps eliminate, the much hoped-for economic gains. The objective of a simpler tax system would also be sacrificed.

It seems likely that Congress and the American public will continue to worry about tax burdens on the poor, the strength of charitable organizations, the viability of home ownership and mortgage institutions, the continuation of health insurance coverage, and the relative losses of businesses with unused depreciation deductions. If Congress retains the EITC, deductions for charitable contributions and mortgage interest, and the exclusion of employer-financed health insurance and offers transition relief to businesses, the flat tax rate necessary to sustain revenue rises to 27.5 percent (see table 7-2). Retaining deductions for state and local income taxes and payroll taxes would raise the rates even further. Other combinations can be seen by adding the required changes in tax rates reported in table 7-2. As the tax rate rises, the appeal of the flat tax declines, since 79 percent of families now pay marginal tax rates of 15 percent or less and only 3 percent pay rates above 28 percent.

Similar dilemmas are raised by the retail sales and value-added taxes. They too would end the tax-advantaged status of state and local taxes, charitable contributions, mortgage interest, and employer-financed health insurance. Under the value-added tax, businesses with unused depreciation would find themselves at a disadvantage relative to firms with newly acquired assets. Under the retail sales tax, the transition issues would be found in the household sector. In both cases, tax burdens would be shifted in a regressive direction. Mechanisms could be devised to moderate these effects, but they would be difficult to administer and would lead to higher basic tax rates. None of these considerations necessarily means that fundamental tax reform is undesirable, but they do mean that it poses some exceedingly wrenching choices that deserve explicit scrutiny and debate.

What Can Tax Reform Do for Economic Growth?

If tax reform boosts growth dramatically, then the difficulties, dislocations, and inequities that would accompany a fundamental change in the tax system would be worth bearing and could be handled fairly easily. Unfortunately, no one knows exactly how fundamental tax reform will affect economic growth. The proposed experiment—replacing personal and corporation income taxes with a consumption tax—has never been tried anywhere, and it would entail a much larger change than any previous modification of the tax system.

Estimates of how much tax reform will increase economic growth depend critically on the "purity" of the reform proposal and on how the current economy and tax system are characterized. As was noted previously, the current tax system is an exceedingly complex hybrid, not a pure income tax. The current system treats capital income and saving in widely varying ways. The effective tax on capital income depends on the type of asset, the owner, how the asset is financed, and whether the alternative minimum tax applies to the income.[19] Some income from capital, such as that from housing, is much more lightly taxed than income from other assets. Most current saving— qualified pensions, 401(k)s, IRAs, and life insurance—now receives tax treatment similar to what it would face under a consumption tax.[20] Moving to a consumption tax would not reduce the tax burden on such saving and could actually reduce the return if interest rates fell. For these and other reasons, characterizing the current system as a pure income tax is wrong. This fact is central to any appraisal of the effects of fundamental tax reform on economic growth.

19. Auerbach (1996).
20. Engen and Gale (1996).

TABLE 7-3. Effects of Fundamental Tax Reform on Economic Growth
Percent

Tax plan	Tax rate	Estimated change in output per person[a]		
		2 years	10 years	Long term
Comprehensive consumption tax with no personal exemptions, no transition relief, and no deductions	12	4.5	6.0	8.9
Comprehensive consumption tax with personal exemptions (Armey flat tax)	20.5	1.0	2.3	5.3
Comprehensive consumption tax with personal exemptions and transitional relief	23.5	−0.6	0.3	2.5

SOURCE: Auerbach (1996).

a. Results assume the presence of adjustment costs in changing investment.

Table 7-3 contains recent estimates of the likely effects on economic growth of replacing the existing corporation and personal income taxes with a consumption tax. A "pure" consumption tax, levied at a revenue-neutral 12 percent rate on all consumption with no personal exemptions or deductions or exclusions, is estimated to raise output per person by about 6 percent after ten years (table 7-3, row 1).[21] Most of this sizable increase would occur in the first two years. If personal exemptions similar to those in the Armey-Shelby flat tax are incorporated in the new consumption tax, the tax rate necessary to sustain revenue rises to 20.5 percent and the effect on growth after ten years falls to 2.3 percent.

Allowing businesses transition relief would necessitate an additional increase in the tax rate. Output would *fall* in the first few years after reform and would be only 0.3 percent higher than under the current system after ten years. These simulations make no allowance for the popular deductions described above. Adding them into the reform plan would raise rates several additional percentage points. Given the meager effect of a 23.5 percent flat tax on growth, a flat tax with deductions and a rate well above 23.5 percent might well *reduce* growth.

As can be seen from this exercise, there is no single answer to the question: "What is the effect of tax reform on growth?" What is clear, however, is that politically realistic fundamental reform analyzed in realistic economic settings may produce little if any added economic growth.

Conclusion

Much as Congress and the American public may yearn to dump the current tax system, the difficult trade-offs in the flat tax and the other types of consumption taxes may make fundamental tax reform look less attractive up close than from a distance. If this is the case, attention could turn to modifying the current income tax rather than replacing it. Certainly at a minimum, this would be a useful interim step while the details and trade-offs involved in realistic fundamental tax reform proposals are analyzed and debated more fully. Useful modifications of the income tax could proceed along the same general

21. This estimate takes account of adjustment costs associated with installing new capital at the business level. Under the assumption that adjustments can be made costlessly, the estimated increase in output after ten years is 9 percent.

lines as proposed in most tax reforms: broaden the base and reduce rates to lessen sheltering activity, make the system simpler, and provide better overall incentives for work and investment. These adjustments could yield small gains in economic growth and perhaps greater simplicity for some taxpayers. But they would avoid the wrenching upheavals and windfall redistributions that might accompany more radical change.

Most of the discussion in this chapter has focused on the flat tax because it is the most well formulated and developed fundamental reform proposal. The other major options for tax reform raise even more formidable difficulties. No tax jurisdiction has ever administered a retail sales tax at rates approximating those that would be necessary if this tax is to replace the personal and corporation income taxes. No tax authority has ever successfully monitored wealth in the detail that would be required during the transition to the USA tax.

The value-added tax is a well-established revenue instrument of almost all developed nations and a growing number of developing nations, but all have used the value-added tax to supplement the personal and corporation income taxes—not to replace them. They have, therefore, been able to use their income tax systems (as well as extensive spending on social services and cash transfers) to achieve distributional equity. When the claims of tax reform advocates have been subjected to the scrutiny that serious consideration of a live legislative proposal inevitably evokes, Congress and the American public may well conclude that the personal and corporation income taxes, reviled and despised as they are, should be remodeled and reformed rather than replaced.

Perhaps because of these considerations, some supporters of fundamental tax reform link their proposals to large tax cuts. If taxes are reduced, reform produces more direct gainers and fewer direct losers. But tax cuts create problems of their own. They require cuts in public spending to achieve any target for deficit reduction beyond those considered desirable on other grounds; otherwise they increase the budget deficit. Reducing government spending would certainly sweeten the pot for tax reform. But cutting spending raises issues that transcend tax reform and that should be considered on their own. Rather than repeat the experience of the early 1980s, when taxes were cut far more than spending and the consequences were a large and long-term budget deficit, it would be prudent to determine spending first this time around.

References

Auerbach, Alan. 1996. "Tax Reform, Capital Allocation, Efficiency, and Growth." In *Economic Effects of Fundamental Tax Reform*, edited by Henry J. Aaron and William G. Gale, 29–82. Brookings.

Brinner, Roger E., Mark Lasky, and David Wyss. 1995. "Residential Real Estate Impacts of Flat Tax Legislation." Lexington, Mass.: DRI/McGraw-Hill (May).

Capozza, Dennis R., Richard K. Green, and Patric H. Hendershott. 1996. "Taxes, Mortgage Borrowing, and Residential Land Prices." In *Economic Effects of Fundamental Tax Reform*, edited by Henry J. Aaron and William G. Gale, 171–210. Brookings.

Clotfelter, Charles T., and Richard L. Schmalbeck. 1996. "The Impact of Fundamental Tax Reform on Nonprofit Organizations." In *Economic Effects of Fundamental Tax Reform*, edited by Henry J. Aaron and William G. Gale, 211–46. Brookings.

Engen, Eric M., and William G. Gale. 1996. "The Effects of Fundamental Tax Reform on Saving." In *Economic Effects of Fundamental Tax Reform*, edited by Henry J. Aaron and William G. Gale, 83–121. Brookings.

Foster, J. D. 1996. "The Flat Tax and Housing Values." Background Paper 15. Washington: Tax Foundation (May).

Gale, William G. 1996. "The Kemp Commission and the Future of Tax Reform." *Tax Notes*, February 5, 717–29.

Gale, William G., Scott Houser, and John Karl Scholz. 1996. "Distributional Effects of Fundamental Tax Reform." In *Economic Effects of Fundamental Tax Reform*, edited by Henry J. Aaron and William G. Gale, 281–320. Brookings.

Ginsburg, Martin D. 1995. "Life under a Personal Consumption Tax: Some Thoughts on Working, Saving, and Consuming in Nunn-Domenici's Tax World." *National Tax Journal* 48 (December): 585–602.

Gruber, Jonathan, and James Poterba. 1996. "Fundamental Tax Reform and Employer-Provided Health Insurance." In *Economic Effects of Fundamental Tax Reform*, edited by Henry J. Aaron and William G. Gale, 125–70. Brookings.

Holtz-Eakin, Douglas. 1996. "Comment." In *Economic Effects of Fundamental Tax Reform*, edited by Henry J. Aaron and William G. Gale, 198–208. Brookings.

National Commission on Economic Growth and Tax Reform. 1996. *Unleashing America's Potential: A Pro-Growth, Pro-Family Tax System for the 21st Century*. Washington.

Slemrod, Joel. 1996. "Which Is the Simplest Tax System of Them All?" In *Economic Effects of Fundamental Tax Reform*, edited by Henry J. Aaron and William G. Gale, 355–91. Brookings.

Sullivan, Martin A. 1996. "Housing and the Flat Tax: Visible Pain, Subtle Benefits." *Tax Notes*, January 22, 340–45.

Tanzi, Vito. 1995. *Taxation in an Integrating World*. Brookings.

U.S. Department of Treasury. Office of Tax Analysis. 1996. "New Armey-Shelby
Flat Tax Would Still Lose Money, Treasury Finds." *Tax Notes*, January 22,
451–61.

Weinberg, Daniel H. 1996. "A Brief Look at Postwar U.S. Income Inequality."
U.S. Census Bureau, *Current Population Reports*, P60-191 (June).

8

HENRY J. AARON &
BARRY P. BOSWORTH

Preparing for the
Baby Boomers' Retirement

LONG-TERM BUDGET CHALLENGES dwarf those raised by the current effort to balance the budget by 2002. The United States is in the early stages of a debate about how to modify public expenditures and taxes to deal with this situation. Most of the long-term budget problem arises from anticipated rapid growth in spending on the elderly. To date, much of the discussion of how to deal with this issue has been divisive. It has been cast as an argument over who should pay: should future retirees bear the burden through reduced benefits and lower standards of living, or should the workers of the next century pay through higher taxes? This bleak trade-off is not inevitable. If the nation plans ahead, it is possible to prepare for the greater future costs of retirement by increasing private or public saving today. Funding a portion of future retirement costs with added saving would expand the resource base, converting what is now a zero-sum game between the working-age population and retirees into a positive-sum game that both groups can win.

The Outlook

The Congressional Budget Office (CBO) has projected that, if policy is unchanged, federal spending on programs will rise from 19.5 percent of GDP in 1995 to 24 percent in 2025 and 28.1 percent in 2050 (see table 8-1). In contrast, revenues are projected to remain at a fairly constant share of GDP—about 20 percent—if tax rates are not changed. Growing budget deficits, fed both by the added program outlays and by rapidly increasing interest on the mounting federal debt, will result. By 2025 the deficit could reach 9.5 percent of GDP, a level likely to exceed private saving. These projected paths of spending and revenues are un-

263

TABLE 8-1. Projected Federal Budget Outlays and Revenues, Selected Years, 1960–2050
Percent of GDP

Outlay or revenue source	1960	1980	1995	2010	2025	2050
Program						
Social security (OASDI)	2.2	4.3	4.5	4.7	5.8	6.9
Medicare	0.0	1.3	2.5	4.4	6.0	8.4
Medicaid	0.0	0.5	1.3	2.4	2.9	3.8
Consumption programs	9.7	7.7	6.3	5.0	5.0	5.0
Other programs	3.8	6.6	4.9	4.3	4.3	4.0
Total program outlays	15.7	20.5	19.5	20.8	24.0	28.1
Interest	1.3	1.9	3.2	3.4	5.3	15.8
Total outlays	17.0	22.4	22.6	24.2	29.3	43.9
Receipts	18.4	20.2	20.4	19.7	19.8	20.4
Budget balance	1.4	−2.2	−2.2	−4.5	−9.5	−23.5

SOURCES: U.S. Commerce Department, National Income and Product Accounts; and Congressional Budget Office, unpublished data, May 1996.

sustainable because, with no net investment, the economy would begin to shrink and living standards would start to fall.

The long-term budget outlook is driven by two circumstances. First, the proportion of the U.S. population that is elderly will increase dramatically in the second and third decades of the next century. As the population mix shifts in this way, the share of national income flowing through the budget increases automatically because the federal budget has become a principal source of income support and medical care for elderly people. A second and less noted but more important force driving up projected federal spending is the expected continuation of the rapid increase in the per person cost of medical services, about one-third of which are now financed through the federal budget.[1]

Budget Projections

The current budget situation—in which, without explicit policy changes, spending on government programs grows faster than GDP and revenues grow at about the same rate as GDP—is a relatively new one. Until the 1980s, federal policymakers were confronted with a quite different and much less vexing problem. In the "good old days," federal expenditures were more controllable because most of

1. Levit and others (1996, p. 234).

them were for discretionary programs whose outlays were governed by Congress's annual appropriations decisions. On the other side of the balance sheet, revenues grew faster than GDP because the personal income tax was progressive and was not indexed—that is, it was not automatically adjusted for increases in the cost of living. Inflation and economic growth steadily pushed families into higher tax brackets and eroded the value of personal exemptions and the standard deduction. With spending growing less rapidly and revenues growing more rapidly than the economy, Congress was faced with the relatively pleasant task, now difficult to imagine, of passing periodic tax cuts and program expansions.

What changed? Three developments created the current, more troubling situation. First, starting in the mid-1970s, economic growth slowed to about half of its pre-1973 rate. Second, a large tax cut, enacted in 1981, cut rates and indexed the personal income tax starting in 1985. The combination of reduced growth, lower tax rates, and the elimination of inflation-related revenue increases drastically slowed revenue growth to roughly 2½ percent a year after adjustment for inflation—roughly the same as the growth rate of the economy. Large deficits ensued because the tax cuts were not matched by commensurate cuts in public spending and the economy suffered the deepest recession of the postwar period. These deficits increased both the national debt and interest rates. Interest payments, which amounted to 1.5 percent or less of GDP before 1975, expanded to 3 percent or more after the mid-1980s.

Third, programs for which outlays are driven by demographic and economic forces, rather than by Congress's annual spending decisions, came to represent an increasing share of total federal spending. Programs enacted in the decade between 1962 and 1972 included medicare, medicaid, guaranteed student loans, food stamps, title XX social services, and supplemental security income. Congress explicitly indexed initial social security benefits in 1972 to the growth of average earnings and subsequent benefits to increases in the cost of living.[2] The costs of medicare and medicaid grew, in part because the number of people eligible for benefits rose, but mostly because the growth of the per person cost of medical services continued to exceed growth of per capita national income. Meanwhile, defense spending fell as a

2. In this chapter the term *social security* refers to the old-age, survivors, and disability insurance programs (OASDI).

share of national output from 9.4 percent, the Vietnam War peak, to 3.6 percent in 1996.

Before the 1980s, congressional stalemate resulted in a *reduced* budget deficit, and consensus was required to expand it. The situation is now reversed: stalemate leads to an *increased* deficit, and consensus is required to reduce it.

The worst is yet to come. As shown in table 8-1, the budget situation is projected to get worse. GDP growth is expected to decline because the growth of the labor force will slow. The CBO projects that annual real GDP growth will average only 1.7 percent between 1996 and 2025. Under the indexed tax system, revenues will rise at about the same rate as GDP.[3] However, program outlays, driven by increased costs of an aging population, are projected to grow faster than GDP, particularly during the second and third decades of the next century.

The major source of rising program outlays is the projected increase in health care spending through the medicare and medicaid programs. As a percentage of GDP, spending on these two programs is expected to more than double, claiming an additional 5.1 percent of GDP over the next three decades. Even these harsh projections of health care costs may prove to be optimistic; they assume that the annual inflation-adjusted growth of federal medical care payments per beneficiary will slow from the 5 percent average rate experienced over the past two decades to about 1 percent after 2020.[4] Contrary to popular impression, social security spending is not expected to grow much faster than GDP through 2015, and in the following decade it is projected to claim only an additional 1 percent of GDP. One reason for this modest growth is because a cut, enacted in 1983, will gradually reduce benefits starting in 2000.

Long-term projections like these are inherently uncertain. Small errors in assumed growth rates compound into large misestimates

3. Despite indexation, revenues from the personal income tax still tend to grow more rapidly than income because growth of per capita income tends to push people into higher brackets. Payroll and excise taxes, however, tend to grow a bit slower than income. The actual projections reflect the effects of expiration of temporary taxes and of other provisions that produce temporary fluctuations in revenues.

4. On the expenditure side, CBO relies on the estimates of the Social Security Administration actuaries for old age, survivors, and disability insurance (OASDI) and the Health Care Financing Administration actuaries for medicare; CBO has developed its own projections for medicaid. The OASDI and medicare projections are updated each year and published as part of the annual reports of the board of trustees of the respective trust funds.

after a decade or two. The uncertainty inherent in the various components of the projections differs. Population projections are among the more certain elements. Except for immigration and emigration, all of those who will be the elderly in the United States in 2025 are alive and resident in the country today. Mortality rates for this group may be higher or lower than those assumed in the projections, but the plausible range leaves little uncertainty about the size of the elderly population three decades hence. Future fertility rates, which are assumed to change little from recent rates, are a bit less certain. Even if the fertility assumptions turn out to be wrong, however, there would be little effect on the size of the labor force over the next three decades because most of those born after 1996 will still be in school in 2025.

Economic projections are more uncertain. For reasons that remain obscure and poorly understood, productivity growth slowed sharply in the mid-1970s. While the projections assume a continuation of recent trends, an unexpected reversal of this slowdown or a new slowdown could occur.

Probably the least predictable element in the projections is the one that is most responsible for expected spending increases: per capita health care costs. Health outlays depend sensitively on emerging medical technologies and on policies that govern the way providers are paid for their services. Both are undergoing revolutionary changes today. Any confidence we have in our ability to project future health care costs should be tempered by the unpredicted sharp decline that has occurred in the growth of private health care spending since 1993.

Despite the uncertainty, there is little question that the budget situation will worsen substantially if policies are not changed. Demographic factors, which are not subject to much doubt, imply roughly a 65 percent increase in federal outlays on the elderly and disabled by 2025. Furthermore, the budget projections presented in table 8-1 are probably optimistic in assuming that the growth in medical care cost per beneficiary, which is responsible for about half of the projected increase in costs, will slow dramatically.

Aging

Aging is a significant factor in the growth of spending on pensions and medical care. The U.S. population is aging because birthrates declined beginning in the early 1960s and because longevity has been increasing for decades. Entry into the work force of children born when birthrates were high and increases in the proportion of women who work outside the home have delayed the effects of these trends on the U.S. economy and federal budget. The aging of the population will become very evident after 2008, however, when the oldest baby boomers reach the age at which they can receive social security benefits.

From the standpoint of the budget, the relevant demographic development is not just an acceleration in the growth of the population over age 65, but also the expected slowdown in growth of the work force. The number of elderly, which is projected to grow at an annual rate of only 1 percent between 1995 and 2010, will then accelerate to 2.9 percent over the next fifteen years. This growth is rapid but not unprecedented: between 1940 and 1965 the elderly population also expanded at a 2.9 percent rate. In contrast, the projected slowdown in the annual growth of the number of workers is truly exceptional. Over the past three decades the work force grew at an average annual rate of 2 percent, but it is projected to grow at only 0.2 percent a year between 2010 and 2025, despite assumed annual immigration of close to 1 million persons.[5] It is this sluggish growth in the labor force, not the surge in the number of retirees, that is primarily responsible for the widely discussed drop in the ratio of workers to social security beneficiaries from the 3.4 to 3.2 range that has prevailed over the past two decades to the projected level of 2.2 in 2025.

A less noted demographic trend is the growth in the proportion of the population that is very old—over 84—which rose from 0.6 percent in 1965 to 1.4 percent in 1995. It is projected to rise to 1.8 percent in 2010, remain fairly stable for the next fifteen years, and then double between 2025 and 2050. The size of this population is important because the cost of health care rises sharply with age (figure 8-1). Average health care spending for those over age 84 is about twice that for persons aged 65 to 74. Much of the increased spending by older people is for home health and nursing home care, which increases significantly with age, especially for the population over age 84.

---

5. Board of Trustees (1996). Under a variant of the social security projections, the U.S. labor force would actually begin to shrink by 2025.

FIGURE 8-1. Public and Private Medical Care Outlays, by Age, 1995

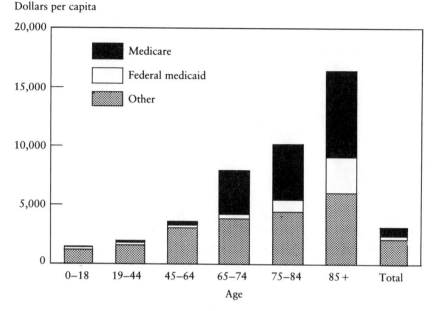

SOURCES: Authors' calculations.

Cost of Health Care

Similar demographic forces drive social security and medicare costs. Nonetheless, spending on medicare is projected to grow more than three times as fast as spending on social security, and the cost of medicaid is projected to grow about as fast as that of medicare. A single statistic illustrates the power of projected increases in health care costs on perceptions of the long-term deficit problem: if spending on medicare and medicaid grew no faster than the cost of social security, the gap between projected program outlays and revenues in 2025 would be less than half as large as the CBO has projected.[6] Rapid growth in the cost of health care *per person* accounts for most of the growth in medicare and medicaid spending.

Breakneck growth in medicare and medicaid and the cost of medical services in general is not a new phenomenon (table 8-2). The

6. This comparison takes account of the 13 percent reductions in social security benefits enacted in 1983 that will take place over the period from 2000 to 2020, when the age at which unreduced benefits can be obtained is raised from 65 to 67.

TABLE 8-2. Annual Growth in Personal Health Care Expenditure, Selected Periods, 1960–94

Percent

Period	Current dollars			Constant dollars[a]		
	Total	Medicare and medicaid	Other	Total	Medicare and medicaid	Other
1960–70	9.9	...	...	7.2	...	...
1970–80	12.2	16.0	11.1	5.4	9.2	4.3
1980–90	10.4	10.9	10.2	6.0	6.5	5.9
1990–94	7.6	11.7	5.6	4.7	8.8	2.7
1992–93	6.1	9.7	4.4	3.6	7.1	1.8
1993–94	5.6	9.6	3.5	3.3	7.3	1.2

SOURCE: Levit and others (1996).
a. Deflated using GDP chain weighted price index.

driving force behind rising health care spending has been the proliferation of new medical technology.[7] Private and public health insurance systems, long bereft of mechanisms to weigh benefits against costs and to promote efficient health care delivery, paid for almost everything that medical science offered. The flood of new medical technology shows no sign of abating, yet growth of aggregate health care spending has begun to slow. After adjustment for inflation, the growth of personal health care spending exclusive of medicare and medicaid slowed from an annual rate of 5.9 percent from 1980 through 1990 to only 2.7 percent in 1990–94. Through 1994, the slowdown occurred largely in private spending. Combined real spending on medicare and medicaid rose at an 8.8 percent annual rate in 1990–94. This discrepancy in growth rates is unprecedented. In 1995 and 1996 medicare spending growth slowed a bit, and in 1996 medicaid spending growth slowed to a crawl.

Whether the slowdown in health care spending will persist and whether it will show up more forcefully in public programs is uncertain. What is clear is that projections of the federal budget are heavily influenced by assumptions that rapid growth of per person health care spending will continue.

The Need to Act Soon

Programs that primarily serve the elderly and disabled—social security, medicare, and medicaid—have replaced national defense as

7. Newhouse (1993); Aaron (1991).

the dominant category of federal budget outlays. If maintained in their present form, these three programs, which accounted for just over two-fifths of federal program outlays in 1995, will claim a bit over half of those outlays by 2010. While social security will contribute little to the problem before 2010, after that, when the baby boom generation begins to retire, its spending will begin to grow rapidly. By 2025 these three programs will constitute over 60 percent of program outlays, or 14.7 percent of GDP.

The fact that so much of the projected increase in budget outlays is associated with retirees and the disabled underscores the need to determine promptly the nature of the changes that will be made in future federal pension and health care policies. If benefits are to be cut so that the elderly will have to pay directly for an increased portion of their own needs, they should be forewarned so that they can adjust their own saving while they are still young enough for it to make a difference.

The oldest of the baby boom generation celebrated their fiftieth birthdays in 1996. As this generation approaches retirement, it will be increasingly difficult to revise the government's benefit commitments. Not only will changes be viewed as inequitable if they are sprung on those who are already retired or just a few years from retirement, but substantial political opposition will mount as beneficiaries and those approaching retirement come to constitute a growing fraction of the voting population. Waiting will eliminate any chance of adopting policies, such as measures to boost national saving, that can actually lighten the future burden of meeting the needs of the elderly. Delay will force the nation into a wrenching and divisive debate over the allocation of a fixed amount of future resources between the young and the old. Delay will also bring another quite tangible cost. The CBO projections indicate that more of the long-run growth of federal outlays comes from increased interest costs—the result of continued deficits—than from increased program outlays.

The desirability of action and the will to act are quite different matters, however. Few elected officials want to talk publicly about measures to reduce social security, medicare, or medicaid benefits or to increase taxes to pay for these programs. Lawmakers have acted in the past, however. Social security has been subjected to major cutbacks three times in the past two decades. Payments to medicare providers have been curtailed repeatedly over the past fifteen years.

Unfortunately, these measures usually have been approved only at the last minute to ward off an impending crisis. They have not been future-oriented initiatives designed to augment the resource base from which retirement benefits could be supported. The remainder of this chapter is devoted to examining the options available to policymakers for dealing with social security, medicare, and medicaid in a more farsighted manner. The discussion focuses on social security because medicare and medicaid are examined in greater detail in chapters 3 and 6.

Social Security

The projected deficit in the social security system has attracted the greatest public attention, but it is only a modest part of the future budget problem and, in many ways, is the most manageable.

Program Structure

Social security covers over 95 percent of the labor force. The program provides benefits through two separate trust funds. Benefits for retirees and survivors come from the old-age and survivors insurance (OASI) trust fund. Benefits for the disabled come from the disability insurance (DI) trust fund. Although legally separate, they are usually considered together.

Revenues to the trust funds come from three principal sources. The most significant is a flat-rate payroll tax—currently 12.4 percent—split equally between employers and employees up to a covered wage ceiling equal to $62,700 in 1996. This tax raised $359 billion in 1995. Interest earnings on accumulated trust fund reserves generated $35 billion. Income taxes levied on a portion of the benefits received by retirees with relatively high incomes yielded an additional $6 billion.[8]

Benefits are related to past covered earnings. Relative to their contributions, those with lower earnings are rewarded more generously than those with high earnings.[9] Benefits can be obtained at age 62.

---

8. Board of Trustees (1996). Unlike other income tax revenues, which are deposited in the general fund, taxes on social security benefits are returned to the OASDI and medicare trust funds.

9. The benefit formula, which rewards low earners more generously than high earners, works as follows. At age 62, each worker's average indexed monthly earnings (AIME) is computed as the average of the thirty-five years of highest covered earnings through age

Those who claim benefits after age 62 receive larger benefits for any given earnings history. Age 65 is regarded as the "normal" retirement age. Those under age 70 who work after they have claimed benefits have their benefits reduced for every dollar they earn above certain thresholds.[10] Married couples can choose between a benefit equal to 150 percent of the higher earner's benefit or the sum of the benefits based on each spouse's past earnings.[11] Surviving spouses receive a benefit equal to the primary earner's benefit. Benefits are increased annually for changes in the consumer price index.

Cost Projections

Social security revenues currently exceed costs. The surplus in 1996 was $66 billion, and, according to the intermediate projections of the social security actuaries, it will rise to $114 billion by 2005. Past surpluses have accumulated in the trust funds as reserves, which amounted to $546 billion at the end of 1996. These reserves are projected to reach a maximum of about $2.9 trillion in 2018, after which the system will run annual deficits. The reserves are projected to be exhausted by 2029.[12]

The best single measure for analyzing social security's financial situation is the "cost rate," the ratio of total benefit payments to taxable wages. If social security were financed on a pay-as-you-go basis, the cost rate would equal the tax rate that would have to be levied on payrolls each year. The cost rate is projected to drift up

---

60. Each year's earnings are adjusted, or "indexed," to reflect changes in general wage levels. Earnings after age 60 can later be used to adjust the AIME, but without indexing. The second step is computation of the "primary insurance amount" (PIA), the basic benefit payable to a single worker who retires at the normal retirement age of 65. In 1996 the PIA equaled 90 percent of the first $437 of the AIME, plus 32 percent of the AIME between $437 and $2,635, plus 15 percent of the AIME above $2,635. The "bend points" in this formula and the ceiling wage are adjusted each year for increases in the average wage.

10. For people aged 62, 63, and 64, benefits are reduced $1 for every $2 of earnings above $8,280 in 1996. For those between 65 and 69, benefits are reduced $1 for every $3 of earnings above $12,500. To the extent that benefits are reduced in this fashion, subsequent benefits are increased. Benefits are paid, regardless of their earnings, to people age 70 or older. Legislation enacted in 1996 will increase the earnings limit for those 65 to 69 from $12,500 in 1996 to $30,000 in 2002.

11. Most industrial countries do not provide a spousal benefit. If it is included, average U.S. benefits are roughly as generous as those of other countries; but the single-earner benefit is substantially less.

12. Board of Trustees (1996).

FIGURE 8-2. Social Security Costs and Income, 1960–2070

Percent of taxable wages

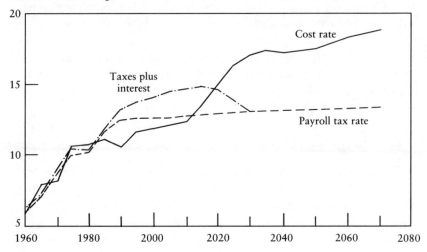

slowly between 1995 and 2010 and to rise sharply over the succeeding twenty years, as the baby boom population retires and the growth of the labor force continues to slow (figure 8-2).

The causes of social security's financial problem can be better understood by examining the trends in two ratios, the dependency rate and the benefit rate, the product of which makes up the cost rate:

$$\text{Cost rate} = \frac{\text{Number of beneficiaries}}{\text{Number of covered workers}} \times \frac{\text{Average benefit}}{\text{Average covered earnings}}$$

The dependency rate, the ratio of beneficiaries to covered workers, is driven principally by demographic factors—birthrates, immigration, and mortality—and the rules establishing the age and other conditions for benefit eligibility. Economic factors play some role through the labor force participation rate and retirement patterns. The benefit rate, the ratio of the average benefit to the average covered earnings, is determined largely by the legislated benefit formula and, to a lesser extent, by economic trends. If earnings growth accelerates, the benefit rate falls because benefits adjust to earnings only with a lag.[13]

13. The benefit rate and dependency rate interact in subtle ways. Beneficiaries include

FIGURE 8-3. Components of the Cost Rate, 1960–2070

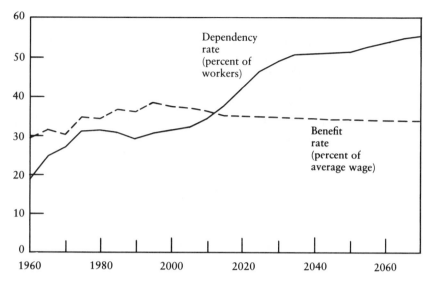

SOURCE: Board of Trustees (1996).

The 1996 report of the social security trustees projects sharp increases in the dependency rate—by 50 percent between 1995 and 2025 and another 20 percent by 2050 (figure 8-3). In contrast, the benefit rate is projected to fall about 8 percent by 2025, largely because of the scheduled increase in the normal retirement age to 67. Thus the cost rate will rise from 11.6 percent of taxable payroll in 1995 to 16.2 percent in 2025 and to 17.5 percent in 2050.

Over the seventy-five-year horizon used in social security actuarial projections, the cost rate exceeds revenues by an average of 2.2 percent of payroll, or 14 percent of benefits. In other words, a tax increase of 2.2 percent of payroll or a one-seventh cut in benefits would restore the system to actuarial balance over the next seventy-five years.[14] But as early surplus years passed into history and future deficit

---

dependents. Since the average dependent's benefit is less than the average benefit of the primary worker, the projected decline in the number of dependents raises the average benefit. This compositional shift offsets a portion of the drop in the benefit rate that results from the increase in the retirement age from 65 to 67 by 2020. The two-year delay in the retirement age is equivalent to a 13 percent reduction in the average benefit.

14. The actuarial balance is the present discounted value of the difference between future income and outgo. Over the past decade, the extension of the forecast horizon,

years entered the seventy-five-year projection calculation, the system again would begin to show long-run actuarial deficits. To maintain balance over successive seventy-five-year periods, either revenues would have to be increased or benefit payments would have to be cut by about 0.5 percentage point every ten years.

While the magnitude of these adjustments may appear to be daunting, they are not exceptional when viewed from a historical perspective. Measured as a share of GDP, instead of taxable wages, the cost of social security is projected to rise from 4.5 percent of GDP in 1995 to 5.8 percent in 2025—a 29 percent increase—and to 6.9 percent in 2050. Between 1960 and 1995, social security taxes increased from 2.1 percent of GDP to 5 percent. Furthermore, the total increase in the cost of social security over the next fifty-five years as a share of GDP is less than the decline in defense spending between 1989 and 1995.

Strategic Issues in Social Security Reform

Financial balance could be restored with modest and gradual benefit cuts or tax increases, or some combination of the two. Nevertheless, the debate that has begun on social security's future goes well beyond these options to raise fundamental questions about whether the social security system should be sustained, contracted, or replaced. Although the debate revolves around the details of specific proposals, at its core it concerns the answers to the following five interrelated sets of questions.

1. What average level of pensions should public policy assure?
2. Should this pension system provide higher benefits in relation to past earnings for low earners than for high earners? If so, through what mechanism should these extra benefits be provided?
3. Should the program provide defined benefits or stipulate defined contributions so that benefits depend on rates of return? In other words, how should the risk arising from economic and demographic uncertainty be distributed between workers and the retired and disabled?

revised economic assumptions, and refinement of projection technique have raised the projected deficit from 0.4 percent to 2.2 percent of payroll. The 2.2 percent of payroll tax increase required to achieve actuarial balance gives an exaggerated impression of the increased burden on future workers because the share of total compensation going into taxable wages is projected to fall and the share going to tax-exempt fringe benefit plans is projected to increase.

TABLE 8-3. Sources of Income for Aged Family Units, Selected Years, 1974–93[a]

Percent

Year	Earnings	OASDI	Asset income	Pensions and annuities	Other	Total[b]
1974	21.3	42.0	18.2	14.0	4.5	100.0
1984	13.3	40.5	28.2	15.0	2.9	100.0
1993	15.1	42.3	18.6	20.5	3.4	100.0
Quintile distribution, 1993						
1st	− 0.2	84.2	6.4	2.1	7.5	100.0
2d	1.8	80.5	7.9	3.3	6.5	100.0
3d	4.0	72.5	11.4	9.7	2.4	100.0
4th	8.7	49.9	15.0	23.0	3.3	100.0
5th	24.1	21.4	24.8	26.9	2.9	100.0

SOURCE: Employee Benefit Research Institute (1995, p. 5).
a. Aged family units include individuals over age 65 plus married couples in which one spouse is over age 65.
b. Totals may not add due to rounding.

4. Should benefits be financed approximately on a pay-as-you-go basis, or should large reserves be accumulated? If reserves are accumulated, should they be invested in private assets or government securities? Who should manage the investment of these reserves?

5. Should benefits be paid as a matter of right to people who have reached a certain age or who meet specified conditions—such as disability or widowhood—or should benefits be conditioned on income or wealth?

The current program answers these questions in the following ways. Social security now constitutes the major source of income for most retirees (table 8-3). It provides those who had low earnings with benefits that, relative to their earnings before retirement, are more than twice as large as those provided to retirees who had high earnings. Benefits are based on past earnings and do not directly depend on investment returns. Current surpluses are now sizable, but total reserves are modest and will remain so relative to those that would be amassed under a fully funded, defined-benefit pension system. These reserves, by law, must be invested in relatively low-yielding government securities. Benefits are paid to all eligible participants without regard to their income or wealth.

Many other answers to these questions are possible. A number entail major modifications or even replacement of the social security system. Not all combinations are under serious discussion, but the following three broad strategies for social security's future provide a sense of the available options.

Strategy 1: Cut Benefits, Raise Taxes, Maintain Structure

Those who believe that the structure of the current social security system is basically sound propose some combination of benefit cuts and tax increases that would restore long-run financial balance without modifying the system in fundamental ways.

Benefit cuts. Benefits can be cut in two ways: by lowering the amounts paid each year or by shortening the period over which benefits are provided. The most straightforward way to cut the amounts paid is to reduce the initial benefits for all new retirees. Since benefits of those who have already reached age 62 would not be affected, this change would take several years to have its full effect. For that reason, an immediate reduction of about 18 percent in initial benefits would be necessary to restore long-run actuarial balance.

Initial benefits can be reduced in many ways. They can be cut proportionately for all recipients, or those of high-wage earners can be cut disproportionately. The scope for closing the financing gap principally by lowering the initial benefits of high earners is limited because the benefit formula is already very redistributional, and deep reductions in these benefits would have to be made to eliminate a substantial portion of the actuarial deficit.[15] Such an approach would further reduce the already low return the system provides to high-wage workers and could generate demands that they be permitted to opt out of the system. In the long run, the exit of those with high earnings would undermine the financing of benefits for low earners.

Another way to cut benefits is to raise the normal retirement age. Under changes enacted in 1983, the normal retirement age will increase by two months a year between 2000 and 2005 and again between 2017 and 2022. This increase in the normal retirement age from age 65 to 67, which is a benefit reduction, could be accelerated and even extended. Raising the normal retirement age to 70 by 2030 would eliminate about one-half of the current actuarial deficit.

Although actuarially reduced benefits will still be available at age

---

15. For example, eliminating an increase in benefits above the second bend point, which is at an earnings level just over half of the taxable maximum, would eliminate only half of the current actuarial deficit.

62 when the normal retirement age increases, Congress could raise the age at which benefits may first be claimed as well. This would have little effect on long-run costs, however, because the actuarially based reduction in benefits for those who opt to retire before the normal age almost exactly offsets the increased costs of their longer payment period. Raising the age at which benefits may first be claimed, however, would force some who want to retire early but have limited personal resources to remain in the labor force. It would also protect the myopic from a lifetime of permanently reduced and possibly inadequate benefits.[16] When the normal retirement age becomes 67, those who retire at age 62 will receive a benefit 30 percent below that which they would receive if they worked until age 67.

In the public debate, modifications in the age at which partial and full social security benefits are available are often characterized as changes in the retirement age rather than as benefit cuts. This characterization has the important rhetorical effect of focusing discussion on how *long* people should work, rather than how *large* benefits should be when they retire. While social security's normal retirement age for men has remained fixed at age 65 since the program began paying benefits in 1940, life expectancy at age 65 has increased by three years and is projected to rise an additional one and one-half years by 2025. Whether added longevity implies working lives have been increased commensurately is a matter of debate. There is little evidence on whether the health condition of the elderly and their ability to continue working at a given age has increased along with the increase in life expectancies.[17] Those with more sedentary jobs may be able to adjust to extended working lives, but those with more physically demanding jobs may find it no easier to work past age 64 in the future than they have in the past. Such workers could be allowed to apply for disability insurance, but it would be very difficult to evaluate equitably the health condition of prospective early retirees to determine whether they should be classified as eligible for the higher-benefit disability insurance program.

Yet another way to cut benefits is to reduce the size of the automatic

16. Benefits are reduced by 0.56 percent for each month (6⅔ percent for each year) a person claims benefits before age 65. A person who claims benefits at age 62 receives a benefit 20 percent smaller than would be payable at age 65 on the same earnings. Workers over age 65 whose benefits are deferred or reduced because they earn more than the maximum allowed for full benefits receive actuarially increased benefits when fully eligible.

17. Bailey (1987). The rate of claims for disability insurance have risen in recent years.

annual cost-of-living adjustment that has protected benefits from being eroded by inflation since 1974. Many analysts have suggested that the consumer price index (CPI), which is used to make this adjustment, overstates inflation for a number or reasons, including a failure to account fully for quality improvements. If the CPI overstates inflation, then social security beneficiaries receive benefits that are not just insulated from inflation, but, in fact, steadily increase in purchasing power the longer they are on the rolls. To correct this alleged bias in the CPI, some policymakers and analysts have suggested that benefits be increased ½ percent (or some other amount) less than the increase in the CPI. Unlike benefit reductions that affect only new retirees, this proposal would impose some costs on current retirees, a group that has received particularly large benefits relative to their contributions. This change would reduce costs by 0.7 percent of taxable payroll, about one-third of the long-run deficit.[18]

Tax increases. The financing gaps of social security and medicare could be closed by increasing the payroll tax. Raising tax rates on wages, however, might accelerate the shift, which has been going on for decades, of labor compensation from cash wages to tax-exempt benefits. As it is, the projected shift in compensation from taxable payroll to nontaxed fringe benefits accounts for nearly half the actuarial deficit in OASDI.[19] Three other options are available: raising the wage ceiling on which the 12.4 percent OASDI tax is levied, extending the payroll tax to currently untaxed fringe benefits, and taxing nonwage income such as interest, dividends, and rents.

Under current law, the wage ceiling, which was $62,700 in 1996, is raised each year by the increase in average covered wages. It could be increased at a faster rate, or lifted entirely, as was done with the 2.9 percent payroll tax that finances part A of medicare. About 12 percent of covered wages are above the taxable ceiling. Although increasing the taxable wage ceiling will eventually raise benefits for the 7 percent of workers who earn more than the current taxable maximum, because of the progressive benefit formula the increase

18. The CPI is used also for indexing the personal exemption and standard deduction and income levels at which tax rates change under the personal income tax. If Congress decided that the CPI incorrectly adjusted for inflation in the social security system, the case would be strong for making a similar adjustment in the indexation of personal income taxes. Such a change would increase revenues.

19. Board of Trustees (1996, p. 189).

would be small.[20] Raising the wage ceiling to make 90 percent of covered wages taxable would reduce the long-run deficit by about one-fourth. The change would substantially increase marginal tax rates for high earners. Like a reduction in benefits for workers with high lifetime wages, this change would favor low-wage workers relative to a general increase in payroll taxes or cut in benefits.

The shift in the composition of labor compensation from taxable payroll to fringe benefits could be countered by broadening the tax base to include some currently tax-exempt benefits. Doing so, however, poses vexing administrative issues. How should one estimate the value to a particular worker of a company-financed health insurance plan? Is it the same for a twenty-five-year-old, a married forty-year-old with three children, and a fifty-five-year-old with chronic emphysema? If not, what is the difference? What is the value of accumulating benefits in a defined-benefit pension program? Many of these administrative problems could be avoided if such nonwage compensation were subjected only to the employer's payroll tax. This approach might also avoid the need to increase benefits to reflect the higher taxable earnings.

A final alternative is to look to other sources of tax revenue. Part of social security benefits are subject to income tax. These income tax collections are returned to the OASDI and the medicare part A (HI) trust funds. Taxing social security in the same fashion that private pension benefits are taxed and returning the additional revenues to the OASDI system would reduce the long-run deficit by about 10 percent.[21] This approach would place some of the burden for eliminating the long-run deficit on current beneficiaries, the actuarial value of whose benefits far exceeds their past contributions. But it extends an anomaly by depositing income taxes on benefits into the social security system rather than into the general fund.

Since its inception, many supporters have argued that general revenues should partially finance social security. Support for this method of financing social security has diminished, perhaps because of a fear that general revenue funding (beyond the allocation of taxes collected on social security benefits) would change the perception of social

20. The proportion of covered earnings above the ceiling was 12.7 percent in 1994. See Social Security Administration (1995, table 4.B1).

21. Private pensions must be included in taxable income, except for the portion that represents the employee contribution, upon which income taxes have already been paid.

security as a self-financed retirement program with earned rights into one of a simple transfer program, subject to annual modification.

Investment policy. How reserves are invested affects long-run financial balance. If benefits are reduced or payroll taxes are increased, social security reserves would grow to far more than the $2.9 trillion projected under current law, and investment policy would become even more important. Under current law, social security reserves are invested in special Treasury securities that yield the same return as the average of securities sold to the public with a maturity of four years or more. The social security actuaries project that these investments will yield an annual return 2.3 percent greater than inflation.

The social return to reserve accumulation is much higher. When social security adds to its reserves, the federal government is able to reduce its borrowing from the public by that amount. As a result, private saving that would have been absorbed by the federal government is freed for private domestic or foreign investment. The return on this investment, made possible by social security reserve accumulation, has averaged 6 percent more than the rate of inflation in recent years. Thus the return to the nation from social security reserve accumulation considerably exceeds the return credited to social security.[22] For this reason, some people have advocated investing part of social security reserves in a broad index of private securities. Doing so would not raise total returns to all investment. If social security allocated part of its reserve accumulation to private investments, the rest of the federal government would have to increase its borrowing from the public by the same amount. Thus there would be no net change in the flow of funds to private investment. But this investment policy would credit social security with the social return that reserve accumulation makes possible. Under one proposal advanced in the 1996 Advisory Council on Social Security, investing 40 percent of social security reserves in private securities yielding 4 percent more than government securities would reduce the long-run deficit by about 40 percent.[23]

Critics of this approach fear that it would enable the federal government to exercise inordinate control over private companies. Advocates respond that reserves of civil service employees' retirement

22. Bosworth (1996).
23. Gramlich (1996).

plans are now invested in three broad index funds that include private securities and no problems of government control have arisen. They believe that institutional arrangements could be established to prevent politically motivated controls on private companies whose shares would be represented in a broad portfolio.

Another concern that relates to any tax or benefit change that would generate larger surpluses is that increased reserve accumulations might encourage Congress to run larger deficits on the rest of government operations, resulting in no net savings. Only if saving occurs privately, the critics maintain, can it be protected from such fiscal indiscipline. On the other side, advocates point out that deficits on general or non–social security government operations increased most rapidly when social security reserves were falling and have fallen when social security reserves have been increasing, a pattern that suggests social security reserve policy is separable from overall fiscal policy.

Strategy 2: Means-Test Social Security

All current social security beneficiaries who live an average life-span, even those who had high earnings during their working years, receive benefits worth more than the payroll taxes they and their employers have paid in plus interest earnings on those payments. To limit such subsidies to those who are in need, some people have proposed an explicit means or income test that would reduce benefits to relatively well-to-do beneficiaries. Peter Peterson, former secretary of commerce and chairman of the Concord Coalition, has proposed subjecting all benefits, including social security, to an "affluence test" that would progressively reduce entitlement benefits for households with incomes above $40,000.[24] Households with incomes above $120,000 would be allowed to keep 15 percent of their benefits.

This and similar proposals have some political appeal but are subject to criticism on several grounds. First, they would discourage saving because the fruits of saving—higher postretirement income—would be indirectly taxed through reduced social security benefits. With private saving as badly depressed as it is, this risk merits serious consideration. Second, means or income testing would raise difficult

---

24. Peterson (1996).

administrative problems. Means testing would encourage potential beneficiaries to conceal assets by moving them abroad, placing them in trusts, or shifting them to children. Income testing would encourage beneficiaries to invest in assets, such as housing, that provide in-kind benefits or that yield little current income but appreciate. Rather than selling assets and realizing gains, wealth holders could borrow against assets and live off loan proceeds. These possibilities are not fanciful. The medicaid means test has fathered quite elegant avoidance schemes employed by some who require nursing home care.[25]

Furthermore, the passage of time is correcting the problem that means testing is designed to solve: that of providing benefits to high-income households that are worth far more than the taxes they paid. This situation is unavoidable in the early years of a defined-benefit pension program, such as social security, that pays adequate benefits soon after the program begins. Social security began collecting payroll taxes in 1937 at a combined rate of 2 percent of payroll up to $3,000 and began paying benefits in 1940. Those who retired in 1940 were bound to receive an enormous return on their contributions. In fact, high returns are inevitable until workers have spent their entire working lives paying taxes under the same system that pays them benefits when they retire. Eventually, when the system is fully mature, the cohort of workers who retire in a given year receives a more modest rate of return. If the system is run on a strictly pay-as-you-go basis, the rate of return is equal to the rate of growth of total wage payments—the sum of labor force and real wage growth.[26] If the system is run on a full reserve basis, the rate of return equals the yield on the investments in which the reserves are invested. Under current law, the rate of return to future cohorts of workers will fall to less than 2 percent (after adjustment for inflation). Since high earners receive relatively less generous benefits than low earners do, there will be no windfall to eliminate.

Of course, means or income testing could always be used to lower the returns to high earners even more than the current benefit formula does. But, as with some of the benefit cut proposals examined above, such a move would lead to negative rates of return and could intensify pressures for high earners to seek ways to opt out of social security

---

25. For a description of these arrangements, see Burwell and Crown (1995); Wiener, Illston, and Hanley (1994, pp. 121–23).

26. Samuelson (1958).

altogether. With their departure, the financial basis for providing relatively generous benefits to low earners would disappear.

Strategy 3: Privatize Social Security

Although social security has been widely popular since enactment, some critics have always questioned one or another aspect of the program. Many economists have questioned pay-as-you-go financing. They have emphasized that social security meets several of the needs for which people customarily save—protection against the death or disability of a breadwinner and accumulation of assets to support retirement—but has led to little public saving. In other words, social security could be an important reason for the fall in national saving. While social security could accumulate much larger reserves than it now does, these economists doubt the will of Congress to renounce use of the annual surpluses to cover deficits in other government accounts. Thus they argue for privatization of the existing system by moving to a system of mandatory individual retirement accounts. An added benefit from such a change would be the ability of workers to invest the savings directly in higher-yielding assets than government securities. Although the social security reserves could be invested in such assets, critics do not trust public fund managers to be guided solely by investment criteria.

Under a pure privatization strategy, all or most payroll taxes would be shifted to individual accounts. Younger workers would eventually claim benefits from such accounts, while older workers would be eligible for a blend of benefits based on the current system and the new one. Individual retirement accounts, it is claimed, would force genuine saving, reduce political risks in the management of such savings, and give individuals increased opportunities to manage their own investments.[27] By their very nature, individual accounts pay benefits proportional to contributions and investment earnings and could not be used for the redistribution that is such a prominent part of the current system.

Most privatization proposals would not be pure, however; that is, they would not rely exclusively on individual retirement accounts. To protect workers with low earnings and those who become disabled,

---

27. For example, see Boskin, Kotlikoff, and Shoven (1988).

whose own accounts might well provide inadequate benefits to support a decent retirement or life with a disability, the individual retirement accounts could be combined with a universal flat benefit and disability insurance.[28] This combination would establish a two-tier system: a reduced public component that provides a low-level uniform benefit and disability insurance and a defined-contribution pension with no redistributional element. Under most privatization schemes, participants would be free to invest the funds in their individual accounts in a range of capital market assets. The selection of assets could be left entirely up to each individual, or choices could be limited to a few funds, as the public employees' retirement system now is.[29]

Critics of privatization voice several concerns. First, they point out that all privatization plans require sizable tax increases over a long transition period to make them function. The tax increases are necessary because few people think it would be good policy or imaginable politics to cut benefits to current retirees or to change the rules for those about to retire. So, for several decades, revenues will be needed to pay benefits to those with substantial accrued claims under the present system. Funds to support accumulations in individual accounts, therefore, can come only from additional taxes. But increased taxes could also be used to build a social security trust fund rather than individual accounts.[30]

Second, critics of privatization doubt that support for the redistributional component could be sustained if it were a distinct program and point to the fate of the welfare programs as evidence for their concerns. Thus they fear that a privatized program would come to provide inadequate support for workers with low lifetime earnings. Third, critics doubt that low-wage workers will make informed investment decisions. Survey evidence indicates that low-wage workers

28. Gramlich (1996). One faction within the Advisory Council on Social Security favors a blended position, consisting of the traditional social security program, scaled back sufficiently to fit within the revenues generated by the current payroll tax, and a mandatory savings plan that would be financed by a new payroll tax equal to 2 percent of payroll. The proceeds of this new tax would be invested in a limited menu of index funds.

29. This type of plan received favorable attention after its introduction in Chile in the early 1980s. See Diamond and Valdés-Prieto (1994) for a thorough discussion of the Chilean program.

30. If taxes are not increased, privatization has no direct effect on funds available for private investment. The payroll taxes diverted from public expenditures boost the federal government deficit and necessitate increased government borrowing that exactly offsets the funds newly deposited in individual accounts.

with IRA accounts make extremely risk-averse investment decisions, frequently opting to put their funds in low-return bank accounts.[31] In addition, administrative costs are likely to increase if there are a large number of small individual accounts, further eroding the return to low earners. Fourth, some of the hoped-for increase in saving from privatization might be offset if mandatory IRAs cause workers to reduce their other private saving. Fifth, individual accounts raise the problem of how to manage the conversion to annuities at time of retirement. If individuals are given the option of accepting lump-sum cash-outs, annuity markets will encounter extreme problems of adverse selection and the price of annuities would have to rise. This problem could be avoided if there were a national system with mandatory conversion of all individual accounts.

Since privatization converts a government-financed, defined-benefit program into a privately financed, defined-contribution program, it eliminates any concern about public-sector costs of the retirement programs; benefits are determined by contributions and market rates of return. But it does so by shifting the risk of poor economic returns from taxpayers at large to retirees and their dependents. Privatization schemes have attracted political support, particularly among high earners. There are concerns, however, about the consequences for low-wage workers.

Advanced funding, that is, the accumulation of additional saving, is essential if the added costs of the baby boom generation's retirement are not going to burden future workers. It would be easiest to implement within the existing public programs because it would leave accrued benefit claims intact. It would require only some combination of an increase in the payroll tax rate or reduction of benefits to create a reserve, and a firm commitment to set the surplus aside from other government accounts. From the perspective of the economic benefits to the nation, it matters little whether the reserve is invested in public or private securities. In either case, national saving increases and the ultimate decisions about where to invest the added saving are made in private capital markets. The economic benefits flow from the increased investment in real capital. If the social security fund purchased government debt, a larger proportion of private saving could go to finance private investment. If the fund chose to buy private assets,

---

31. Employee Benefit Research Institute (1996b); Congressional Budget Office (1994, p. 12).

more of the private saving would be used to cover the public-sector budget deficit.

Medicare

Medicare, which is discussed in greater detail in chapter 6, accounts for over three-fifths of the federal government's health care outlays. Medicare serves most of the social security beneficiary population: people over age 64 and the disabled (but not their dependents who are neither aged nor disabled or those between the ages of 62 and 64) and some others, notably those suffering end-stage renal disease. It consists of two parts. Part A, hospital insurance (HI), is financed through a payroll tax, currently 2.9 percent, but without a ceiling on taxable wages. Part B, supplemental medical insurance (SMI), covers physician fees, outpatient hospital services, laboratory charges, durable medical equipment, and certain other services. Premiums paid by participants cover only 25 percent of part B costs, and general budget funds cover the rest. SMI is voluntary, but more than 97 percent of those eligible to join do so because it is a very good buy. Over two-thirds of the medicare population carries supplemental private insurance to pay deductibles and coinsurance charges for services that medicare does not cover. Another 15 percent are covered by medicaid.

Medicare outlays per enrollee rose at an annual rate of 5.5 percent (after adjustment for inflation) between 1975 and 1995, compared with 4.6 percent for per capita national health expenditures and 1.8 percent for per capita GDP. Thus the problem of rapid increases in the cost of health care, common to both public and private health systems, is most severe for medicare.[32] That growth has occurred in spite of intense government efforts to control costs and a considerable degree of cost shifting from medicare (and medicaid) to private insurance patients.[33] Although medicare pays for a significant portion of health outlays for those over age 64, about half of their spending is paid for by direct out-of-pocket payments, supplementary private insurance, and medicaid (figure 8-1).

The annual outlays of the hospital insurance trust fund exceeded

32. The faster growth of medicare expenditures has recently been concentrated in home health and skilled nursing, two components of medicare with characteristics similar to those for long-term care.

33. Congressional Budget Office (1993, p. 8).

TABLE 8-4. Annual Change in Real Medicare and Medicaid
Expenditure, by Source of Change, Selected Periods, 1980–2050
Percent

Program	1980–95	1995–2010	2010–25	2025–50
Medicare				
Caseload	1.8	1.0	2.9	1.3
Age distribution	0.2	0.1	−0.2	0.3
Intensity	5.1	4.9	1.7	0.5
Total	7.0	5.9	4.4	2.1
Medicaid				
Caseload	3.5	2.0	0.6	0.3
Age distribution	−0.5	0.5	0.6	0.2
Intensity	5.6	4.3	1.7	1.8
Total	8.6	6.8	2.9	2.3

SOURCE: Authors' estimates. Totals may not add due to rounding.

its revenues in 1995 and 1996, and the fund has begun to draw down
the $130 billion reserve that had accumulated from previous sur-
pluses. The gap between income and outlays is expected to grow in
future years, and by 2001 the reserve will be exhausted. In 2001
outlays will exceed revenues by $56 billion, or 40 percent. The mag-
nitude of this shortfall means that even significant errors in the projections would not avoid the need to modify the medicare program
substantially to close the HI deficit. Over the long-term seventy-five-
year horizon, the HI deficit is projected to average 4.5 percent of
payroll, twice that of the social security program. This projection
does not include the costs of the SMI program, which, if not modified,
will place a roughly equal burden on the budget.

Sources of Rising Costs

Medicare costs will be driven by three factors. The first is the
increase in the number of beneficiaries, which will in turn be driven
largely by the retirement of the baby boom generation, the oldest of
whom will begin to participate in 2011. Between 1995 and 2025
medicare enrollment is projected to increase at about the same rate
as the social security population: 2 percent a year (see table 8-4). The
second factor is the changing age distribution of the medicare population. This shift matters because medical expenditures rise sharply

with age (figure 8-1).[34] The average age of the medicare population will increase over the next decade and a half and then, as the baby boomers begin to participate, it will fall. Over the full period of 1995 to 2025 changes in the number of participants and their age distribution will raise medicare spending by 60 percent.

Daunting as the demographic trends are, they should not divert attention from the fact that increases in the cost per beneficiary (shown as intensity in table 8-4) will continue to be an important determinant of the total growth of medicare outlays. As was mentioned earlier, this aspect of the projections is highly uncertain. The projected slowing of the growth in cost per beneficiary reflects the view of the medicare actuaries and others that current trends are unsustainable, rather than any knowledge of the specific forces that could reduce the increase in intensity after 2010. Health care spending per person will depend critically on the pace and cost of advances in medical technology, which are difficult to forecast. It also will depend on market developments, such as the spread of managed care, and legislated changes in reimbursement policies.

Proposals for Reform

Medicare is a defined-benefit program, which means that government is committed to pay the cost of a specified set of services for the eligible population. Decisions on whether to use these services reside with medicare beneficiaries and their physicians (or other providers). Under such arrangements, the federal government can control only the prices it will pay for covered services. Medicare could be changed into a defined-contribution program to limit the federal government's financial exposure. Alternatively, the age of eligibility could be increased or taxes raised.

Reimbursement cuts. The Health Care Financing Administration (HCFA), the government agency that administers the medicare program, has been implementing controls on prices for over a decade. First the growth of payments made to hospitals, which are based on diagnoses at admission, was limited. Later the increase in the fees paid

34. The sharply rising health care costs for the very old are heavily influenced by nursing home care. These costs are overstated because they include nonmedical, normal day-to-day living expenses. Per capita medical care costs, excluding nursing home care, rise much more gradually across the over-65 age categories than do total outlays covered by medical programs.

to physicians for their services was restricted. Additional reimbursement cuts have been proposed. For example, the payments that medicare makes to support graduate medical education and to assist hospitals that serve a disproportionate share of indigent patients could be curtailed. The payments made for home health services, which are growing at double-digit rates, could also be reduced. Savings such as these can postpone the exhaustion of the HI trust fund, but they can not prevent eventual insolvency. In a similar fashion, tight limits on physician reimbursement can achieve a one-time reduction in the growth of SMI spending. Both the Clinton administration and the Republican budget plans include such specific cuts as well as further reductions in the growth of hospital payments.

Change to defined contribution. Republican budget plans have proposed a more far-reaching modification, the creation of a defined-contribution component in medicare.[35] Under a pure defined-contribution plan, the federal government would provide eligible beneficiaries with a voucher that they could use toward the purchase of any private health insurance plan. Beneficiaries could supplement the voucher with their own funds if they wished to buy insurance that cost more than the value of the voucher. The hope is that competition among insurance vendors and heightened cost consciousness by insurance purchasers would slow the growth of health care spending and improve the quality of care.

The Republican plan included in the Balanced Budget Act of 1995 would not have established a pure defined-contribution component to medicare. Medicare would have paid insurance plans directly rather than providing vouchers to participants; the extent to which beneficiaries could supplement the voucher would have been limited; insurance plans would have been required to cover the medicare package of services; and the traditional medicare fee-for-service program would have been retained as an option. Under this proposal, the voucher amounts were specified in law, and the spending in the traditional program was restrained by limiting the fees paid to providers. Critics feared that the reimbursement limits in the fee-for-service component might have been so tight that many physicians and other providers would refuse to offer care at those rates.

Defined-contribution plans raise a host of technical and program-

---

35. Ideologically diverse private analysts have also supported the idea of converting medicare to a defined-contribution plan. See Butler and Moffit (1995); Aaron and Reischauer (1995).

matic problems, which are examined in detail in chapter 6. The first issue concerns the adequacy of the voucher. By limiting the value of the payment that the federal government makes, the growth of medicare spending can be held to any target. But if the payments are too low, the voucher may not be sufficient to purchase insurance that provides adequate protection, and many elderly and disabled may not be able to afford to supplement this amount. Other problems relate to assuring that the elderly and disabled, who may suffer from preexisting conditions of various kinds and or be frail or incapacitated, can actually buy insurance at fair prices. The transition from the current medicare system to a new one also poses difficult administrative problems.[36]

Increase age of eligibility. Some observers have suggested that the age at which individuals are eligible for medicare be increased from 65. The rationale is that, under current law, the age at which unreduced social security benefits will be paid is scheduled to increase from 65 to 67. As noted previously, however, the age at which reduced social security benefits can be claimed (62) will not change. However, eligibility for medicare and social security status have never been closely linked. In fact, most workers retire and start receiving social security benefits before they reach age 65, the point at which they first become eligible for medicare. Pushing back the age of first eligibility for medicare to 67 would reduce medicare costs in 2025 by only 5 percent. The effect is relatively small because people aged 65 and 66 tend to be healthier than older medicare recipients. Delaying the medicare eligibility age to 70 would cut medicare costs by 2050 by about 15 percent.[37]

As is the case with proposals to increase the age at which reduced social security benefits can be received, some have criticized this proposal on the grounds that, although life expectancies have increased, the evidence is much weaker that the health of the elderly at a given age has improved. Increases in life expectancy can occur because medicine or rising incomes free people of conditions that cause both death and debility. Alternatively, medicine may keep alive people who previously would have died, but leave a population at any given age that is, on average, less healthy. Evidence on which phenomenon is dominant is quite mixed.[38] If the age of medicare eligibility is raised,

36. For a discussion of these issues, see Aaron and Reischauer (1995).
37. Congressional Budget Office (1996, p. 465).
38. Poterba and Summers (1987).

people aged 65 and 66 whose health keeps them from working may face difficulties obtaining affordable health insurance. The ranks of the uninsured and medicaid costs would increase. One way of ameliorating this problem would be to let younger retirees buy into medicare at an actuarially fair price.

Revenue increases. It is hard to see how insurance that provides the elderly and disabled with significant protection against large medical costs can be sustained in the long run without some increase in payroll or other taxes. The projected deficits are just too large. Payroll taxes could be increased, but using a revenue source other than the payroll tax has more appeal for medicare than it does for social security. Unlike social security benefits, the value of medicare benefits an individual receives is not linked to past earnings or to payroll taxes paid. As a result, there is no strong reason to rely on a wage tax to finance a system that provides medical insurance to retirees, many of whom made little or no past contributions to the system. Some analysts have suggested that medicare would be better financed out of a broad-based value-added tax.[39] Furthermore, participants could be required to shoulder more of the burden by increasing part B premiums. The original financing arrangement for SMI envisioned that costs would be split equally between premiums levied on the retired and disabled and the general fund. In response to political pressures, however, premiums have not been raised to keep pace with rising program costs and currently are about 25 percent of costs. Returning to the original division of costs would reduce net medicare costs by about 1.3 percent of GDP in 2050.

Summary

The core problem in charting reforms of medicare centers on the uncertainty regarding the future growth of health care spending in general and medicare in particular. Most research on health costs concludes that cost increases are driven principally by technological innovations that have broadened the range of potential medical interventions. Within a few decades, organ transplants, bypass surgery, and other major medical interventions have become commonplace. Noninvasive diagnostic tests, such as magnetic resonance imaging, have become routine. Because they are less risky and less painful,

---

39. Schultze (1992, pp. 310–14); Aaron (1991).

these tests are employed far more frequently than the procedures they replaced. In addition, health care outlays are concentrated on high-cost episodes, suggesting that incentives to shop wisely will have only limited effects. Reducing payments to providers may generate a one-time reduction in spending. So may shifting medicare beneficiaries into managed care plans. Such savings may delay the exhaustion of the HI trust fund by a few years and reduce SMI outlays somewhat. But, unless managed care organizations successfully limit access to high-cost interventions over a lengthy period, the underlying forces driving up health care costs—new technology and population aging—will cause the rapid growth of health care spending to resume.

The budgetary problems of medicare could be made similar to those of social security by converting to a voucher system that provides assistance in the purchase of private health insurance. However, although such a change could control growth of medicare spending, it would not solve the problem of rising medical care costs. It would highlight the fact that growth of medicare spending will not be solved without restraint of health care costs for people of all ages.

Medicaid

Medicaid supports health care services for a significant fraction of the low-income population. Chapter 3 discusses its current operation, as well as proposals for converting it from an open-ended matching grant into a block grant or a matching grant with per capita limits. The projected growth of medicaid spending, shown in table 8-1, illustrates that, one way or another, health problems of poor Americans cannot be ignored in framing a full picture of long-run health care costs. Under current law, most of these costs show up in public budgets. Federal medicaid spending is projected to rise from 1.3 percent of GDP in 1995 to 2.9 percent of GDP in 2025. In addition, state spending on medicaid, now 1 percent of GDP, is projected to rise commensurately.

A great deal of uncertainty surrounds these projections. Like medicare spending, future medicaid costs will depend critically on the course of medical technology and per capita health spending for the general population. In addition, medicaid spending will depend on decisions that states will make concerning the populations and services they choose to cover under their medicaid programs and the pace at which they raise payments to providers. Although states are required to offer medicaid coverage to certain populations and to cover certain services, most states go well beyond these federal minimums. Less than half of medicaid spending in 1993 represented mandatory services provided to mandatory participants. If the program's fiscal burden becomes too onerous in the future, states could decide to ratchet back their programs.

Medicaid spending is divided among acute care services for the nonelderly, nondisabled (32 percent), acute and long-term care for the blind and disabled (36 percent), and acute and long-term care for the elderly (32 percent). The enactment of medicaid in 1965 significantly increased the access of these groups to health care. But coverage of these groups remains incomplete. In particular, only about 58 percent of the nonelderly poor are covered by medicaid, and 28 percent of this group are currently uninsured.[40]

The medicaid caseload remained relatively constant between 1975 and 1988. However, it jumped by over 50 percent between 1988 and the mid-1990s as a result of court decisions and legislation that extended coverage. The medicaid caseload is projected to grow at almost twice the rate of the total population over the 1995–2025 period. Changes in the age distribution of the medicaid population will exert a modest upward pressure on projected spending (table 8-4).

The shadow of long-term care hangs over medicaid and health care spending more generally. As the population aged 85 and over increases, the costs of long-term care will grow commensurately. Direct payments by individuals account for about half of total nursing home spending. Medicaid now accounts for most of the other half. The poor qualify directly for medicaid financing for long-term care. The majority of middle-income Americans with modest assets find that they are not eligible for medicaid until they either deplete those assets or divest them. Adequate long-term care insurance policies are expensive, unless they are purchased well before an individual reaches retirement age, which rarely happens. Only the relatively wealthy, therefore, can afford to purchase long-term care insurance or to pay for sustained long-term care themselves.

Changes in the medicare program would affect future medicaid costs. State medicaid programs are required to pay the part B premiums, deductibles, and coinsurance of poor medicare beneficiaries and the part B premiums of participants with incomes between the poverty

40. Employee Benefit Research Institute (1996a).

threshold and 120 percent of that level. If medicare reforms require participants to shoulder more of that program's costs, some of the burden will therefore be shifted back onto medicaid. Alternatively, if increasing proportions of medicare participants choose to receive their health services through medicare HMOs, many of which have little or no cost sharing, the growth of medicaid costs for the elderly would be attenuated.

The Role of Funding

Advanced funding, that is, increased saving by current generations, emerges as the most effective means of paying for the burgeoning future costs of an aging population. This increased saving can be done under public or private auspices. For example, the current surplus of the social security system could be expanded by increased taxes or reduced benefits. If deficits in the rest of government operations are unchanged, the added surplus would add to national saving. Alternatively, the increased saving could take place within private retirement or pension accounts. The imperative for economic growth is that the increase in retirement saving actually translate into an increase in national saving and not be offset by reduced private saving or increased public deficits.

If today's large working generation raised its saving, either publicly or privately, this generation would not impose an increased burden when it retires or becomes disabled, despite its size. This is because, by raising its saving and capital formation, the current generation would have increased the wages and incomes of future workers from which the taxes to support retirement and disability pensions and health benefits will have to be paid.[41] If national saving is not increased, the resource base from which these costs will have to be paid will not be larger. A divisive battle will ensue because either the benefits expected by the elderly will have to be reduced sharply or increases in spending on the elderly will have come at the expense of active workers.

The current interest in funding a portion of future retirement costs is motivated in part by evidence that the saving rate has fallen, not increased, at a time when demographic factors suggest the need for

41. Some aspects of partial funding were examined in Aaron, Bosworth, and Burtless (1989).

TABLE 8-5. Net National Saving and Investment Balance, Selected Periods, 1960–94

Percent of net national product

Category	1960–69	1970–79	1980–84	1985–89	1990–94	1995
National saving[a]	11.9	9.2	6.4	5.2	3.5	4.7
Private	9.7	9.8	9.4	7.8	7.0	6.7
Households	5.6	6.3	6.7	4.6	4.1	3.6
Corporate	4.1	3.5	2.7	3.2	2.9	3.0
Government	2.2	− 0.7	− 3.0	− 2.6	− 3.5	− 1.9
National investment	11.6	9.8	7.0	5.1	4.1	5.0
Domestic	10.9	9.6	7.7	8.2	5.3	7.3
Private	8.0	8.2	6.4	6.5	3.9	5.8
Government	2.9	1.3	1.2	1.7	1.4	0.9
Net foreign	0.7	0.3	− 0.7	− 3.0	− 1.2	− 2.4
Statistical discrepancy	− 0.3	0.6	0.6	− 0.1	0.5	0.3
Addenda:						
Capital consumption allowance	12.0	13.0	15.3	14.1	13.6	12.8

SOURCE: U.S. Commerce Department, revised National Income and Products Accounts.

a. State and local government employee pension accounts are moved from government to the household sector to match the treatment of private pension programs.

more saving (table 8-5). The national saving rate in 1995 was less than half that of the 1960s. The net private saving rate, which averaged 9 to 10 percent of net national product (NNP) in 1960–80, fell to 7 percent in the 1990s. Meanwhile, the public-sector (federal, state, and local) deficit (dissaving) rose to more than 3 percent of NNP in the early 1990s. More recently, the federal deficit has been reduced sharply, but private saving remains depressed.

How much would saving have to increase to finance the increase of 5 percent of GDP in federal government program outlays that is projected to take place between 1995 and 2025 (table 8-1)? To fund those outlays at no cost to future workers, the United States would need to increase its capital stock enough over the next thirty years to raise income 5 percent. Since 1960 the real return on physical capital in the United States, net of depreciation, has averaged about 6 percent, suggesting the need to raise the capital stock by approximately 80 percent of output over the next thirty years.[42] In comparison, the national wealth of the United States in 1995 is estimated to have been about 2.8 times GDP, or $19 trillion.[43]

42. Bosworth (1996, pp. 98–100).

43. Board of Governors (1995). National wealth is domestic wealth minus net foreign liabilities.

In practice, however, the situation is somewhat more complex. First, if all additional saving is invested in the United States, the return on both new and existing capital will fall. Part of the decline is not a problem from a national perspective, since total labor compensation would increase as the capital stock rises. This added labor compensation would partly offset the declining return to owners of capital. However, the total increment to national income from an additional unit of investment can be expected to decline gradually if capital formation accelerates.

The decline in the domestic return to capital could be moderated if some of the increased capital were invested abroad. U.S. residents now earn returns on foreign investments comparable to domestic yields. Investing the increased saving in other countries would avoid most of the decline associated with increased domestic investment because the additional U.S. saving would only be a small part of total world capital formation.[44] However, increased foreign investment raises another problem. Such a strategy would require the United States to convert its current account deficit with the rest of the world into a substantial surplus. Initially, U.S. terms of trade would deteriorate. In other words, export prices would need to fall and import prices to rise to affect the reallocation of trade flows. Thus only some of the decline in the rate of return can be offset by access to a larger global economy.

The bottom line is this: if national saving is increased by a little more than 5 percent of GDP, the added saving should boost growth enough to raise GDP by the increase in government spending that is projected to occur over the next thirty years. This represents more than a doubling of the current saving rate. Looked at in a historical perspective, it is about equivalent to reversing the decline in saving that has occurred over the past quarter century. Whether the added saving and the increased spending on retirement occurs in the public or the private sector is important for many purposes, but the burdens of caring for the dependent population will be the same whether this population is supported publicly or privately.

---

44. This assumes that not all of the economies with aging populations are trying to raise their saving and invest in the global economy.

Conclusion

The projected costs of pension and health benefits for the elderly and disabled are high. With prudent planning, however, they will be manageable. The greatest problem for the United States is that as these future liabilities have been mounting, the American propensity to save, both publicly and privately, has fallen. The most effective way to address the financing problem involves partial funding of retirement and health programs to help boost saving in anticipation of the greater transfers future workers will have to make to a growing elderly and disabled population.

The controversial aspect of a shift to partial funding revolves around the question of whether it can be done within the framework of public programs in which the costs and risks are shared or requires a shift to private programs where workers own and control their own retirement accounts and bear increased risk. Those who object to a funded public program express doubts that trust fund surpluses would truly be saved, that is, add to national saving and increase national income in future decades. To many, privatization would curb the risk that politicians would squander this nest egg.

The existing public system, however, has many advantages that justify a major effort to save it. The system is progressive in offering larger benefits relative to lifetime earnings for low earners than for high earners, while maintaining a proportionate wage tax. In providing old-age annuities to all of the retired population, it avoids the high-cost adverse selection problems of private annuity markets. Its administrative costs are lower than private plans, and it can offer benefits that are indexed for inflation. These features are difficult to duplicate in a private system. Privatization has always had an appeal to those who disliked the redistributional aspects of the public program; but recent interest in the funding of future retirement costs has also stimulated interest in privatization.

Skeptics will have no difficulty explaining why elected officials will not adopt a program of partial funding, public or private. Political leaders have been unwilling so far to look much beyond the next elections. They may well ignore financing problems until they reach crisis proportions. Even if they act, and added capital formation raises the incomes of future workers, those who work and vote in the future will still have to transfer more current production to support a growing elderly and disabled population. To be sure, building up a sizable social security reserve and investing part of that reserve in a mixed public-private portfolio with a yield approximating the social return generated by the trust fund accumulation will eliminate much of the need for future tax increases. But future generations may not recognize that the income gains they are enjoying resulted from increased saving and investment by their parents and grandparents. They will find, however, that the transfers they are called upon to make need not force them to accept a significantly diminished living standard. There is not much more that the current generation can do to help future generations bear these costs.

References

Aaron, Henry J. 1991. *Serious and Unstable Condition: Financing America's Health Care*. Brookings.

Aaron, Henry J., Barry P. Bosworth, and Gary T. Burtless. 1989. *Can America Afford to Grow Old? Paying for Social Security*. Brookings.

Aaron, Henry J., and Robert D. Reischauer. 1995. "The Medicare Reform Debate: What Is the Next Step?" *Health Affairs* 14 (Winter): 8–30.

Bailey, Martin Neil. 1987. "Aging and the Ability to Work: Policy Issues and Recent Trends." In *Work, Health, and Income among the Elderly*, edited by Gary Burtless, 59–102. Brookings.

Board of Governors of the Federal Reserve System. 1995. *Balance Sheets for the U.S. Economy, 1948–94*. C.9 release (June).

Board of Trustees. Federal Old-Age and Survivors Insurance and Disability Insurance Trust Fund. 1996. *Annual Report*.

Boskin, Michael J., Lawrence J. Kotlikoff, and John B. Shoven. 1988. "Personal Security Accounts: A Proposal for Fundamental Social Security Reform." In *Social Security and Private Pensions: Providing for Retirement in the Twenty-First Century*, edited by Susan M. Wachter, 179–206. Lexington, Mass.: Lexington Books.

Bosworth, Barry P. 1996. "Fund Accumulation: How Much? How Managed?" In *Social Security: What Role for the Future?* edited by Peter A. Diamond, David C. Lindeman, and Howard Young, 89–114. Washington: National Academy of Social Insurance.

Burwell, Brian, and William H. Crown. 1995. "Medicaid Estate Planning: Case Studies of Four States." In *Persons with Disabilities: Issues in Health Care Financing and Service Delivery*, edited by Joshua M. Wiener, Steven B. Clauser, and David L. Kennell, 61–92. Brookings.

Butler, Stuart M., and Robert E. Moffit. 1995. "The FEHBP as a Model for a New Medicare Program." *Health Affairs* 14 (Winter): 47–61.

Congressional Budget Office. 1993. "Responses to Uncompensated Care and

Public Program Controls on Spending: Do Hospitals 'Cost Shift'?" *CBO Papers* (May).

———. 1994. "Implications of Revising Social Security's Investment Policies." *CBO Papers* (September).

———. 1996. *Reducing the Deficit: Spending and Revenue Options* (August).

Diamond, Peter, and Salvador Valdés-Prieto. 1994. "Social Security Reforms." In *The Chilean Economy: Policy Lessons and Challenges*, edited by Barry P. Bosworth, Rudiger Dornbusch, and Raúl Lábán, 257–320. Brookings.

Employee Benefit Research Institute. 1995. "Sources of Income of the Elderly Population." Washington (June).

———. 1996a. "Sources of Health Insurance and Characteristics of the Uninsured." Issue Brief 170. Washington (February).

———. 1996b. "Worker Investment Decisions: An Analysis of Large 401(k) Plan Data." Issue Brief 176. Washington (August).

Gramlich, Edward M. 1996. "Different Approaches for Dealing with Social Security." *Journal of Economic Perspectives* 10 (Summer): 55–66.

Levit, Katharine R., and others. 1996. "National Health Expenditures, 1994." *Health Care Financing Review* 17 (Spring): 205–42.

Newhouse, Joseph P. 1993. "An Iconoclastic View of Health Cost Containment." *Health Affairs* 12 (Supplement): 152–71.

Peterson, Peter G. 1996. "Will America Grow Up Before It Grows Old?" *Atlantic Monthly* 277 (May): 55–86.

Poterba, James M., and Lawrence H. Summers. 1987. "Public Policy Implications of Declining Old-Age Mortality." In *Work, Health, and Income among the Elderly*, edited by Gary Burtless, 19–58. Brookings.

Samuelson, Paul A. 1958. "An Exact Consumption-Loan Model of Interest with or without the Social Contrivance of Money." *Journal of Political Economy* 66 (December): 467–82.

Schultze, Charles L. 1992. "Paying the Bills." In *Setting Domestic Priorities: What Can Government Do?* edited by Henry J. Aaron and Charles L. Schultze, 295–318. Brookings.

Social Security Administration. 1994. *Annual Statistical Supplement, 1994, to the Social Security Bulletin*.

Wiener, Joshua M., Laurel Hixon Illston, and Raymond J. Hanley. 1994. *Sharing the Burden: Strategies for Public and Private Long-Term Care Insurance*. Brookings.

Appendix

PROPONENTS of regulatory reform argue that the level and growth of the nation's economy are being depressed by excessive and inefficient regulation and that economic growth could be spurred by deregulation. In 1995 the newly elected Republican majority in Congress launched a series of legislative measures designed to redesign, restrain, and, in some cases, reduce the federal regulatory apparatus, most particularly in environmental protection and workplace safety. They attempted to use both substantive legislation and appropriation cutbacks to achieve these objectives. In assessing the impact that such measures might have on the growth of potential GDP, it is useful to examine separately the two kinds of regulation—economic and social.

Economic Regulation

As its name suggests, economic regulation involves placing restrictions on business behavior to further some economic objective. Most economic regulation of the past has been directed at spurring competition, that is, restraining monopoly power in industries that, by their nature, are not subject to the forces of competition. Typically, once such regulation is established it begins to lose its usefulness. New technologies introduce competition into industries once thought secure for monopolies: trucks threaten railroads; cable companies encroach on the markets of broadcasting networks while satellite receivers eat into cable markets; innovations in long distance transmission destroy the economic foundations of the telephone monopoly; and gas turbines and solar applications undercut the scale economies that large coal-fired and nuclear electric generating stations were once believed to have. But almost invariably, the old regulatory apparatus not only persists but is transformed into an institution devoted to keeping prices high and sheltering the old industry from the assaults of potential competitors.

303

Starting in the mid-1970s, the United States took the lead among the world's industrial powers in scaling back its economic regulations. Airline deregulation was first, followed by deregulation of trucking and railroads. Regulation of banking and many other financial institutions was eased. Competition was introduced into the long distance telephone industry. And, in recent years, new information and communications technology has been forcing a combination of deregulation and regulatory redesign in the telecommunications industry. The same pattern is developing in the electricity industry.

Although the political struggles with and among the relevant special interest groups have been fierce, the battle has not been waged along partisan lines. Broadly speaking, both political parties have supported scaling back, relaxing, and modernizing economic regulation. Given the rapidity of technological advance, especially in the information- and transaction-processing industries, continued updating of the remaining areas of economic regulation, and most likely some further scaling back, will be appropriate in the future. But the continued deregulation that is in prospect is unlikely to be so much greater than that in the recent past that it could produce a significant increase in economic growth.

Social Regulation

Whereas economic regulation places restrictions on some aspect of business behavior, most social regulation involves a governmental mandate on firms to undertake expenditures directed toward meeting environmental, health, and safety standards. Such regulation requires economic resources that might have been used to produce standard goods and services to be diverted toward producing a cleaner, healthier, or safer environment. The standard goods and services given up are measured and counted in the official GDP statistics; but a large part of the environmental benefits are not. Cleaning up the environment, therefore, lowers GDP. Conversely, reducing the costs of environmental cleanup tends to raise GDP.[1] The following discussion

---

1. The actual accounting for environmental costs as they affect GDP is much more complicated than the text indicates. If a firm invests in pollution control facilities, that investment is counted as part of GDP. But to the extent that environmentally mandated investment crowds out productive investment that business firms otherwise would make, the production of future GDP is lowered. If environmental regulations cause a firm to incur

concentrates on the environmental controls of the Environmental Protection Agency, since both their costs and their benefits bulk largest among the various types of social regulation.

In 1990, economists Dale Jorgenson and Peter Wilcoxen developed a relatively comprehensive estimate of the economic impact of environmental regulations. Using an elaborate econometric model, they estimated that GDP would gradually rise by 2.6 percent if all the mandatory controls that were in place from 1972 to 1985 were removed.[2] Subsequently, they raised their estimate of the gain in GDP to 3.2 percent to reflect the increased stringency and costs of controls imposed by the Clean Air Act Amendments of 1990.[3] This, however, may be a slight overestimate because some of the 3.2 percent GDP loss represents their estimate of costs associated with mandated installation of emission control devices for motor vehicles, part of which are already accounted for in official GDP estimates.[4] Adjusted to take

---

additional operating expenses for labor or raw materials, to switch to more costly fuels, or to employ more production processes, and if the economy is operating at close to high employment, those resources must be diverted from the production of other goods, thereby reducing measured GDP. Some environmental costs are incurred by units of government—for example, the operating costs of local waste treatment plants. According to the conventions of national income accounting, such government spending is counted as part of GDP. But governments must pay for this spending. Paying for it with taxes will reduce consumer income and consumption; financing it with cuts in other spending will reduce government services. Again, standard goods and services are sacrificed for environmental benefits, except that in this case the cost is not reflected in a lower GDP.

2. The Environmental Protection Agency (EPA) estimated in 1990 that the annualized costs of all environmental regulations amounted to 0.9 percent of GDP in 1972 and 2.1 percent in 1990 and could significantly exceed 2.8 percent in 2000. (EPA's 2.8 percent estimate for 2000 excludes part of the costs added by the 1990 amendments to the Clean Air Act.)

3. See Jorgenson and Wilcoxen (1990, 1993). Their methodology may not have identified some of the subtle and indirect costs of complying with regulations. On the other hand, they make no allowance for the fact that the cleanup of the environment by some industries may have lowered production costs of other industries, thereby increasing GDP. To take some obvious cases, the fishing industry benefits from the cleanup of the nation's waters, as do those food industries that depend upon the large-scale availability of clean water. It is difficult to know whether the net effect of these two considerations makes the "true" effect on GDP higher or lower than their estimate.

4. In an exception to the general rules of national income accounting, the statisticians make an upward addition to GDP equal to the cost of motor vehicle emission control devices, to reflect the environmental benefits of those devices. And so, the resources used to produce mandated emission control devices, unlike those devoted to most other environmental controls, add to measured GDP. I have subtracted a rough estimate of this amount from the overall Jorgenson-Wilcoxen result.

account of this fact, the estimate of the GDP losses from current environmental controls would be roughly 2.9 percent.

Clearly, not even the most radical advocates of reforming and scaling back regulation propose scrapping all environmental controls. But how much of the GDP "loss" might be recovered through a reasonable and politically feasible set of cost-reducing regulatory reforms?

There are two ways to reduce regulatory costs. The first is to scale back the stringency of environmental cleanup requirements on grounds that current regulatory statutes and the processes of the regulatory agencies tend to produce excessively ambitious targets and standards. The second is to devise more efficient methods of meeting the existing environmental standards.

Starting from a highly polluted and unhealthy state, the social and health benefits of the first steps to improve the environment are very large and the costs of doing so are typically quite low. But once a substantial degree of cleanup has been accomplished, the benefits of further increments of cleanup get smaller while the costs of additional cleanup start to rise, often sharply. At some point the benefits of additional environmental stringency begin to exceed the extra costs. Yet many of the statutes under which current environmental regulations have been issued do not require regulators to give economic costs any weight in making their decisions about how stringent environmental standards should be, and a few statutes explicitly forbid considering costs. Since it is often difficult to assign a quantitative economic value to environmental benefits, and since there are divergent views among Americans about the worth of those benefits, just where to draw the line beyond which further environmental gains are not worth the costs has to remain essentially a political decision, subject to debate and controversy. Nevertheless, installing procedures that require regulatory agencies to be more explicit and transparent about weighing benefits against costs in their decisionmaking, and removing existing statutory barriers to doing so, could well reduce the regulatory costs imposed on the economy without a commensurate decrease in environmental benefits (so long as those procedures themselves do not hamstring decisionmaking or sharply increase environmental litigation).

It is impossible, of course, to predict just how much of a reduction in environmental costs such a procedural change might produce. In a recent study of fifty-four major environmental, health, and safety regulations promulgated between 1990 and mid-1995, Robert Hahn of the American Enterprise Institute concluded that only twenty-three of the regulations would produce benefits exceeding their costs.[5] If all of the thirty-one regulations with benefits less than costs had not been issued, costs with a present value of $115 billion would be saved over a twenty-year period (0.1 percent of GDP). But this estimate covers only regulatory activity that occurred over four and one-half years. If new regulations with costs in excess of benefits continued to be issued during the twenty-year period with the same frequency as in the period studied by Hahn, the total costs would amount to 0.5 percent of GDP. These results, of course, depend on a host of complex calculations and highly uncertain estimates of such matters as the number of lives saved, illnesses avoided, or accidents prevented by various regulations.

There are several reasons to think that Hahn's results might be an upper-bound estimate of what could be achieved by procedural reforms. His $115 billion cost saving assumes that if a proposed regulation did not meet the cost-benefit test no regulation would have been issued and no costs would have been incurred. In reality, a scaled-back regulation that met less ambitious targets and a cost-benefit test might be adopted, resulting in smaller but not zero costs. More important, it is not realistic to assume that regulatory mandates would be scaled back according to a bloodless cost-benefit calculus, ignoring both the regulatory enthusiasms and the industry opposition that produced the present system.

For many years economists have argued that environmental objectives could be achieved at much lower costs than the nation now pays if detailed government regulation were reduced and greater reliance were placed on various economic incentives, through such devices as levying taxes on pollutant discharges or auctioning off the rights to use the environment.

Traditionally, environmental regulations have specified that each polluting source achieve relatively uniform reductions in the emission or discharge of particular pollutants. Often they have also required that those reductions be achieved by installing a particular technology

---

5. Hahn (1996). Since the ones that did pass his benefit-cost analysis tended to have very large net benefits, the aggregate benefits of all the fifty-four regulations were still greater than their aggregate costs. Forty of the regulations covered by Hahn's study were issued by the EPA; fourteen were concerned with other health, safety, and consumer protection matters.

specified by the regulators (such as catalytic converters on motor vehicles, "best achievable technology" for waterborne effluents, or "scrubbers" to reduce sulfur dioxide from coal-fired generators). But different firms and industries face quite different costs to reduce their environmentally damaging discharges.

To achieve any given level of pollution reduction at the lowest cost, sources with the lowest cleanup costs should do the most reduction, while those with the highest costs should do the least. Similarly, it makes little sense for society to specify the use of a particular cleanup technology for a firm so long as the desired pollution reduction is achieved, since in their own self-interest firms would search for the lowest-cost approach, including attempts to discover new technology.

If polluting firms were charged a fee for each unit of pollutant they discharged (effluent or emission fees), those that could avoid pollution cheaply would cut back substantially while those facing high costs of reduction would do less and pay more in fees. The level of the fee could then be set to achieve the desired environmental goals, minimizing the total economic costs of achieving the goals.[6] Alternatively, the regulatory agency could establish an overall volume of pollutants of various kinds that would be allowed in an area and auction off to individual firms the rights to emit that amount. The same kinds of efficiency gains would be realized. Various less comprehensive means of harnessing economic incentives to promote low-cost pollution reduction have also been devised. Some of these more limited incentive-based schemes have gradually been introduced into the regulatory process in recent years.[7]

Over the years a number of studies have examined how large the cost savings might have been if particular environmental objectives had been pursued though the use of economic incentive mechanisms such as emission fees or auction markets. T. H. Tietenberg assembled the findings of eleven such studies dealing with various air pollution regulations. Most of these studies estimated the cost saving from a single regulation in a specific locality, but several made estimates for a particular regulation on a nationwide basis.[8] In all but one study

6. In many cases the fees would have to be differentiated by location, so that particular areas would not become highly polluted by the presence of firms with above-average costs of pollution reduction.

7. See *Economic Report of the President, 1996*, pp. 146–49; Burtraw (1995, especially pp. 1–2).

8. Tietenberg (1990, table 1, p. 24).

the savings were estimated to be very large. In seven of the studies the traditional regulatory approaches were estimated to have cost from four to twenty-two times more than an incentive-oriented solution.

As Tietenberg explained, these numerical estimates are subject to great uncertainty. Many may overstate the cost saving that might realistically be expected from incentive-based approaches to regulatory reform. Moreover—especially in the Clean Air Act of 1990—a number of partial incentive techniques have recently been authorized and are already in the process of being implemented. However, opposition to these approaches is strong. Under effluent fees and emission charges the overall cost of cleanup for the nation would be lower, but many business firms would end up paying more than under the existing regulatory system.[9] Business organizations have never been major proponents of a shift toward environmental incentive schemes, and many environmental interest groups think of them as licenses to pollute.[10] The recent conservative-led thrust for regulatory reform has focused more on scaling back regulatory objectives and requiring cost-benefit analyses rather than on promoting adoption of economic incentive approaches to regulation.

The Jorgenson-Wilcoxen estimates, as adjusted, set the economic loss due to the costs of environmental regulations at about 2.9 percent of GDP. Optimistically, these costs might be reduced by 25 percent if the nation adopted procedural changes that weighed costs as well as benefits and continued to infuse economic incentives into the traditional regulatory system. That would gradually increase the level of GDP by 0.7 percent by the early years of the next century. Given how hard it is for government policy to raise the long-term level of GDP, this is not an insignificant amount. But GDP increases of this magnitude will contribute only marginally to what is required to balance the budget.

9. Under full-blown economic incentive schemes, business firms would pay fees or be required to buy permits for any pollution they discharged into the environment, whereas under the current system once they meet the regulatory standards they have no further cleanup costs. But what business firms paid in effluent fees or in permit auctions would be available to the government as a substitute for other taxes, thereby offsetting, for the nation as a whole, some of the control costs.

10. Some time ago, however, the Environmental Defense Fund adopted a position more favorable to incentive approaches. See Tietenberg (1990, p. 18, n. 3).

References

Burtraw, Dallas. 1995. "Cost Savings *Sans* Allowance Trades? Evaluating the SO2 Emission Trading Program to Date." Discussion Paper 95-30. Washington: Resources for the Future.

Hahn, Robert W. 1996. "Regulatory Reform: What Do the Government's Numbers Tell Us?" In *Risks, Costs, and Lives Saved: Getting Better Results from Regulation*, edited by Robert W. Hahn, 208–53. New York and Washington: Oxford University Press and AEI Press.

Jorgenson, Dale W., and Peter J. Wilcoxen. 1990. "Environmental Regulation and U.S. Economic Growth." *Rand Journal of Economics* 21 (Summer): 314–40.

———. 1993. "The Economic Impact of the Clean Air Act Amendments of 1990." *Energy Journal* 14 (1): 159–82.

Tietenberg, T.H. 1990. "Economic Instruments for Environmental Regulation." *Oxford Review of Economic Policy* 6 (Spring): 17–33.

Index

311

Index